F

The Nurse Leader

The Nurse Leader:
Philosophy and Practice

Charlotte Epstein
Temple University

Reston Publishing Company, Inc.
A Prentice Hall Company
Reston, Virginia

Library of Congress Cataloging in Publication Data

Epstein, Charlotte
The nurse leader

Bibliography: p. 291
1. Nursing service administration.   2. Leadership.
I. Title.   [DNLM: 1. Leadership.   2. Nursing, Super-
visory.   3. Philosophy, Nursing.   WY 105 E64n]
RT89.E6   610.73'68   81-15853
ISBN 0-8359-5027-1   AACR2
        0-8359-3969-3 pbk.

© 1982 by Reston Publishing Company, Inc.
A Prentice Hall Company
Reston, Virginia 22090

10 9 8 7 6 5 4 3 2 1

Printed in the United States of America

Contents

Preface . . .   ix

Chapter 1   Leadership: A Conceptual Framework . . .   1

A.   A Functional Concept of Leadership . . .   1

Teaching, **3**; Rational thinking, **4**; Interdisciplinary communication, **4**.

B.   Leadership in Nursing . . .   4

C.   Philosophical Underpinnings of Leadership—Humanism and Democracy . . .   8

D.   Practicing Leadership Skills . . .   16

Assessing the needs of a situation, **16**; Interdisciplinary mobilization, **18**.

Chapter 2   The Nurse Leader As Teacher . . .   25

A.   Professional Education . . .   25

The missing factor, **26**; The clinical experience, **28**.

B.   In-service Education . . .   28

Commitment to education, **29**; Planning for teaching, **30**.

C.   Teaching in Nursing Care . . .   33

Learning from patients and clients, **34**; Teaching patients and clients, **35**.

D.   Research and Writing . . .   36

E.   Practicing Teaching Skills . . .   38

Writing behavioral objectives, **38**; Analyzing the instructional milieu, **42**.

Chapter 3   Leadership and Systems . . .   45

A.   The Systems Approach . . .   45

A plan for change, **48**.

B.   Components of the System . . . 51

The interdisciplinary context and the informal organization, **51;** Unanticipated consequences, **54;** Information gathering, **62;** Defining objectives, **64;** Mobilization, **66.**

C.   Practicing Systems Skills . . . 66

Gathering information, **66;** Strategy for identifying feelings and values, **70;** A note to
the prospective leader, **73.**

Chapter 4   The Interdisciplinary Component of Leadership . . . 75

A.   The Basis for Interprofessional Interaction . . . 75

B.   Interdisciplinary Communication . . . 80

Providing opportunities, **82;** Status and communication, **84.**

C.   Inter-Role Interaction . . . 86

Role clarification, **88;** Functioning, **88;** The nurse, the patient, and the team, **91.**

D.   Interpersonal Interaction . . . 93

Assuming leadership, **94;** Modeling behavior, **96.**

E.   Practicing Small-Group Skills . . . 99

Self-disclosure, **100.**

*Chapter 5   The Independent Nurse Practitioner: A Leadership
Route . . .* 103

A.   Impeding Factors . . . 103

Fear of change, **104;** Sexism, **105;** Ignorance of nursing, **105.**

B.   Personal/Professional Factors . . . 106

Leadership qualities of practitioners, **107;** Resistance in nurses, **110.**

C.   Practitioner Roles . . . 112

Leadership functions, **114;** Planning for change, **120;** Leadership abroad, **126.**

D.   Developing Trust and Acceptance . . . 129

Defining the nurse's role, **129;** Assessing a non-traditional competence, **131;** Encouraging consciousness-raising, **132;** Reading needs messages, **134;** Accepting negative
feedback, **136.**

Chapter 6   Leadership in the Institutional Setting . . . 141

A.   The Dynamics of Changing Organizations . . . 141

Principles of change, **143;** Conflict and cooperation, **146;** Instituting change, **146.**

**B.   Leadership in Bedside Nursing: A Care Plan Based on Special
Knowledge . . .** 150

Intergroup relations, **150;** The problem, **150;** General information, **151;** Acquiring
specific information, **152;** Moving toward readiness to plan, **153;** Consequences, **154.**

C.   Leadership in Nurse-Patient Relationship . . . 154

Behavioral objectives, **154;** General knowledge and communication skills, **154;**
Establishing trust, **155;** Patient input, **155;** Listening, **156;** Understanding, **156;**
Assessing the situation, **157;** Feedback, **158;** Looking at causes, **158;** Indepen-
dence, **158;** Evaluation, **159;** Follow-up, **159.**

D.   Leadership in Nurse-Unit Manager Relationship . . . 160

Asking for a change, **160;** Assessing the other's knowledge level, **161;** Planning for
leadership, **161;** Establishing communication, **162;** Maintaining ego safety, **162;**
Achieving collaboration, **163.**

E. Leadership in the Nursing Team . . . 164

The team meeting, **164;** Group goals, **167;** Self-fulfillment, **167;** Leadership functions, **168;** Ambivalence and confusion, **169.**

F. Leadership in Primary Nursing . . . 171

Staff development and supervision, **172;** Nurse-physician communication, **175;** Preservice education, **176.**

G. Increasing Sensitivity and Empathy . . . 178

Analyzing small-group dynamics, **178;** Vicarious experiences for increasing understanding and acceptance of others, **178.**

Chapter 7   The Nurse Leader in the Community . . . 187

A. Leadership Functions of Nurses . . . 187

Unique contributions of nursing, **187;** The linking function, **191;** The teaching function, **195.**

B. The Nature of Community . . . 197

Living and working in the community, **197;** Assessing community needs, **200;** Community defined, **203;** The future of the community, **204.**

C. Nursing Leadership for Neglected Groups . . . 205

The aged, **205;** Women, **212;** Children, **214;** Patients as patients, **215;** Minorities, **216;** The poor and the middle class, **218.**

D. Community Institutions for Nursing . . . 222

Health centers, **222;** Mental health centers, **224.**

E. Becoming Involved in the Community . . . 227

Initial observation in the community (1), **227;** Initial observation in the community (2), **237;** Initial observation in the community (3), **239;** First steps in community involvement, **239.**

Chapter 8   Political Leadership . . . 245

A. Political Activity . . . 245

Attitudes toward political activity, **246;** The nature of political activity, **248;** The political leader and her constituency, **251.**

B. Opportunities for Political Leadership . . . 253

Employing institutions, **253;** Professional organizations, **256;** Educational institutions, **260;** Citizen policy and planning boards, **261;** Action in local government, **265;** Action in national government, **266.**

C. Political Problems in Nursing . . . 268

Maintaining professional independence, **268;** Third-party payment, **269;** Allocation of professional resources, **270;** Quality of health care, **271;** Dissemination of new nursing data, **272.**

D. Taking Action . . . 273

Self-assessment on some leadership behaviors, **273;** Assessing the setting, **284;** Identifying a problem for political action, **288;** Preparing a plan for action, **288.**

Suggested Readings . . . 291

Preface

A review of almost half a century of leadership observation and systematic study makes it clear that we can formulate no consistent theory of leadership that predicts all relationships and explains all phenomena. We are not even in agreement about what constitutes leadership behavior; our observations run the gamut from the Blackfoot Indians, who had different leaders for different functions (who had no power except that which was permitted them by the people in a particular situation), to the contemporary elementary school teacher in the "back to basics" school who talks about "guiding" children while she tells them exactly what they must do.

This kind of theory vacuum leaves us all free to define leadership operationally, in terms of a philosophy of life and an explanation of human development that is consistent with that philosophy. This is what I have tried to do here.

But I have gone beyond behavioral descriptions of leadership behavior to explore the answer to the age-old question of the clinician: What do I do on Monday? Merely to say that it is a well-documented fact that people resist change and that the successful leader minimizes that resistance and achieves commitment to change, omits the all-important answer to the question: How?

The point of this book is that, if you accept the concept of self-actualization* as an *explanation of human development*, then it follows that

*Self-actualization is pinnacle of Maslow's needs hierarchy—not "Explanation of human development."

you wish to function democratically, communicating openly with the other people in your universe, teaching them and learning from them, and even daring to blast out of your accustomed orbit to explore other systems and contemplate the existence of other universes. The book will prepare you to change the world if that is what you want to do. But, even more immediately, it will convince you that you—because of your knowledge and your skill, because of the good ideas you have and the good will you bear others—can be a leader today. You may even be helped to recognize that, without ever having realized it, you are already a leader and, with a little more preparation, you can lead the people around you to even more exciting changes.

The last section of each chapter provides exercises and guidelines for action that will take you where you want to take others. You need not be overwhelmed or disheartened because you are not ready to do it all. Getting involved in a single exercise can be useful in your work. And success with it will bring you back to a second exercise and a third.

Take it at your own pace. No one ever goaded a really democratic leader into leading against her will.

Acknowledgement

My thanks to Temple University for the six-week summer research fellowship that freed me from the necessity for teaching so that I might complete this book.

chapter one

Leadership: A Conceptual Framework

A Functional Concept of Leadership

As long as problems exist that need solving, then leaders will be needed to help solve them. Which era in the history of the world, which profession since its inception has not suffered from too few leaders? Every profession wants more and better leaders, but little is ever done, beyond exhortation, to help people identify and practice specific skills of leadership behavior. Books identify people who are leaders in the profession; students are taught the various theories of leadership; sometimes traits of known leaders are discussed in courses and leadership behaviors are described.

Studying theories of leadership is helpful in understanding the framework within which leaders function. To identify leaders and, in a general way, to appreciate their behavior can be encouraging to those contemplating an attempt at leadership. But such information is, in the balance, more frustrating than helpful. Sensitive, caring professionals who recognize the need for change in health care delivery and who are willing to risk the dangers of leading the way, inevitably—when faced with a first step or a next step—find that they do not know *what to do, what to say*. Treatises on leadership generally end at this point, when the reader decides that she wants to be a leader. And now, what? she asks. But she has come to the end of the book, or the end of the course.

Students of leadership, after successfully passing examinations on which they feed back the information just described, are expected to get their first practical experience as leaders in the clinical setting—with patients, with superiors, with other professionals. Here they begin to discover that knowing about leadership is a far cry from being a leader. They find that the definitions of leadership need to be more functional and that leadership traits cannot be donned like work clothes. When they attempt to use leadership behaviors, they discover that they are awkward, inept, and unskillful, and that their errors interfere with their grand purposes.

The intermediate step in learning to be a leader must be the systematic, intensive practice of specific behaviors in a setting where mistakes may be made safely and where time is available after practice for retrospection and feedback from peers and other teachers. Then, when the time comes for practice of leadership in the real world, the margin for error has been substantially reduced and the chances of success have been increased. Such initial success is vital if leadership behavior is to persist, if the individual is to live her professional life as a leader. Too often what happens is that the unpracticed leader fails at the outset and is so disheartened that she believes that failure is inevitable, that change is impossible, and that it is wiser and more comfortable to play the old conforming games.

This book attempts to take up where other books end by proposing that leadership involves three essential behavior categories: (1) rational thinking, (2) educating, and (3) interdisciplinary communication. Within each category specific behaviors are described and exercises are provided for practicing those behaviors. If practice does indeed make perfect, the student or the practicing professional using this book should finally be equipped to function as a leader in her own sphere of professional life.

I propose that leadership means influencing individuals or groups to take an active part in the process of achieving agreed-upon goals. If one accepts this definition of leadership, one also accepts the implications: (1) that real leaders have conscious, autonomous followers who understand the relationship between leader and followers as one in which everyone retains control over his own life; (2) that much of the literature purportedly dealing with leadership discusses other processes that should not be labeled leadership.

There are other implications of this definition that proceed from the idea that followers are aware, active, and self-controlling:

1. At different points in the development of a situation, at different times during the process toward goals, one or more followers may become significantly influential, and may be identified as leaders. Such influence depends on what is needed at that moment: some special knowledge, some interpersonal skill, some insight that can move the group closer to its goals.

2. Though an organization may, through its formal structure, hold a supervisor or administrator accountable for achieving organizational goals, the supervisor or administrator who accepts this definition of leadership functions in such a way that responsibility and accountability are shared by the people doing the work. There is nothing to be gained by protesting that

when one is employed in a managerial capacity, then one must assume responsibility for getting the job done; that this is the nature of management and one cannot argue with axioms. It is well to bear in mind that it was once accepted as axiomatic by organizational analysts that workers were merely parts of a machine, and that the goal of management was to keep those parts working in the most efficient way possible, achieving maximum production at minimum cost. We have come some way from this concept of production, but, perhaps, not far enough. Side by side with the data on human development, human needs, and human rights, exists the traditional belief in the need for "strong" leaders to assume most of the initiatives for organization, creativity, insight and satisfaction of others' needs. It is time that we used some incisive thinking to cut away the necrotic material of the past and clarify the idea of leadership.

3. The leadership literature often makes the distinction between a leader who is task oriented and one who is group oriented.[1] The distinction—for an understanding of leadership—is, I believe, a specious one. If the purpose of leadership is the achievement of human goals, then the task must be addressed, or no goals will be reached. And, if goals are reached at the expense of the people involved, then there is no leadership worthy of the name. A leader of human beings is both task oriented *and* people oriented, and, if he makes a choice of one or the other, he is no longer worthy of the appellation leader. He may be a boss, a manager, a supervisor, or a dictator, but not a leader.

There are three essential functions of leadership as I define it: one is teaching, the second is rational thinking, and the third is interdisciplinary communication. The essence of teaching is providing opportunity to help people grow into everything they can be, to provide an environment that permits them to change their behavior so that they act productively on the basis of knowledge. Rational thinking is subsumed in the systems approach: identifying objectives and planning for the achievement of those objectives. Interdisciplinary communication is related to holism in interacting with others in all aspects of living.

Teaching

Motivating people to become involved in the gathering of information, in defining objectives, and in planning processes for effecting change is a teaching function. The job of the teacher is not to disseminate bits of information. This is a concept that we learned from our experience with not very competent teachers when we were children, when they fed us information and forced us to give it back to them on examinations. The essential function of teaching is motivation; the central function of leadership is motivating other people to behave in certain ways. Of course, if you know something that other people need to know in order to solve a problem or make a decision, part of your leadership function is to communicate this knowledge to them.

If they are unable to use the knowledge (and "unable" to some people can mean "unwilling"), then the leader must try to identify the impediments to the others' use of the knowledge and help to remove them. Identification and removal of impediments to using new information is teaching.

Rational thinking

Rational thinking requires the best available information, awareness of one's own needs and propensities for selective perception, and a commitment to honesty. Unless one has a real commitment to honesty, one will not profit from introspection. That is, where there is no honesty, there is no real search for self-understanding. There is a tendency, then, to ignore the ways in which our own needs make us overlook the needs of others, the ways in which our beliefs blind us to errors, the ways in which our emotional investment in the things we have learned prevent us from using new knowledge.

Without the ability to use the best available information, we cannot understand ourselves, or the people and situations around us; we cannot distinguish between real objectives and rationalizations; our planning is simplistic and ineffective; our processes create anxiety and hostility in the people involved in them.

Interdisciplinary communication

Communication across disciplinary lines is necessary for effective teaching or really rational thinking and planning. Nobody knows this better than the nurse who, in her holistic approach to nursing, is aware of the need to understand the knowledge of such disciplines as psychology and medicine, human relations and sociology, education and social work. Not only must she cross disciplinary lines in order to make effective contact with clients, but she must also make effective contact with physicians, dietitians, peers and aides, and politicians and administrators.

A leader approaches knowledge in the same way a nurse leader approaches patients—recognizing that knowledge is whole and data in all fields are interrelated. Using data in one field without understanding their relationship to the data in other fields, may cause damage to people and to the environment.

Leadership in Nursing

Much is written by nurses about the low self-concept of nursing, the need to change nurses' self-image, and the history of the profession that has left it with doubts about its ability to make a unique contribution to health independently of the other health professions. If all this is only partly true, it still has implications for the kind of leadership that is needed. In the final analysis, the leaders in a profession lead the members of their own profession. If nurses are forever led by authoritarians—no matter how knowledgeable and benevolent they may be—those being led are condemned to further ego damage. If people are convinced that they have neither the knowledge nor the skill to run their own lives and professions, then they cannot maintain a sense of self-worth.

It is not unusual for people to equate leadership with supervision and administration. Recently, when I discussed with a physician my interest in identifying leadership skills for nurses, he asked me, "If all good nurses become directors, who'll do the nursing? Administrative nursing and direct patient services seem quite different to me." He was quick to admit, however, that the *assigned* leadership of administrators and supervisors is not always accepted by those they are supposed to lead—often with sad results for the product, the patient, the education of the child, or any other system outcome.

The kind of leadership we are concerned with here goes beyond the job description. It is a role assumed by people wherever they find themselves in contact with other people, and it involves influencing those others to learn, to grow, to be and to become everything they are capable of.

Nurses studying the concept of leadership and the skills related to it should understand that the conventional literature on leadership needs some basic alteration if it is to be applied to the nursing profession. Most leadership studies deal with situations in which the "leader" is in a management position, and the effectiveness of his leadership is defined in terms of increased productivity and employee satisfaction. The result of effective leadership in such situations is generally the maintenance of the status quo, with major changes coming from the top and being imposed on the lower levels of the organizational hierarchy.

In nursing, leadership is needed at present to effect changes, and the history of nurses in supervisory and administrative positions has been the usual management history of maintaining the status quo. For nurses, effective leadership must clearly be identified in terms of those professional goals that have generally not been realized, and there is little worth in discussing many of those leadership theories that are so dependent for their validity on acceptance of businesses and institutions as they have been established.

(Perhaps the group of high school youngsters who recently informed their principal that they intended to burn down the school were the real leaders, whose followers knew that the 80-year-old firetrap, the outmoded rules, the ineffective teaching and the absence of financial support required burning the place down and starting from scratch. Any leadership exercised by the principal, even if it were "effective" enough to keep the students attending school, was leading them up a path to disillusionment and failure.)

No one is suggesting here that nurse leaders engage in arson. The point is that leaders in many situations who are able to foster satisfaction in their followers may be doing the profession a grave disservice by perpetuating practices and goals that violate the real aims of the profession.

The whole matter of values in organizational leadership has been virtually neglected. No matter what style of leadership one espouses, if employees and groups in an organization are resisting the leadership efforts of their supervisors and administrators, it may be that the goals of the organization are essentially antithetical to the goals of the people it employs, to general humanistic goals, and to the very nature of the human being.

For example, attempts to lead people to engage in hospital practices that violate the dignity of patients may succeed with some employees. But those who reject the leadership, respond with hostility to the directives or suggestions, and score low on measures of "loyalty" to the institution, are demonstrating their own leadership behavior. They are disruptive and interfering with the institution's effectiveness; their behavior leads to low marks for the assigned leaders of the institution. However, the essential factor in the situation is the difference in values between assigned leaders and other leaders. Which leaders ultimately prevail depends partly on their leadership skills and partly on which leadership skills are being supported by the total environment.

Leadership is concerned not only with conflicts over institutional goals and values, but also with personal needs. When the needs of people in an organization are not fulfilled, they must look elsewhere for satisfaction. Professionals' search for need satisfaction outside the organizations that employ them can result in the virtual destruction of that organization or—at the least—the subversion of its stated objectives.

One current case in point is what is happening in many universities. In the panic surrounding the falling off of the student population, the faculty—heretofore the ones who governed the university—have abdicated the governance role to administrators. The result has been the erosion of viable educational objectives, which are being replaced by dollar values.

Faculty, unable to find satisfaction in setting personal and professional objectives determined by how much money can be brought into the university, and whose special skills are generally underutilized in university governance, threatened also by possible loss of jobs because their courses do not bring in enough money (even though they may be teaching very important subjects), have found alternative means of satisfying those objectives: they spend more time off campus sharing their expertise with other business and professional groups; they retreat to libraries and laboratories and study and write without university support; and many, in spite of the shortage of positions, are leaving the universities.

In many cases, nurses have had neither the opportunity to follow effective leadership nor the skills to be effective leaders in traditional settings. So, though some have carved out for themselves viable alternatives in various types of independent practice, very many of them have fallen away from nursing. The conventional wisdom has it that people leave nursing because they are mostly women who choose not to combine careers with motherhood, but I reject this analysis outright. Women in other professions do not generally give up their professions when they decide to have a family; they make all kinds of temporary arrangements for managing both aspects of their lives. Why, then, does the profession lose so many nurses? I submit it is because nurses are prevented from practicing their profession in the best ways and feel powerless to change what is happening.

Realistic assessment of a situation is one vital aspect of rational thinking. It may give some needed support to nurse leaders who are being bombarded with misinformation that is threatening to undermine their efforts. The ability to assess a situation realistically is important not only in solving everyday problems, but is vital if one is to venture into uncharted waters where predictability is almost impossible. One facet of accurate assessment involves those who are antagonistic to what the leader is trying to do. Such people will—sometimes in the guise of friendship, out of "concern" for the leader's welfare—assure him, "That will never work." This kind of remark is relatively easy to discount; we know about people who believe that anything new "will never work," and anything they have not the courage to try will never work. However, when they add that "Everyone is talking about it"; "They all agree that you're wrong about this"; "No one will support you; they're saying you have no right," we need all the skill of rational analysis to neutralize the effect of these comments.

In many cases, these comments are not based on fact. The commentators may not be consciously attempting to discourage the leader's effort by lying about the opinions of the target population. At least two psychological processes may be operating in the commentary; knowledge of them may help the leader keep an eye on the real situation. The first process is projection; the other is selective perception.

A person who believes something very strongly may also think that everyone else believes the same thing. Priding herself on her good sense, seeing her position as a natural outcome of logical thinking, she cannot imagine that most people do not see the matter in the same light. And, especially if she has not been forcefully confronted with data to the contrary, she lives her life thinking everyone—or everyone who matters—agrees with her. In other words, she projects her own convictions on to everyone else, assuming that, when she expresses her opinion, she is also expressing the opinion of her listener.

Selective perception reinforces the projection process. The individual, emotionally committed to a belief, actually does not see or hear evidence contradicting the belief. If she says to someone that she believes that independent practice for the nurse is wrong, and that person disagrees with her, she checks that person off as an exception to the prevailing point of view. She is able—so desperately do some of us cling to our illusions—to say about ten or twenty or even fifty people who disagree with her, that they are exceptions. After a while, she may actually forget about them, and remember only those who agreed with her, just as she will forget other information that contributes to the proof that she is wrong.

Being prepared with information that indicates that "everyone" is *not* saying these things can bolster our confidence in the undertaking. It is helpful to give the nay-sayer the names of individuals—preferably some in positions of influence and power—who have indicated that they support the new venture. If the venture is an independent practice, the names of clients who have come back for a second visit is good information. If the venture is a campaign for changing over to primary nursing in the hospital, the knowledge that this supervisor, that administrator, these nurses and physicians have already approved of the idea can help the leader maintain his equilibrium.

We might also bear in mind that if he has, on the basis of his knowledge and experience, concluded that change is necessary, the chances are good that there are others who agree with him. Identifying those others and organizing for mutual support is one of the best antidotes to the "Everybody's saying . . ." comment.

Philosophical Underpinnings of Leadership—Humanism and Democracy

Humanism is the belief in the essential worth of all human beings. The psychology of humanism draws its data from an understanding of the human being's drive for satisfaction not only of basic biological needs, but also of needs for love, self-acceptance, autonomy, and creativity.

Democracy as a sociopolitical concept is consistent with humanistic values and humanistic psychology. It is based on the right of human beings to be involved in the decisions that affect their lives—a right that is rooted in people's need for autonomy.

All through the literature on leadership, though there is discussion of democratic leadership, and the needs and rights of people who are led, the belief persists that the leader is the one who makes the decisions; the leader is the one who does the planning; the leader is the one who identifies the objectives. This is inconsistent not only with a basic democratic approach to life but with the humanistic, holistic approach to dealing with people that characterizes the whole nursing profession.

An example of this kind of inconsistency may be found in the conclusions of McClelland and Burnham,[2] who identify the characteristics of good managers: Good managers want power and influence over others far more than achievement or being liked by their subordinates; a democratic, coaching, managerial style is the other characteristic of all good managers. These researchers discuss the importance of having power tempered by maturity and self-control. They suggest that maturity implies little or no egotism or a freedom from preoccupation with one's own needs and problems.

How does one logically equate a desire for power over others with a democratic approach to interpersonal relationships? If ever two ideas canceled each other out, these do! The democratic personality has no need to exert power over others. He is free to try to persuade others of the validity of his point of view, just as he leaves others free to try to persuade him to their point of view. Sometimes one, sometimes the other prevails, and it is probably only human to derive satisfaction from success at persuading another person. But the satisfaction is not rooted in a need for power over that person; rather the satisfaction lies in the ability to present a point of view clearly and authoritatively, in the ability to open an intellectual or affective door for another person, even in the ability to persuade without the use of power and authority.

It seems to me that a need for power over others implies a monumental egotism; thus it is contradictory that researchers and writers maintain that the "best managers" want power but are mature enough to be free of egotism. Only an egotist can be so sure of his rectitude, so sure he knows what other people ought to do that he uses power to make them do it. The really mature individual has self-confidence, but he also has confidence in the ability of other people to lead their lives effectively and to reach the goals to which they commit themselves. If they sometimes need help from others, so does the mature individual and, as much expertise as he has in an area of life, he keeps an eye open always to the possibility that there are aspects of the subject he still does not know.

"Authoritarian" and "leadership" are mutually exclusive terms, notwithstanding the fact that "authoritarian leadership" has been the subject of study since Kurt Lewin's work in 1939,[3] and has been identified as one of several leadership "styles." It is time, I think, to stop repeating the propositions and conclusions of these old researches and to redefine leadership in terms that are consistent with goals of optimum human development.

If an individual forces others to do what he wants by means of overt threat or threat implied by the power vested in him by his position, he is an autocrat, but he is not a leader. And if he gets people to do as he wishes by means of cajolery, flattery, and rewards or promises of rewards, he is just as autocratic—though not, on the surface, unpleasantly so—but, again in terms of human needs, not a leader. (The Pied Piper of Hamlin was not a leader; he was a monstrous user of people.)

The human being's drive toward mental health is analogous to the constant movement of the physical mechanism toward homeostasis. All kinds of environmental factors interfere with this drive—from early learning experiences that create needs for dependence, destroy curiosity and discourage a healthy skepticism, to experience of economic poverty that fosters fear and reluctance to plan for the future. The authoritarian takes advantage of people's damaged egos and underdeveloped personalities to force them to his will, just as he is forced to do the bidding of those he perceives as more threatening or more nurturing—depending on his susceptibility to sharp or sweet authoritarianism. This is not leadership; it is destructive exploitation. A leader would assist in removing the impediments to the self-actualization drive—to the movement toward optimum development.

I doubt that authoritarianism is ever justified in societies of adults—and serious questions may be raised about its justification in interactions between adults and children. Often commentators on leadership concede that, though authoritarianism is generally undesirable, it is necessary in times of crisis when one person must give the orders and all others follow in the interests of safety and saving time. This is sloppy thinking. Unless authority has been delegated to an individual by his peers and the exercise of that authority previously delimited by consensus, the assumption of authority is *not* justified; it is not leadership.

If such previous consensus has never been achieved and an individual, on his own initiative, has saved lives by virtue of giving orders and having them carried out, we have an instance of inadequate planning. When the crisis is over, people need to look back at what happened and make decisions about leadership in future crises, not depend on fortuitous assumption of autocratic powers by someone who may give the right orders and be labeled a leader or someone who gives orders that result in tragedy and who is labeled a fool or worse.

Leaders are not elected officials. They are not administrators or supervisors who have been hired by other administrators and supervisors. Leaders are people who influence other people. People are willing to go along with them. Leaders are people who can motivate other people to do what has to be done. But all of this must go in a framework of humanism and democracy.

There are differences between democratic leaders and authoritarians. Democratic leaders permit other people to assume leadership roles as they perceive the need for them. The authoritarian permits no encroachment on his leadership function; he owns the leadership.

What the democratic leader does not do is try to convince the profession that the old ways were the best, that the old criteria should be maintained, that the old concepts should remain unchanged. Nor does the leader demand that everything new must be accepted, that the profession must go wherever the pressures from outside push it. Deciding which changes are viable and which are not, which current changes should be accepted and what kinds of changes should be planned for the future should not be the leader's decision; it should be the decision of all the people who will be affected by the changes.

There is an idea extant that democratic leadership and democratic functioning generally are not as efficient as authoritarian functioning, not as efficient as being led or administered by a single, strong individual who can make decisions expeditiously. It has become almost a truism that democracy is inefficient, and—incredibly—there are still those who insist that the efficiency of the Italian railroad system should be considered in the evaluation of the dictatorship of Mussolini.

I deny categorically that democracy is inefficient. If we view the nature of the human being, what his needs are, then there is no more efficient way to live than democratically.

If we start with the premise that a human being is important, that his importance neither increases nor decreases by his numbers, that the destruction of a single person is as outrageous, as wrong as the destruction of a thousand people, then it must follow that there are no small murders. Any action that prevents a person from expressing his feelings is a murder. Any action that interferes with a person's physical growth and development is a murder. To "lead" by murdering is not efficient. By definition, efficiency is the achievement of goals without waste, and what is more wasteful than the destruction of a human being?

Authoritarian rearing interferes with the physical growth of children as well as with the development of their ability to think and to feel. Typically, the authoritarian adult decides when a child shall sit and when he shall stand, when he will run and at what time of the day he will use the toilet. Though there are times when it is clear that the child is unequipped to make a decision governing his behavior—as when a two-year-old wants to do his walking out in traffic—making almost all such decisions for a child prevents optimum growth. When a teacher plans the school day so that the child must sit at certain times and move at certain times, with no concession to individual needs for stretching and bending growing muscles, the physical development of the child cannot proceed at optimum level. (So great is children's need to move at will that many authoritarian teachers are beset with "disciplinary" problems—that is, children who risk the dire punishments in order to continue to grow. It becomes almost a fight for survival in the face of authoritarian constraints.)

We have evidence that authoritarian imposition of teaching strategies that are not compatible with individual learning styles of children destroys curiosity and damages for life the individual's motivation to learn and change. Too many children, bright and curious when they start to school, shortly become dull and uninterested.

Children who do not participate in planning their lives, who must submit to the plans of others, too often without understanding what is happening to them, may develop feelings of worthlessness that prevent thinking and learning. Children who are asked only questions of limited "fact," and must respond with "factual" answers that will shortly no longer be factual may never learn to use data productively to solve problems. They may never have the ability to think on more complex levels than merely recall of recently learned information.

Since almost all of us has been subjected to authoritarian rearing and teaching and to the practices that go along with such teaching, it is likely that most of us are not functioning at the level that our human structure makes possible. That is probably why so many of us are willing to permit others to tell us what to do, to run our lives for us. So inadequate do we feel, so agitated at the thought of becoming involved in ordering our own lives and having to find our own solutions to the problems of living, that we clutch at the delusion that authoritarian management is more efficient than democratic problem solving.

The authoritarian model of interaction is taken from relationships of people with other animals, whose level of thinking must remain low and whose expression of feeling is primitive and untempered by reason. The people who prefer this model are usually those who have been subjected to it in their formative years, when they learned that one either rules or is ruled by others. This model violates the nature of the human being, in that it prevents the achievement of that potential level of function to which the human race has evolved.

There are times in the life of a working group, times in the group's progress toward solutions to problems, when no leadership is needed. At those times the individuals who make up the group are involved in practicing their own skills, responding to each other's needs and in other ways moving the group toward mutually agreed-upon goals without the direct and immediate influence of a leader. It may be that the group has arrived at this pattern of operation because the leader has been influential in freeing it from various impediments to optimum functioning. As other impediments become apparent, special leadership skills may again be needed, and at that time, the leader will become prominent again.

Some students of leadership may identify the period of time when the group's leader is not prominent as evidence of a "style of leadership" called laissez-faire. That is, there is a leader but he has decided that his style is to permit the group to function independently of his leadership. Generally this "leadership style" is rejected as unproductive, with the implication that the people want and need leadership and cannot achieve their goals without it.

The error in all this lies in the premise on which the analysis is based: that leadership is vested only in the person hired to manage or supervise or teach the group. Thus, the teacher who does not actively manage her class is said to be engaging in laissez-faire leadership; the supervisor who permits her supervisees to set their own goals and plan to achieve them without her active participation is said to be a laissez-faire supervisor.

If we look at leadership as behavior characterized by certain skills used to move a group toward its goals, the concept of laissez-faire must be rejected as a leadership style, since it is nonleadership. Anyone who has the job of supervisor, manager, or teacher and who does not exercise leadership skills is not a leader and is not doing the job for which she was hired. By the same token, the employee, the pupil in a classroom, and every other human being in a group who does not exercise leadership skills—that is, behaviors that imply the individual's responsibility to move the group forward—is not a leader.

Situational leadership ideas propose that the effective leader provides the kind of leadership demanded by the particular situation and the needs of the people involved. The inference is that if the group members "need" to be told what to do, to have their plans laid out for them and their decisions made by others, then that is the kind of leadership that should be provided. One can see most clearly the results of such a concept of leadership in the situation of teachers and children. Children who have not learned the skills they need to identify objectives and to cooperate on plans for reaching those objectives; skills for recognizing the needs of other people and providing support for them; or skills for identifying and communicating their own needs and satisfying them in productive ways, will never learn them as long as they are dominated and their lives ruled by an authoritarian teacher. They need opportunity and help in developing skills for making their unique contributions to the group's work. The teacher (leader) must provide that help.

Though the responsibility of the leader of adults is not quite so clear-cut, the general observation is the same: As long as a group is subjected to autocratic rule, it cannot learn to function autonomously. One does not learn the skills and responsibilities of democratic living while living in a dictatorship. What generates the dissatisfactions and unproductiveness of people in autocratic groups is not their inability to function democratically, but what seems to be the drive for self-actualization, a human need for health, the essence of which is democratic, humanistic interaction with others. Because people may have the drive but not the skills for democratic functioning, initial attempts at self-rule immediately after the overthrow of a dictatorship are often disastrous. But reimposition of autocratic rule obviously does not cause them to learn what they need for living autonomously.

It is interesting that it is generally conceded that professionals and others on the professional level of knowledge respond best to nonauthoritarian leadership; that is, if they are free to supervise themselves and make their own decisions. Conversely, there are management professionals who believe that people in lower level jobs need more authoritarian management.[4] Though the writers in the field have moved some way from the original conception that workers were just cogs in the production machine and had nothing to contribute but their mechanical movement on the assembly line, the implication is often still made that what is called democratic leadership is something they should have in very small doses.

In this way, managers become agents for fulfilling their own prophecy—"these people" cannot handle participatory democracy, so we will not provide them opportunity for it, so they never get the chance to learn how to handle it. This process, sad to say, starts in the kindergartens of our public schools. The attitude pervades our culture, with too many people quite willing to assume responsibility for running the lives of their fellow human beings.

To the extent that authoritarianism adjures people not to think, not to act on the basis of their own decisions, to relinquish control of the decision-making processes that govern their own lives, to that extent it is against the essential nature of human beings, of their need to achieve a level of functioning that requires autonomy and a sense of unity with all humankind.

A problem often arises in organizations that causes difficulty in clarifying both leadership and followership roles; that is, there is inconsistency between the overall institutional system and both the subsystems and the individual roles. For example, an institution may have objectives that are clearly articulated and publicized. These objectives are socially desirable and generally laudable. However, workers in the institution who know how the organization functions, know also that there are real objectives that are not so laudable, but that units and individuals are obliged to work for if they are to keep their jobs and get the rewards that go with the jobs. What, then, is the function of the leader in the situation? Which goals does he work for—those that are publicly accepted, and to which he committed himself when he came into the organization, or the hidden ones that have since been revealed to him? Is he a leader if he leads people to resist the hidden goals? Or is he "unproductive" and "inefficient" in terms of those hidden goals?

In research and literature, leadership is generally evaluated in terms of the organization's goals. Little space is devoted to the role of the leader in raising questions about the validity or morality of the real goals, and to the integrity of organizations whose apparent goals are quite different from their real goals. Much of the writing also deals with satisfaction of personal needs on the job, again without devoting much thought to the relationship of that satisfaction to immoral, destructive, or otherwise reprehensible organizational goals.

A startling example of this is being acted out, as university professors who have frequently taken antiwar stands become part of a million dollar grant to their university for helping the army to function more efficiently by training teachers of soldiers. (The army, discovering that many soldiers cannot read and write well enough to do their jobs, has contracted with universities to train teachers who will, in turn, teach soldiers basic communication skills.)

The professors have assumed leadership positions in this endeavor and have never questioned the inconsistency between professed values and the values associated with maintaining armies. Their responses to questions about this have ranged all the way from: "If we don't do it, someone else will," to "We can't afford to give up so much money; the university is in desperate straits." And they continue to be lauded for their "leadership" in this matter, because they undertake such a difficult task and help the army to reach its goals.

And, closer to home for most of us, perhaps, is the "leadership" behavior of supervisors and administrators in one hospital who, while publicly subscribing to the goals of community service and improvement, worked to force neighborhood people from their homes to make way for a larger parking lot for hospital employees.

Drawing on the available researches, Moloney states: "Since the leader is one of the sources for supplying rewards or punishments, he is in an excellent position to provide considerate behavior and satisfy followers' needs for recognition, advancement, belongingness, and competence, as well as for pay and security. Moreover, if he demonstrates high initiating structure, indicating the paths that he wants followed, and if he connects reward to successful following of these paths, such behavior will have a positive impact on the followers."[5]

Nothing I have read in the leadership literature so clearly implies a belief in the paternalistic nature of leadership and the essential dependency of those who are led. The idea seems to be that the leader is responsible for identifying the needs of potential followers, and then getting them to do his bidding by satisfying their needs. Here the concept of leadership smacks decidedly of manipulation.

And what happens to those same followers who are one day subjected to the "leadership" of a villain who, by satisfying their needs for recognition, advancement, and security, induces them to travel paths toward immoral goals? What did they ever learn from their experience with the first leader that can help them to resist the second one, that is, to get satisfaction of their needs without abandoning their integrity?

Again, I do not think Moloney is talking so much about leadership as she is about people in supervisory and administrative positions. People get into such positions for a variety of reasons that have nothing to do with leadership skills (though some, of course, *are* leaders). However, if you have had any experience with the procedure by which people are hired as head nurses, hospital administrators, department chairmen, deans and associate deans, it will be clear that leadership skills are rarely identified accurately. A series of two or three interviews by individuals or search committees, a perusal of past job descriptions, and a casual call to a former colleague are hardly adequate to assess leadership qualifications. The proof of this is that most people appointed in this way are not leaders, though they may sometimes be effective producers. The data that reveal such widespread dissatisfaction with work must be related in part, at least, to the quality of supervision and administration.

Though coordinated effort of the individuals in an organization is necessary to achieve the goals of that organization, I disagree with Moloney that

". . .such coordinated effort can only be achieved through authority . . . ."[6] To corroborate her observation, she cites Benne: ". . . all men engaged in common enterprises, the most mature, rationally autonomous, self-directing persons . . . need commonly accepted rules, norms, or principles of orders to guide and direct the processes of their cooperation."[7]

To suggest that common agreement on an order of principles and rules is the same as the command authority of individuals in positions of power and prestige is specious. In our system of law, for example, authority is invested in the law, not in people, and those who obey the law do so because it is consistent with their own values, and because they have the right to institute a process of change when it no longer satisfies them.

The contemporary organization falls somewhat short of this rule of law; no administrator's authority can be equated with the authority of the law.

If, as a culture, we value the concepts of democracy, humanism, individual autonomy and acceptance of differences, then the person who is able to influence people toward antidemocratic and antihumanistic goals cannot be considered either an efficient leader (efficient because he achieves the antidemocratic goals of the organization) or an effective leader (effective because the people who cooperate with him in achieving those goals feel satisfied and happy about what they are doing). The element of values—of morality and integrity—must be included in the evaluation of a leader, or we are left with a mechanistic model that is good because it works.

Moloney says, "If the authority figure utilizes his leadership talent and applies it to the legitimate authority position, he should be effective in influencing the behavior of subordinates toward goal achievement."[8] But what if the authority position is legitimate within the parameters of the organization, but the organization itself is engaged in immoral work? Can we still evaluate the authority figure as an effective leader? In terms of the values and goals we espouse as a society, I think not. If we do, we confuse the concept of leadership as it is conceived in a democratic, humanistic milieu.

Practicing Leadership Skills

Assessing the needs of a situation

Jane Brown is one of three nursing team leaders in the large medical-surgical unit of Blank Hospital. She has almost no contact with the personnel of the other teams, except for the two other nurse leaders. The three of them have lunch together whenever they can manage it. At those times, their conversation is always about the work: the problems of understaffing, the new residents who have to be broken in, which team has more than its fair share of uncooperative patients this week, where things seem quiet and routine—at least for a little while.

At one of these lunches, Jane brings up a problem on her team that has been bothering her for some time. One of the R.N.'s (there are two besides Jane on the team) is very hostile. Though she is a competent nurse and is caring and humane with patients, she responds to Jane and other nursing personnel tersely, with anger, always with a frown on her face. Jane has had difficulty confronting the situation because there seems to be no professional handle to get hold of. The nurse does her work very well, follows orders and directions, and does more than her share of giving when it comes to professional matters. Jane rather hesitantly adds an additional comment: The hostile R.N. is Black. (Jane is White).

When Jane finishes her story, one of the team leaders says she knows exactly how to deal with someone like that. She had a similar experience with an obnoxious personality and she . . .

The other team leader suggests that the single similar experience may only be the same on the surface, that this nurse may be quite different from the nurse the other leader knew. She thinks Jane should . . .

Jane listens and wonders if either approach is adequate. She begins to think she needs more information concerning . . .

Have at least two other people working on this with you. One person should write down an analysis of the needs of the situation based on personal experience—what the first leader might have said when she heard Jane's story. In your analysis, include a plan for ameliorating the situation.

The second person of the triad should write down a plan for approaching the solution of the problem. This plan should include questions she would ask the hostile R.N. and other procedures for getting additional information about her that can be used in resolving the problem.

The third person should write down a plan based on general information about individual psychology; about the experience and behavior of people in small groups and people in large social groups such as racial, sex, and nationality groups; and about the feelings and attitudes of nurses as a profession.

The three people in the triad should now compare their plans and try to come to some general conclusions about the experience. The following questions may serve as guides for your discussion:

1. What good reasons can you give for utilizing your particular source of information? How, for example, do you think that source will provide some important data for the problem's solution?
2. What limitations have you discovered in the information source you used?
3. Are there other sources of information, that might be used? How are they important? How is their value limited?

When you have completed your discussion, perhaps you would like to share some of the generalizations of your group with the total group, if you are part of a class or team engaged in the exercise.

Interdisciplinary mobilization

The term mobilization has been used to identify the process whereby people are brought into the process of planning for change. Communities are mobilized by leaders to demand a voice in political and economic decision making. Professionals reach out to people in need of service and mobilize them to use available resources.

It seems appropriate here to extend the use of the term to describe a process that the nurse leader can engage in for the purpose of involving other professionals in the direct planning of patient care.

These exercises provide guides and opportunities for interdisciplinary mobilization. Initially, they require a certain amount of courage, because they require behavior that may not be expected in many settings. But the beginner can ease her way into the unexpected in a number of ways:

1. If she is a student, she has the support of her course instructor. Saying something is "required" for a course can make most harried nursing service supervisors relent, even if they do so reluctantly.

2. If she is a staff nurse, she can keep the mobilization so informal at first that the social aspects of the interdisciplinary conference will almost obscure the professional functioning that is occurring. The interdisciplinary team can meet for lunch, or even for a cocktail party at the nurse's home.

3. If she is a nursing supervisor or administrator, she may start the mobilization process when members of different disciplines are already assembled for other purposes. Raising a question almost casually during a lull in a budget meeting may plant a seed and start a process. For example, when the committee members have just made a difficult decision and feel pleased with themselves, it may be a good time to say, "We ought to have meetings like this downstairs, to solve some of our patient care problems." Even if only one or two of the other people seem interested enough to pursue the suggestion, there is a nucleus for forming the first interdisciplinary care planning team.

EXERCISE 1

To prepare yourself for taking the first step to mobilize an interdisciplinary team, try role-playing a difficult situation to test behavioral alternatives.

If you are students, you have a ready-made group of peers with whom to do this exercise. If you are a staff nurse, some of your colleagues might be interested in joining you in the room behind the nurses' station during a coffee break or with a brown-bag lunch. If you are a supervisor or administrator, sound out some of the nurses you know and see if there are any who are receptive to the idea of practicing mobilization.

A. Start by reading the following story:

Jane Burke is a nurse in a primary care medical-surgical unit. She believes that, during case and care-plan presentations, it would be useful to have people from other disciplines present to give their input and help utilize all available data in the development of the care plans. Up to this point only registered nurses, licensed vocational nurses and, occasionally, nurse's aides make up the audience and provide additional relevant information to the presenter.

Miss Burke has a presentation to make on Thursday and she decides to get reactions from some of the other people concerning the plan she will present.

Today is Tuesday. At lunchtime, standing in line in the staff cafeteria, she sees Ms. Hanlon, the dietician, behind the steam table checking the entrees. Behind Miss Burke is one of the hospital social workers. They get into a conversation and sit down at a table together. At the next table is Paul Singer, a busy, competent internist who often has patients under Miss Burke's care. Miss Burke smiles, thinking to herself, "We have all the ingredients here for an interdisciplinary meeting. I sure would love to present my plan for Mr. Cohen to those three!"

The social worker, Gracy Levy, asks her, "What's so funny? You look as if you're hatching up something."

B. Now, three of you take the parts of Miss Burke, Ms. Hanlon, Mrs. Levy, and Dr. Singer in the cafeteria situation. Play out the scene any way you like, while the rest of you watch. Jot down some of your observations of what happens. For example:

1. Does Miss Burke act on her vagrant wish?
2. Which of the other people does she approach?
3. What are their responses?
4. How is she able to deal with refusal?
5. How prepared is she for acceptance?

C. After the scene is played, let each role player say a word or two about how she felt.

D. The audience now discusses what happened, using the questions above as a guide.

E. After about ten minutes of discussion, have different people take the roles (unless one or two want to play them again) and try other tactics that may have occurred to you while watching the role-play or during the discussion.

F. Again, let the players say how they felt.

G. Discuss this version of the scene, using the same guide.

H. Replay as many times as there are ideas in the group for different ways to get the desired results.

I. Now that you have tried out and discussed the alternative strategies for approaching people from different disciplines and trying to get them interested in listening to presentations and giving input to nursing care plans, what generalizations can you derive from the experience?

1. What skills have you identified as necessary for involving people in other disciplines?
2. Are some ways more useful than others to involve people in interdisciplinary communication?
3. What generalizations can you make about people in other disciplines?
4. What generalizations can you make about nurses?
5. Does the idea of initiating a process for forming interdisciplinary health care teams seem less difficult now?

EXERCISE 2

A. If you prefer not to try mobilization on your own, try this before you do Exercise 3: Among your classmates or your colleagues on the job, identify one or two who may agree with you about the value of interdisciplinary collaboration in planning for patient care. They need not be as enthusiastic as you are about the matter; it is important only that they be willing to discuss it and then, perhaps, participate in the initial step of the process. They can, at first, become involved in some of the gathering of information on interdisciplinary collaboration. Then they can share in developing the plan for approaching people in other disciplines and raising questions with them concerning a particular patient.

The support provided by like-minded people can get you all through the discomfort of the first stages of initiating change. In addition, all of you can make up the steady nucleus of the group that continues to provide leadership for the change process.

B. When you first get together, you might start by discussing the question: What are my feelings when I talk to a physician? (Or to a dietitian, a social worker, a psychiatrist, an aide, etc.)

C. When you have revealed your feelings with candor and have discovered shared feelings, identify the feelings in yourself you would like to change, to reduce in intensity, or to eliminate altogether.

If, for example, you have all the physical and psychological manifestations of fear when you speak to a senior physician, to what do you attribute this fear? Are you afraid of the consequences of speaking to him? Can you identify these possible consequences?

1. Are you afraid he will snub you, ignore what you say?

1. Plan to approach him when there is no one else near him. Plan to face him when you speak. This would generally require that he be sitting down or standing still. Do not initiate the conversation when he seems to be very involved in an activity, such as writing complicated orders. Try to engage his complete attention with a provocative opening statement like, "Doctor Blank, can you help me?"

2. Are you afraid he thinks you are not important, that your function is not worthwhile?

2. Review what the literature and your own experience have taught you about the effects of nursing care on patients and the effects of lack of such care. Clarify for yourself those aspects of care and treatment that are uniquely nursing— quite independent from medical or other treatment.

Review humanistic philosophy (refer to Maslow[9], for example) and deduce the humanist's assessment of anyone who thinks another person is not important. The point is that if you get cues that a physician, or anyone else, believes you are not worthwhile, you may confidently conclude that the problem is *his,* that there is something wrong with *him.* There are people who have such profound feelings of inadequacy that they cannot live with themselves unless they are forever reassuring themselves that others are inferior.

3. Are you afraid he will think you are ignorant or incompetent?

3. Make sure that the question you ask him is so clearly within the area of his own special competence that he could not reasonably expect someone in another discipline to have the answer.

4. Are you afraid he will misunderstand your approaching him?

4. Whatever motives he may attribute to your approaching him will sooner or later be reflected in what he says and does. If he has any misconceptions, you can correct them then. In the meantime, plan to focus on the question and on the objectives of your change plan, maintaining a pleasant but serious demeanor in all your interactions.

EXERCISE 3

In your clinical setting, prepare a number of questions about a particular patient the answers to which can make significant contributions to the patient's care. Each question should relate to the area of knowledge represented by a different discipline. For example, if the patient has had a colostomy, the questions might be:

For the social worker. What kinds of problems does a patient with this kind of disability often have with members of his family when he returns home?

For the physician. What is generally the nature, location, and frequency of pain both pre- and post-operatively in cancer of the bowel and permanent colostomy?

For the psychiatrist. What are the data on the contribution a well-rehabilitated ostomate can make to a patient's post-operative adjustment?

For the nurse's aide. How do you think people feel when they have to look at or care for a person who has had a colostomy? (This kind of question may give the nurse some clues to feelings and attitudes that the patient may experience immediately after the operation. If he is not prepared to cope with these attitudes, no matter how subtle the clues are, he may experience shock and dismay.)

For the dietitian. What foods are more likely to cause gas and offensive odor after permanent colostomy?

For the pharmacist. What is the current state of the art and the future of drug therapy to help make management of colostomy easier?

Approach each one of these people and ask the appropriate question. (This kind of approach is rarely difficult to make. Generally, we are able to make a request for knowledge from someone who knows more than we do about something. Part of the reason for this is that we know that the other person will probably be pleased to answer, because we are implying by the request that we appreciate his expertise. In addition, we ourselves are not usually threatened by such an approach, because we are asking questions about a subject not in our own area of expertise; that is, we are not betraying an inappropriate ignorance.)

Each time you get an answer from someone, ask him if he would mind letting one or more of the other people hear his answer, because there seems to be a need for some exploration of the relationships between the answers. Say that you don't think it's a good idea to try to communicate the other people's answers because you may not do them justice. For example, if the social worker tells you that the patient's wife and family must be included in the plan to care for the patient, and the nurse's aide tells you that she—and, she believes, most people—feel horror and disgust when they must care for a colostomy patient, consider how this information can be reconciled to achieve optimal care of the patient.

Ask if they can make time—ten or fifteen minutes at 1:30 that afternoon—to exchange information. Don't be concerned if all of them are unavailable; meet with those who can make it. Stopping at this time to go through the frustrating procedure of finding a time that is convenient for everyone may abort the whole project. Some people may get scared off because it begins to sound too formal and time-consuming; others may feel annoyed at being left out when, after all the juggling of times, a meeting is arranged when they are unable to attend. So, just keep it as casual as possible. What comes out of that first meeting should serve to motivate people to continue with the process.

After this first meeting is set up, report back to your class or to those colleagues with whom you role-played in preparation for initiating the change. Together, you may review what you said and the responses you got. Perhaps you feel that you would have said or done some things differently, given a second chance. (You might role play alternative behaviors and see what responses you get.)

Now you may want to plan a procedure for the interdisciplinary meeting, so that:

1. The meeting is reasonably short. Long meetings are not appreciated by busy people, and may make them reluctant to continue the process.

2. You are clear about what you want to achieve. Since the meeting was your idea, you ought to be able to communicate to the others just what you hope to get out of it. At the end of the meeting you should be able to make a statement indicating how the patient's care will be affected by the meeting.

3. You can review your own function in the meeting. Bear in mind that

people in meetings have personal as well as professional needs, and, unless those needs are satisfied, they will not seek out this experience again. Watch to see that everyone gets the opportunity to speak, that he is listened to and responded to with appreciation. When controversial issues are aired, sum up the points made as objectively as possible, keeping the focus on the scientific data and off the personal feelings involved. If the group continues to meet, such feelings must be dealt with openly and honestly, or they will impede the work of the group. At the outset, however, it may be preferable to enable everyone to come away from the meeting with the conviction that his point of view has been given a fair hearing.

Eventually you or another member of the group may raise the question of instituting interdisciplinary collaboration as an integral part of patient care. It is at this time that the process of information-gathering, carried on by interested people, can begin. In the information-gathering exercises in Chapter 3, not only do you gather relevant information about the people affected by a specific change, but you as the initiator involve them in the first steps of the process. You raise questions with them concerning current practices in an attempt to start them thinking about those practices. You identify a variety of behaviors and start them thinking about the relationship of those behaviors to their professional goals. Sometimes people seem to be disagreeing about a desired outcome when they are really disagreeing because (a) they are not all aware of what is really happening; (b) they don't all agree on what is important or most important; or (c) they don't all have the same scientific information. Getting as many people as possible involved in gathering information helps them fill gaps in their knowledge and contributes to developing a commitment to planning for change. The preceding exercises have provided strategies for getting people involved in the change process— the process of mobilization.

NOTES

[1] Fred E. Fiedler, *A Theory of Leadership Effectiveness*, (New York: McGraw-Hill Book Company, 1967) pp. 240-246.

[2] D.C. McClelland and D.H. Burnham, "Power is the Great Motivator," *Harvard Business Review*, 1976, Vol. 54, 100-109.

[3] Kurt Lewin, Ronald Lippett and Robert K. White, "Patterns of Aggressive Behavior in Experimentally Created 'Social Climates,'" *Journal of Social Psychology* (1939), Vol. 10, pp. 271-299.

[4] John Cowan, *The Self-Reliant Manager* (New York: AMACOM, 1977), p. 122.

[5] Margaret M. Moloney, *Leadership in Nursing—Theories, Strategies, Actions*, (St. Louis: C.V. Mosby, 1979), pp. 62-63.

[6] Ibid., p. 171.

[7] K. Benne, *A Conception of Authority*, (New York: Teachers College, Columbia University Press, 1943), p. 158.

[8] Moloney, op. cit., p. 71.

[9] Abraham Maslow, *Motivation and Personality*, (New York: Harper and Row Publishers, Inc., 1954).

chapter two

The Nurse Leader As Teacher

Professional Education[1]

The essential problem for teachers of the professions appears to be the difficulty of integrating professional school experience with work experience. Almost all new graduates of professional schools are faced with the realization that the people they encounter on the job, even those with less schooling, often seem able to make more competent decisions merely by virtue of their experience. Also, those professionals who have been on the job for some time are quick to inform the new person that what she was taught in school will not serve her very well on the job. The nurse on the job who assumes leadership in education can significantly raise the level of nursing practice in her immediate sphere of influence and, perhaps, in the profession as a whole, not only by encouraging change on the job, but by supporting new nurses in their use of the most recently developed data and skills.

The concept of school as "ivory tower" and the perception of the teacher as "idealistic" and unaware of the demands of "the real world" is probably the most uneconomical concept in the preparation of professionals—uneconomical of time and of professional effectiveness. To spend two to six years learning a profession only to be compelled to unlearn, modify, and adapt what has been learned is disheartening, and can result in cynicism and a diminution of commitment to excellence in practice. Even more significant, the quality of service to the client or patient is inevitably diluted in the name of "realistic" compromise. We teach the best of what we know, often only to see it subverted because of "lack of time," "lack of money," "lack of competent staff," "lack of space," even lack of "good" patients, students, or clients. I propose that most of these reasons are merely rationalizations that develop because students are not permitted to use all they know and are not helped to deal with the fears of change, inertia, cynicism, and hostility they encounter on the job.

The leadership function in educating professionals, then, would take two forms: (a) developing a system of professional education that will insure the carry-over to the work site of the professional principles and practices taught in school; (b) developing a system of in-service education for people on the work site to reinforce practices learned in school.

The missing factor

The strategies of higher education, including professional education, have gained nothing from at least a century of accumulation of knowledge and skills in teaching. Most instructors in college classrooms stand at the front of the room and talk to a sea of faces blurred by reading glasses. Occasionally a more or less intelligible illustration is made on the chalkboard; occasionally, a question is asked by the instructor or an assertive student. The information read from the instructor's notes is more or less accurately transcribed into students' notes, then memorized for transfer to examination papers.

The teaching of leadership follows this pattern. Theories of leadership, research in leadership, presumptive leadership skills, and evidence on the need for leadership are all presented. However, students are rarely given the opportunity to make creative inferences from the literature (and thereby, perhaps, to see ways for assuming leadership that are uniquely their own). Nor is there time allotted for them to practice identified leadership skills before they go into the clinical setting, so that they may start their work experience at a reasonable level of ability.

The competency-based movement in education has urged the incorporation of this intervening step in professional education between the acquisition of knowledge and the field practice. Provision is to be made, in the sheltered setting of the college, university, or hospital education site, for students to use their knowledge and try out their skills in simulated situations, where errors are not dangerous to the client or threatening to the student's self-concept.

There are a number of difficulties associated with providing such opportunity for skill development, but they are not insurmountable. One is the obvious need to increase the length of time between entrance into a professional program and the beginning of clinical experience. Perhaps this can be offset by decreasing the time needed for precertification experience in the clinical setting. Students coming into the hospital or other health agency with a fairly high level of competency should be ready sooner to assume independent responsibility for doing the job.

Having time for simulated practice does not mean that the student should be denied experience in the field until he is professionally competent. On the contrary, very early opportunity to systematically observe the on-site operation of a profession is important in reinforcing the student's decision to become a part of that profession (or, conversely, convincing the student early enough that the wrong decision was made in choosing the profession). Early experience is also important in helping the student assess his own developing knowledge and skills, comparing them to the knowledge and skills demonstrated by seasoned professionals. Nor should the student be compelled to wait until he has reached a certain level of all the needed knowledge and skills before beginning to practice in the field. He should be permitted to practice a skill in the clinical setting as soon as competency is gained in that particular skill.

The second difficulty with insisting on skill before clinical experience is the problem of defining clearly the minimum level of competency necessary, so that students will know exactly what they are working toward. Students should be assessed in such a way that they know exactly where they fell short and what they need to do to reach the required level of competency. All of this requires the breaking down of complicated professional behaviors into simpler skills that can be learned in sequence. It also requires that plans and materials be provided for the learning of each skill. Often, there must also be alternate strategies so that students with different learning styles and different levels of cognitive and skill development may use different routes to achieve competency.

For example, when a nursing teacher tells a student that she must be able to get all members of her team to participate in discussions of care plans, the teacher needs to analyze the "ability to get people to participate in discussions," and identify the specific skills that make up the ability. One such skill is formulating nonthreatening questions to ask the group. The student should actually write such questions and submit them to a factor checklist to see if they meet the specifications for encouraging responses: for example, the question does not single out a particular person in the group to answer; the question is phrased so that there is no right or wrong answer; the question is phrased so that it does not require merely a yes or no response; the question is phrased so that everyone can answer from the perspective of her own knowledge and experience.

When the student practices writing questions, she is able to check them against the list and make the necessary changes. She will know when she has the skill.

After she has learned several such skills, she may be ready to lead a small discussion group and practice the learned skills. If the group is made up of her classmates rather than her supervisees or clients, any errors she makes in attempting the integration of the various skills can be checked and opportunity provided for a second or a third chance to succeed. Only when the student, her peers, and her instructor agree that the minimum level of competency has been demonstrated can the student proceed to the clinical setting where she may lead small-group discussions when the appropriate opportunity arises.

The clinical experience

In most professional education today, time is allotted for clinical experience, to give the student an opportunity to practice what he is learning in his classes. From what we know about learning, we can identify certain factors that must be a part of the clinical experience if the student is to get the optimum benefit. For example, the student needs systematic opportunity to relate specific practices to professional objectives and knowledge in the field, to generic skills developed and used in human relationships, to specific objectives of the agency or hospital and the special information developed there, and to the distinctive skills of the agency or hospital.

Systematically making such relationships helps to reduce the effects of the disorganized nature of on-site practice. That is, in a hospital, one does not always have the opportunity to practice skills in order of difficulty or logic. The skills needed during any single affiliation period may range from simple to complex. The knowledge required may be basic or highly specialized. Generally, the situation must be dealt with as it occurs. Only by going back over it and examining it in retrospect can the student clarify the knowledge base and the outcomes of his behavior. Such repeated introspection helps him add to his knowledge and refine his skills.

In addition, the student needs experience not only in situations that are common in the work situation, but also in situations that do not occur often. "The essential problem is that day-to-day demands of the job come into conflict with the systematic pattern of instruction-practice-feedback-instruction-practice so necessary in education. For example, student nurses are often exposed to the conflict between what their clinical instructors expect them to practice and what the director of nursing service expects of them in the hospital, where patient care rather than teaching/learning is the primary concern."[1] Leadership in this area involves working with the affiliation agency to resolve the conflicting demands of service and education. It also involves working in the professional school to obtain the necessary commitment to adequate clinical experience.

In-service Education

Of course, the directors of nursing service and nursing education are strategically situated to teach the technical aspects of nursing by modeling. Their leadership function can easily include time allotted for working side by side with the other nurses on the staff. Their credibility in teaching and in requests for optimum levels of service can be enhanced by the quality of the nursing they provide themselves. If they are not directly involved in practicing nursing, the leadership roles assigned to them by virtue of their positions may never become true leadership roles; they will forever be fighting against beliefs that "those front-office managers" don't really know what the requirements of the job demand.

Education leadership by administrators of nursing service and nursing education requires the same kinds of structural amenities as education leadership of students. If regular times are not scheduled for education, if plans are not regularly developed for dealing with the various topics of knowledge and skill, then in-service education becomes one of those things that we ought to have but we never quite get to. It becomes a piecemeal, hit-and-miss affair of lectures on discrete topics that may or may not be well attended, or lectures in the disciplinary sense of scoldings for deficiencies of one kind or another.

Generally, nursing supervisors should have the main responsibility for ongoing education of the staff in their area of supervision. The supervisor whose supervisees feel free to raise questions, to request special topics for systematic exploration and, finally, to assume the responsibility for their own in-service education, is an education leader in the best sense of the concept. She is also a supervisor whose staff members perceive her as a colleague and are encouraged to profit from her knowledge and experience by consulting her when problems arise. Thus she is a leader not only because she has been hired to fill a certain position, but because the people around her accept her as their leader.

Commitment to education

Educators of nurses—whether they work at education full time in a school setting or educate as part of their administrative and supervisory duties— have similar problems vis-à-vis their organizations. These problems involve getting total commitment to optimum education from institution policymakers, and then getting action on the commitment.

Even in institutions where education is the ostensible objective, a gap often exists between the commitment to optimum education and educational practices. We all know that schools for children often form classes too large for effective education, hire unqualified teachers, and practice management policies (for example, employing "permanent substitutes" to avoid paying regular fringe benefits) that mitigate against good professional practice. Universities, too, fail to provide many elements of good education, though their spokespersons maintain that good education is the reason for their existence. They may remove courses from their curricula because a minimum number of students do not enroll in them, even though the courses are known to provide significant learning options for those who can profit from them. They crowd enormous numbers of students into classes, so that a sheaf of lecture notes can be used as a substitute for a viable learning experience.

In nursing programs, as in other professional programs, more students are assigned to clinical instructors than can be effectively supervised. In addition, institutions are often selected for clinical affiliation on the basis of expediency rather than because they can provide the best kind of educational experience. Above all, people who educate professionals may not have the knowledge and skills necessary for effective teaching. Many of them realize this and struggle alone to gain the needed skills. Unfortunately most of them do not realize this, and use as teaching models their own teachers who were similarly unprepared.

Planning for teaching

How can the nurse educator provide leadership in getting what is necessary if her students are to be educated?

1. *She must systematically identify others in her institution who agree with her that the commitment to optimum education must be made and then honored in education practices.* There is nothing to be gained by operating on the premise that the nurse educator is alone in her concern about the quality of education being provided. Nor is such a premise likely to be accurate. What so oftens happens is that when we become aware of the deficiencies, we neglect the next step: checking to see who is also aware of them. This neglect is relatively easy in a hospital setting, for example, where most people are not directly concerned with education. It is not so easy, but nonetheless common, in educational institutions, where faculty members do their teaching in isolation from other faculty members and come together for functions unrelated to the ideal objectives of the university. Often, each teacher believes that the others are content to operate ineffectively, and they rarely meet to share their mutual discomfort.

2. *The educator and those who agree with her must set up priorities of educational practice and develop a plan for instituting the desired practices.* Before starting this, they need to gather information that makes clear the relationship between effective professional functioning and the factors in optimum education. Some of the available information is based on systematic research. For example, we have research data that indicate that teachers who provide more opportunity for students to speak about what they are learning, to identify their own learning objectives and plan for reaching them, to use subject content to solve relevant problems, and to ask questions are more likely to have students who understand and retain what is being taught. Learning situations involving so many students that instructors rely on lecturing to "cover" the content are not likely to result in the most competent professional practice.

Another example is the evidence we have that rewards reinforce behaviors. The rewards on a hospital unit that always has two staff fewer than it should may go to those who work fast. The approbation of supervisors and preferred work schedules may go to those who quickly carry out the assigned tasks and have neat and physically-cared-for patients. All the nursing principles we subscribe to about treating the whole person, all the care plans we study that include providing for patients' affective needs, will not change the limited approach to nursing practice on this unit, will not get nurses to take the time to sit at a patient's side and let him cry out his grief.

Other information is based on logical reasoning and a general knowledge of human behavior. An example of this is the realization that extremely anxious people are less likely to learn efficiently. Thus, a rigid, authoritarian supervisor who enforces her regulations by intimidation interferes with the learning of supervisees.

The group of people who have identified each other as uncomfortable enough to begin to plan for change can initiate the process by speaking to others about what they have already discovered concerning the discrepancies between what is happening and the institution's stated objectives. They can start by identifying priorities in terms of those objectives, drawing into the deliberations as many people as possible who will ultimately be affected by any changes.

3. *Part of the plan must include monitoring and feedback devices to maintain control over the system, so that it does not slip back into old ways because of the pressures of customary contingencies.* For example, when money is tight, sound educational practice should not be the first thing sacrificed to economy. When there are internecine power struggles, educational principles should not be subverted. When new people come into the system, they should not be permitted to operate in violation of the best available knowledge in the field. Above all, there should be continuous feedback from every element in the system; no factor—especially, no human being is so unimportant that he does not have valid information for maintaining the self-correcting properties of a good system.

As we learn from the systems approach to thinking, objectives of any system must be defined operationally or there is no viable way of ascertaining whether or not they have been achieved. If we look at an instructional system—a plan for teaching—as a device for enabling a student to do something that he could not do before he entered the system, then we can begin to see what a behavioral objective is.

Nor is it only the student for whom the teacher must define behavioral objectives. Objectives for the patient, too, need formulation so that the nurse may evaluate the outcomes of any treatment modality.

Many times, teaching objectives sound like the kinds of systems outcomes that are used for publicity purposes and to make systems managers feel good. A health maintenance organization (HMO) whose stated objective is to teach its clients to "appreciate the importance of preventive medicine" sounds laudable. But how does the HMO find out whether clients do, indeed, "appreciate"? They must do or say things that indicate such "appreciation," or no one can know that they appreciate. If ninety per cent of the HMO's clients come regularly for a medical examination, even when they have no discomfort or other symptoms of illness, then one may infer that they appreciate the importance of preventive medicine. The objective, then, would be better defined in terms of the clients' behavior: Ninety-five per cent of the HMO's membership will undergo routine medical examination every twelve months. This is an objective that is easy to evaluate. If the objective is not achieved, the system may be reexamined and corrected on the basis of the feedback data.

Similarly, the nurse who includes in her nursing care plan a plan for teaching must be sure that her teaching (or, more properly, learning) objectives are stated in terms that provide accurate feedback, so that she may determine the success of her teaching plan. How can anyone tell when the patient has learned not to be afraid of exerting himself lest he bring on another heart attack? We can only observe certain behaviors; we cannot see a lack of fear. Objectives in this instance may be: The patient will list the causes of heart attack. The patient will describe what he must do to minimize the risk of heart attack. The patient will do certain exercises each day. The patient will volunteer the information that his fear of bringing on another heart attack is virtually gone.

The supervisor, too, must plan for teaching, whether it takes place in a formal, scheduled meeting or is done in a one-to-one situation where either she or her supervisee initiates the teaching/learning process. There is little to be gained by complaining, "I keep *telling* her and *telling* her how to do it!" Obviously, the "telling" is not resulting in a change of behavior. Identifying the desired target behaviors and sharing this identification with the learner, can remove some of the confusing background "noise" that interferes with learning. The fear of failing, the fear of losing face, the feeling of embarrassment, the fear of reprimands and even loss of a job constitute psychological "noise" that tends to drown out the teacher's communication.

However, when both supervisor and supervisee can agree on the target behavior, preferably not the total procedure all at once, then it becomes easier to devise methods that lead to that behavior. When the behavior has been demonstrated, the feeling of success makes it easier to learn the other behaviors that make up the total procedure.

For example, when a nurse must develop a teaching plan as part of her nursing care plan, she may feel overwhelmed at the prospect of having to ascertain the readiness of the patient to learn, the significant sociocultural data, and the specific steps in the teaching process. There seem to be so many things she needs to know how to do in order to complete a teaching plan! However, if we take one part of the planning process at a time and identify specific behaviors that the nurse needs to demonstrate in completing the process the learning is easier to contemplate and to manage.

What must the nurse do or say to find out whether the patient or the supervisee is ready to learn? First, the nurse must listen. The clearest sign of anyone's readiness to learn is that he asks specific questions requesting information. Often, teachers ignore questions because they want to communicate certain information that is not covered by the questions. Though they may feel that what they have to teach is more relevant to the patient's problem, teachers should remember that nothing is more relevant than what is on the learner's mind, if only because what is on his mind may block out other communication. It is more efficient to respond to the learner's questions and then find some way of connecting his concerns with what the teacher thinks he ought to know.

Readiness to learn may also be indicated by the learner's level of knowledge. A quick question or two can ascertain whether the learner knows the relationship between exercise and the circulatory system, or if he thinks that being very quiet and moving as little as possible will keep his heart working longer and so keep him alive.

The learner's general perception of himself and his life situation also provides evidence of readiness to learn. Someone who is reluctant to assume responsibility, someone who wants to be told what to do on the job instead of using his own judgment, someone who wants to be tended rather than be independent will give hints of this to the teacher/observer/supervisor. Sometimes a direct question will bring this to light: Would it make you more comfortable if I gave you one job at a time, or would you like to list everything that has to be done and plan the whole day for yourself? Or a leading comment may be made: After rearing a family, I'll bet you don't mind letting people take care of you for a change. If someone wants to be dependent, he will resist efforts to teach him skills that will make him independent. He is just not ready to learn them.

Once the teacher determines the patient's—or the supervisee's— readiness to learn, she can take the next step: define objectives that indicate readiness, or define objectives that indicate learning that is more directly job related or health-related.

Thus, taking one component of planning at a time, the teacher can lead the learner to recovery and health, or to providing optimal health care.

Teaching in Nursing Care

The essential leadership function in the nurse-patient relationship is an educational one. If the nurse leader is truly an effective, humanistic teacher, she also becomes a learner in the relationship.

Learning from patients and clients

Take, for example, the case of the patient who is convinced that he cannot move about the way he did before he became ill. Effective leadership here means that the patient will learn that he can move and will begin to do so. However, in order to achieve this objective, the nurse must permit the patient to teach her about himself. That is, she cannot just develop a care plan that includes exercises and expect that the patient will learn to do those exercises because she says he will. She must first *learn the patient,* read him to discover what must go into her care plan: (a) What, exactly, does he believe would be the consequences of his moving about? Is he afraid his condition will become worse if he resumes his normal activity? Is he afraid he will feel pain if he moves? Does he believe that when he feels pain it means that he is doing himself irreparable damage when he moves? (b) What does he want out of life that requires his moving or his not moving? Does he hate his job? Has he realized that being ill gives him a legitimate reason for not working, and now is he consciously or unconsciously prolonging his illness? Does he enjoy the pampering and attention that he never gets when he is well? Is he happy to be relieved of family responsibilities that have become increasingly burdensome? (c) Who are the people in his life about whom he care most? Does he have a child with whom he loves to play baseball or go on trips? Does he love his wife very dearly? Has he a sister or a good friend whose esteem he values? Does he feel a great sense of responsibility for the welfare of an aged parent or a younger brother?

Learning the patient may not be a simple process of asking direct questions and obtaining clear answers. The patient may not want to give the answers directly, and questioning may be resented and resisted. But the nurse leader knows that a good teacher is an excellent listener, and that the patient will teach her what she needs to learn if she is willing to wait.

How does the patient teach the nurse what she needs to know about him? What are the clues she must listen for? If, every time he makes a move, he stops with the comment, "It hurts too much; it's worse when I move," it may indicate that he is fearful that there will be no top limit to the pain he will feel if he continues to move. He imagines that the pain will increase in intensity until it is unbearable and that he must at all costs avoid causing himself such anguish.

Or, when urged to move the patient may say, "It doesn't hurt now; I don't want it to start hurting the way it did before." He has equated pain with the onset of the illness, and is reluctant to change anything in the current situation now that he no longer has the pain.

Like so many people, he may believe that his own inappropriate behavior was the immediate cause of the illness and the pain: "I worked too hard; I ran around too much." He is unwilling to resume his pattern of behavior for fear of a recurrence of the illness.

He may think that the pain he feels is a message that his body is being damaged each time he moves, and that only keeping still will prevent this damage. He tells a story about the time he cracked a rib and was told by the doctor long afterwards that, if he hadn't kept very quiet and breathed very carefully, he might have punctured his lung. He may believe that keeping quiet is the way to give his body "a chance to heal."

None of these viewpoints may be very clear in a person's mind. He may be unable to articulate them when asked a direct question. But if the nurse listens while giving routine care and doesn't push too hard to institute the rehabilitation plan, she will learn what strategy can be used to get the patient to share in defining objectives for recovering his health.

Teaching patients and clients

At this point it is the nurse leader's turn to teach. The giving of accurate information is a part of teaching, but a person with an emotional investment in holding on to what he thinks he knows will not accept the new information. A vital part of teaching is providing experiences for the learner that will make him receptive to new data. Introducing him to a patient who is recovering successfully from a similar condition and leaving them alone to share experiences is one way of preparing him to take an active part in his own recovery. Giving the necessary information to the person he cares most about or respects greatly, and letting that person relay the information to him is an effective strategy.

Though it may sound cumbersome for a hospital setting, an audiovisual aid can provide an effective vicarious experience. For example, a film depicting the recovery of someone with the same illness can influence the person to reevaluate his beliefs and consider changing his behavior. (Making such films is a research and education function that few nurses think of. Yet what could be more useful in our television era than good video materials for teaching?)

When the patient begins to ask questions and make statements that indicate a readiness to consider planning for health objectives, the change may commence. Questions like, "Do you think if I tried to move my arm, I could get it to work the way it used to?" show that the patient is beginning to ponder cause-and-effect relationships in his condition, and he may be ready to identify outcomes that he desires.

Comments like, "I guess when it hurts it could be just that I'm not used to moving any more," reveal a changing perception of the causes of pain that may lead to a decision to change behavior.

It is at this time that the nurse can raise the question, "How many steps do you think you could take by the end of the week if you started with just one step today?" Such cooperative goal-setting can reduce anxiety in the patient because he remains in control of the objective. If he sets it too low, the nurse should not insist on her own more realistic goal for him. When he succeeds in taking the first few steps, that success will motivate him to raise his own sights without pushing from anyone else. What the nurse can do is remind him periodically of how far he has come, so that his success remains fresh in his mind. There is no more motivating factor in learning than previous success.

It may seem that such deliberate planning for teaching is unrealistically time-consuming; busy professionals, with their own clear objectives in mind, consider the approach inefficient and become impatient with it. Perhaps those who undertake to lead others should consider that, ultimately, the success of leadership depends on the willingness of followers to be led. An inordinate amount of time is spent by professional teachers in trying to teach people who are neither ready nor willing to learn. Most of us are aware of the end result of this: the large numbers of people who leave school early and the even larger numbers who leave uneducated. What a waste of time and lives! Better to put some of that time into planning and motivating for learning. Then, long after teachers are gone from their lives, people will continue to learn and grow.

For nurses, evaluation of their teaching function must be intimately related to their definition of nursing. If nursing merely means doing things to people, then an enumeration of the nurse's activities is adequate evaluation of her competence and success. But contemporary nursing rejects this concept of the profession. Rather, the democratic, humanistic philosophy of nursing requires that nurses lead people to assume responsibility for achieving and maintaining their own health. Just getting people well enough to leave the hospital is not a nursing function. Getting them well enough to function at a minimal level of wellness is not competence. If people are to live their lives at the highest level of wellness possible, the only appropriate health care approach is one that motivates them to become involved in identifying their own objectives and in planning their own processes for achieving those objectives.

Research and Writing

There is another leadership function that may be considered a part of the education role of the nurse leader. This involves defining hypotheses based on experience in the field, systematically researching the validity of those hypotheses, and then writing up the results of the researches and publishing them for the use of the rest of the profession. Pushing back the frontiers of knowledge is a leadership function that few people undertake, yet without it the profession stagnates. The only significant new data are adopted from other fields, and problems unique to the profession go unsolved.

Unfortunately, many nurses view research as an esoteric endeavor, requiring mysterious skills and selfless commitment. Actually, research is merely a systematically managed thinking process that anyone who is reasonably knowledgeable can learn. The scientific method is the rational approach to problem solving, the systems approach to thinking. It does not require any more special training than does learning how to think clearly.

You may remember from your reading in introductory science courses that the scientific method has the following steps: (a) Identify a problem, (b) gather all the available information concerning that problem, (c) set up a plan for gathering new data, (d) analyze the data, (e) draw conclusions, (f) test the conclusions where feasible, and (g) suggest additional research if needed.

Problem solving has the same steps. Systems approach to planning has the same steps. As professionals we are aware of the unsolved problems that prevent us from moving to where we need to be, prevent us from addressing the needs of individuals, of institutions, of our society, and of the world. Refining our skills in taking those steps in the scientific method will make competent researchers of us. Even more, it will contribute to the solution of the problems that plague us.

Research does not always require huge sums of money or even time away from the routine of daily work. Rather, it requires an acute awareness of a problem, determined application to observing events and phenomena that relate to the problem, and the willingness to formulate a hypothesis that may be tested for validity. Recently, two nurses, using as subjects infants and mothers in their clinical practice, tested systematically to see "whether or not the addition of sugar to foods consumed by babies early in their feeding significantly alters later preference of sweetened or unsweetened foods." They were able to contradict the common misconception that babies prefer sweet foods. They may have contributed to the reduction of the sugar addiction so prevalent in our society. This was a small, inexpensive, uncomplicated research project that may have far-reaching consequences, done by professionals who were particularly sensitive to the problem.[2]

Another recent study tested an attempt to teach compliance with standards for handwashing and found that "neither knowledge of fundamental asepsis nor attitudes toward infection control necessarily determined whether or not a nurse would comply with the handwashing policies of the unit. The visual evidence of microbial growth also did not affect compliance." The researchers' recommendation that new ways should be investigated to increase compliance with scientific principles is a serious one, based on a small but tight study conducted by two nurses, and having practical implications for nursing care and education.[3]

It is not always necessary to do research before writing for publication. Often, acute observation may reveal new insights from which the rest of the profession may profit. For example, one nurse pulled together the available information on cold-weather injuries and compiled practical lists of "Susceptibility Factors" and "How to Prevent Cold Injury," an invaluable aid for nurses who see prevention of illness and the maintaining of wellness as a major professional emphasis.[4]

We know that writing is difficult for many people. There is something about a blank page to be filled that chills the blood of the bravest individual. Also, many people have never learned to write clearly. Learning to write is worth the effort it requires. Struggling to communicate clearly on paper helps to clarify thinking. However, while we are trying to learn, it is not always necessary to delay contributing to the profession the results of our unique experiences. We can discuss our experiences with skillful writers in the field and collaborate with them to inform the profession. Competent researchers in all fields avail themselves of the writing skills of their colleagues. The objective is to get the new data into circulation for the purpose of improving professional practice—if not immediately, then ultimately.

I recently read a letter from a nurse who stated that reading the nursing journals kept her involved and interested in the profession while she was not practicing. She calls the writers she read "nursing's leaders, highly visible nurses," who helped her maintain her sense of place in the profession.[5]

Writing for publication lets the teacher use her knowledge and skill to change the whole profession, rather than just the people in her immediate work setting. A typical example is the article by Mary Lynch Fortin, who describes teaching nursing students about alcoholism. This article should have meaning for the many health professionals who encounter alcoholics on the wards and react to them with distaste, moral condemnation, and, perhaps, a reduction of motivation to give optimum care.[6]

Practicing Teaching Skills

Writing behavioral objectives

The objective of the following exercises is: You will define behaviorally objectives of teaching in your own situation.

First, think of a procedure that you would like someone to learn.

EXAMPLES OF PROCEDURES

1. Repositioning a patient regularly to avoid cubitus.
2. Establishing open, peer-status communication with other staff members traditionally perceived as having higher or lower status.
3. Substantially reducing the patient's fear of being discharged from the hospital.

Second, list all the behaviors that make up the procedure to be learned. (Remember, an attitude is not a behavior, a feeling is not a behavior. Only what a person says or does is a behavior.)

Each of these behaviors must be intrinsically rational. The learner is not likely to be motivated to learn a behavior that makes no sense to her.

EXAMPLE OF BEHAVIORAL ANALYSIS OF A PROCEDURE

Procedure. Establishing open, peer-status communication with other staff members traditionally perceived as having higher or lower status.

Behaviors required Greet a nonpeer with more than the customary open greeting of "Good morning."

The different levels of familiarity and openness leading to peer communication may be illustrated by the following comments:

Level 1 "How are you today?"
"Isn't the weather beautiful?"
Level 1 communication is generally stereotyped and conventional, asking not-quite perfunctory questions that offer the other person some choice of staying at Level 1 or going to a higher level of self-disclosure.

Level 2 "You're looking very well."
Level 2 communication offers a slightly more personal observation, and an implicit invitation to respond in kind. However, there is almost no risk involved; nonresponse from the other person may be interpreted as the usual kind of response to a perfunctory greeting.

Level 3 "I like that tie you're wearing!"
"Every bed is filled today—a full house!"
"I've been running since eight this morning. It's going to be one of those days!"
Level 3 expresses a feeling that is to the other person, to oneself, or to the work situation. The self-disclosure at this level carries some element of risk, since no response communicates indifference to the speaker's feelings.

Level 4 "Can you show me how to do this procedure? I'm not sure, but I think I'm leaving something out."
Level 4 is a direct request for communication. Not only does it require a response, but it reveals a need for information or a desire for help, and consequently entails some risk. The speaker is revealing that he is not perfect; he

is also implying that the other person is more competent, at least in the one area covered by the question.

The risk is reduced somewhat because most people are receptive to this kind of appeal; it gives them an opportunity to show what they know, and positive feelings are generated in teachers toward receptive students. There is also very little ego threat to the person who is asked to teach what he knows.

Level 5 "I really think the way we treat terminal patients here is superior to any other place I've worked."

Level 5 communication offers a positive, accepting opinion about an aspect of the work. It suggests, in fact, that not only is the speaker competent to judge in this area, but that her judgment is important enough to matter. It also intimates that the other person is himself important enough to have this judgment shared with him. The implication is that a negative judgment by the speaker would necessitate some reconsideration of the matter and might result in change.

These implications are of different kinds of significance, depending upon whether the person being addressed is of traditionally higher or lower status than the initiator of the communication. For example, the implication that the speaker is competent to judge may be more difficult to manage when speaking to a person of higher status. When speaking to a person in a lower-status role, the significant implication is that *he* is important enough to talk to about this.

Level 6 "I don't believe that we adequately prepare people for surgery or for what to expect after surgery. I think all personnel should participate in the preparation, and some planning and teaching should go on to develop skills for this kind of preparation."

Level 6 also offers an opinion, but a negative one. As with the positive opinion, it implies competency on the part of the speaker. It suggests that the speaker has the right to initiate a process of change, and that this communication is the first step in such a process.

There is a certain amount of risk in this level of communication. If the receiver of the communication is of higher status, he may perceive the criticism as a personal attack and he may counterattack. The counterattack could range from merely saying something hostile to arranging for the speaker to be removed from her job. However, experience has shown that the risks have been overestimated; though there may be an immediate angry or defensive reaction, the sincerity of the communication and the unhostile, self-confident delivery more often arouses interest and respect in the listener.

Level 7 "I have been reading the available evidence on the new bypass surgery, and there seems to be growing doubt that it is useful, except in relatively few cases."

Like Level 6 communication, Level 7 implies equal status between sender and receiver. The sender offers information that the receiver may or may not have, implying that both people have the right and the responsibility to be concerned about complicated work procedures and to discuss them openly. It implies a desire to learn more than basic job skills and the right to go beyond one's own discipline in trying to understand a job.

If the sender of the communication is of higher status than the receiver, it conveys the unspoken message that the receiver also has this right, this responsibility, and this desire.

All in all, it establishes a significant change in the pattern of communication between health personnel.

Third, determine the most appropriate order for learning the behaviors.

The behaviors for learning this procedure have been put down here in the order of difficulty. That is, each succeeding behavior violates to a greater degree the traditional etiquette between ranks in the hierarchy of the medical social order. Though they do not necessarily have to be learned in this order, it is probably easier for the learner to establish the less difficult levels of communication before going on to the more difficult ones.

Each new level is not entered upon "cold." The particular communication that typifies that level should be part of a longer conversation that goes on during work, during a meeting, during lunch or dinner, during a coffee break.

The "teacher" cannot always be present to hear a new level broached by the "student," so her teaching plan should include a step providing for systematic feedback: The student may report verbatim the conversaion that illustrates the achieved level of communication; the student may keep a daily log that records various relevant conversations and submit this log to the teacher; or the plan may provide for a "buddy system" in which peers observe each other and make notes of the significant conversations.

Fourth, now you are ready to develop a step-by-step process for teaching the first behavior. Only when the learner has demonstrated that first behavior should she be taken through the next step-by-step process for learning the second behavior on the list.

The learner who has achieved success in demonstrating several of the behaviors and been given explicit recognition by the teacher may leap ahead and demonstrate the total procedure without need for further systematic teaching. This happens when the learner knows some of the required behaviors but has not heretofore recognized their relevance to the total procedure. It may also happen when initial successes in learning encourage the learner to risk trying the other behaviors.

However, it probably will not happen if the learner does not know what all the target behaviors are and how they relate to the total procedure.

Consequently, one of the objectives in the step-by-step process for learning the first target behavior should be that the learner will list all the target behaviors and tell how they relate to the total procedure.

Analyzing the instructional milieu

One thing the effective teacher must do, whether she teaches children in a classroom or nurses on a hospital unit, is to analyze the teaching/learning situation to determine what may interfere with learning and what changes may be instituted that will improve the opportunity for learning.

One analytical approach has to do with changing inappropriate behavior. We may look at such behavior as a deliberate attempt to make us unhappy or to interfere with our professional performance. Whether represented by the child who refuses to stop talking or the patient who insists upon getting out of bed when total bed rest is prescribed, the problem faced by the professional is how to teach appropriate behavior.

Three factors may be examined as influencing the patient's behavior:

1. His motivation, what need he is trying to satisfy by his behavior.
2. The ability he has to satisfy that need.
3. His physical environment.

(This analytical process was suggested by Ojemann.)[7]

For example, look at the behavior of a patient who shouts at nurses and other staff people, demanding that they open the window, close the window, get his lunch, remove his tray, improve the food, open the door, shut the door, etc. From what we know about men in our culture and, perhaps, from what little more we know about this particular man, we may conclude that he is attempting to assert himself, to reassure himself by "proving" to everyone around him that he is still in control of his own life.

If we assign a weight of 100 to the observed behavior, and evaluate the other factors in terms of how strongly they influence the behavior, giving all three factors a total weight of 100, then we have a system that looks something like an equation:

$$\text{Motivating Forces} + \text{Resources} + \text{Immediate Physical Surroundings} = \text{Behavior}$$

If the patient's Motivating Forces (MF) are high, if for example he has a strong need to feel independent, then we would say that his MF was 70 (The values are, of course, not exact. This analytical system is not really an equation; it just approximates relative values for the purpose of having a model that facilitates understanding of the problem.)

When he is forced to lie flat on his back and accept the ministrations of other people—*a condition that is new for him*—his resources for maintaining a sense of independence are obviously very low. He simply does not know how to act independently enough to keep his self-esteem, without doing himself harm. We may value his resources at 5.

The physical surroundings, which include not only the hospital but the arrangement of the room furniture and even the people, probably contribute substantially to his dependence. The nurse aide who finds it more efficient to bathe him than to permit him to attend to his own bathing; the cleaner who manages to place his night table just out of his reach; the nursing supervisor who addresses him in the third person, very much the way some adults speak to children: "And how is William today?"; the staff physician who discusses him with the resident as if he weren't there—all add to his feelings of helplessness.

The result is behavior that only simulates independence. It makes the patient feel a little less helpless, but it doesn't really make him feel good about himself. It also interferes with his treatment in that it disturbs the people around him and reduces their effectiveness in his behalf.

The resulting analysis looks like this:

$$\underset{\substack{\text{MF} \\ \text{(Need for} \\ \text{independence)}}}{70} + \underset{\substack{\text{R} \\ \text{(Ability to} \\ \text{satisfy need)}}}{5} + \underset{\substack{\text{IPS} \\ \text{(People,} \\ \text{furniture and} \\ \text{hospital setting)}}}{25} = \underset{\substack{\text{B} \\ \text{(Demanding,} \\ \text{shouting,} \\ \text{characterized by} \\ \text{frustration and} \\ \text{anger)}}}{100}$$

From what we know about human behavior, it is not likely that we can reduce the strength of the drive to be independent. I, for one, would not want to do so if I could. We can see from the "equation" that the factors to be addressed are the individual's resources and his surroundings. It is well within our professional purview and our ability to add to his resources and to change his environment so that he can adequately satisfy his need for greater independence. We can give him clear signals that we understand and appreciate this need. We can provide him with opportunities to make his own decisions and control those aspects of his life that he is quite capable of controlling. In this way we help him to use appropriate ways of acting independently, thus increasing his resources for satisfying his need in ways compatible with his treatment. We can avoid behaving as if to imply that he is not the most important factor in the whole treatment process; we can arrange the furniture so that he can reach and use materials without asking for help, thereby adding still more to his resources.

Now, the chances are that his behavior is less demanding, less characterized by frustration and anger. The "equation" may now look like this:

70		25		5		100
MF	+	R	+	IPS	=	B
(Need for independence)		(Ability to satisfy need)		(Hospital setting)		(Non-demanding, quieter)

Dealing successfully with inappropriate behavior—of patients, of supervisees, of administrators—is a form of leadership behavior, in that it influences others to follow this approach. Rather than complaining, gossiping, and griping about the recurring inappropriate behavior and the person displaying it, the leader views the situation as an education problem to be solved. This approach reduces the level of annoyance and resulting personal animosity directed against the perpetrator of the behavior and frees the nurse to perform at an optimum level of professionalism.

NOTES

[1] Charlotte Epstein, *An Introduction to the Human Services*, (Englewood Cliffs, N.J.: Prentice-Hall, 1981), pp. 284–285.

[2] Marie S. Brown and Carol C. Grunfeld, "Taste Preferences of Infants for Sweetened or Unsweetened Foods," *Research in Nursing and Health* (1980), Vol. 3, No. 1, pp. 11–17.

[3] Maureen Moore and Nellie Kuhtik, "Can Handwashing Practices Be Changed?" *American Journal of Nursing*, Jan. 1980, p. 80.

[4] Tina Davis DeLapp, "Taking the Bite Out of Frostbite and Other Cold-Weather Injuries," *American Journal of Nursing*, Jan. 1980, pp. 56–60.

[5] Carol Ray, "Letter to the Editor," *American Journal of Nursing*, Feb. 1979, p. 245.

[6] Mary Lynch Fortin, "Detoxification: Then What? A Community Nursing Course in Alcoholism," *American Journal of Nursing*, Jan. 1980, pp. 113–114.

[7] R.H. Ojemann, *Personality Adjustment of Individual Children*, (Washington, D.C.: National Education Assn., American Educational Assn., No. 5, 1954).

chapter three

Leadership and Systems

The Systems Approach

The familiar poem that follows is often referred to in the systems literature as an example of how nonsystematic thinking can lead to gross error.

THE BLIND MEN AND THE ELEPHANT[1]
A Hindoo Fable

It was six men of Indostan
To learning much inclined,
Who went to see the Elephant
(Though all of them were blind),
That each by observation
Might satisfy his mind.

The *First* approached the Elephant,
And happening to fall
Against his broad and sturdy side,
At once began to bawl:
"God bless me! but the Elephant
Is very like a wall!"

The *Second,* feeling of the tusk,
Cried, "Ho! what have we here
So very round and smooth and sharp?
To me 'tis mighty clear

This wonder of an Elephant
Is very like a spear!"

The *Third* approached the animal,
And happening to take
The squirming trunk within his
hands,
Thus boldly up and spake:
"I see," quoth he, "the Elephant
Is very like a snake!"

The *Fourth* reached out an eager
hand,
And felt about the knee,
"What most this wondrous beast is
like
Is mighty plain," quoth he;
"'Tis clear enough the Elephant
Is very like a tree!"

The *Fifth* who chanced to touch the ear,
Said: "E'en the blindest man
Can tell what this resembles most;
Deny the fact who can,
This marvel of an Elephant
Is very like a fan!"

The *Sixth* no sooner had begun
About the beast to grope,
Than, seizing on the swinging tail
That fell within his scope,
"I see," quoth he, "the Elephant
Is very like a rope!"

And so these men of Indostan
Disputed loud and long,
Each in his own opinion
Exceeding stiff and strong,
Though each was partly in the right,
And all were in the wrong!
The Moral:
So oft in theologic wars,
The disputants, I ween,
Rail on in utter ignorance
Of what each other mean,
And prate about an Elephant
Not one of them has seen!

John Godfrey Saxe

Here the elephant, supposedly a clearly-defined system with unmistakable boundaries, is misperceived by "analysts" who come to conclusions based on inadequate information. The real joke, however, is on the author—the "systems scientist"—who, seeing more clearly than the blind men, thinks he truly understands the system. However, other scientists might legitimately raise such questions as: Does the skin of the elephant actually constitute the borders of the elephantine system, or are there other elements that must be included? Is what the elephant eats a part of the system? Are the flies that light on him and the microbes that live in him part of the system? To the extent that he affects other living things, including the human beings who care for him in captivity, are they part of the elephantine system?

In the final analysis there is only one system, a universal mechanism of interrelated subsystems. Perceiving the total system, identifying all its measurable outcomes, and planning comprehensive change is, at present, beyond us. We are not able to conceptualize and analyze everything at once. The best we can do is to identify a part of the system and call it our target or internal system, then work to understand it as completely as we can. We analyze it and plan to make it work better and more efficiently.

In dealing with systems that include human beings, as with mechanical systems, efficiency requires that the stated objectives coincide with the outcomes—the real objectives—of the system. Those outcomes must be observable and measurable if the validity of the system is to be established.

As an example, nurses learn early in their professional education that the major objective of hospital nursing is to bring a patient to optimum functioning while helping him to maintain his dignity and sense of self-worth. Yet many hospital procedures and practices, such as concealing from the patient information about his condition and details of treatment, make him dependent, violate his sense of self, and make him feel powerless. These are outcomes that are contrary to the stated objective. If the stated objective is indeed desirable and attainable, then changes must be instituted in the system so that it may be attained. This requires a clear picture of how the system works, as well as skill in instituting change.

Carol Taylor, in her study of a hospital, revealed that often the stated objectives are not consistent with the real outcomes and that often people are not even aware of the inconsistencies:

> I moved into other parts of the hospital in order to examine all the departments that directly or indirectly support the central function of the hospital which is to diagnose, to treat, and to care for patients.
>
> In each part of the hospital I did what I had done in the patient-care units: I began with structure, both formal and informal; and then examined the processes that gave the structure its purpose. In order to do so, I looked for four kinds of information. Information confirming and contradicting the institution's notion of how it had organized each of its parts to function. Information about how each part did, or did not do, whatever it was supposed to do. Information about what the people who worked in each department actually do and what they said they were doing, as well as each department's functional relationship with various departments and other parts of the hospital. In all parts of the hospital I found that people had organized themselves to function in ways that were different from those suggested by the organization chart. I also found that individuals described what they did, and what their departments did, in such a way as to contradict what I could observe being done. In a sense my study of the hospital was patterned on the contradictions that I found in it.[2]

A system is a model of operation—real or ideal—or an operating mechanism. It is a description of a pattern of interlocking events, or a machine made up of interlocking parts.

A systems approach is a process of observing what is, of thinking about what ought to be, and of planning for change. It is not completely new, nor is it an old approach dressed up in new terminology. It incorporates the principles of logic, the integration of Gestalt perceptions, the clarity of the scientific method, the honesty of the true humanist, and the language of the new technology. It is based on information: information about what is, information for defining realistically what ought to be, information to keep the process changing as necessary.

Beginning students of the systems approach often complain that the terminology and mechanics of systems analysis unnecessarily complicate what they would do in any case; that is, identify what needs changing and do something about it. However, if they stop to compare their old approach with a systems approach to solving a problem, they find that the old approach has usually omitted important information or a vital step, omissions that significantly increase the margin for error and the chances of failure. A systems approach to thinking is a necessary discipline for most of us, who may never really have been educated to think clearly. Rather, the emphasis in our education has been on conforming, following directions, and memorizing the results of other peoples' thinking.

People who are systemic in their approach to problem solving may have an advantage in their attempts to lead others toward more efficient and more humanistic functioning. The gathering of information and the systematic identification of alternative solutions is basic to the systems approach. The possibility of failure is taken into consideration in the building of the system, so the systems scientist or planner is not caught totally unprepared when the solution does not work. The planner may consequently be spared at least some of the emotional trauma resulting from failure.

Thus, armed with information, the systems planner/analyst is able to respond with confidence to most challenges to the validity of the plan. Able to project in advance a number of alternate routes to a solution, she can help sustain activity to change. Accepting the possibility of some failure before a successful solution is found, she is less likely to become discouraged and abandon her position of leadership.

A plan for change

Let us examine a particular problem faced by nurses and see how systemic thinking can lead to useful solutions. We can see also how a nurse leader can be instrumental in motivating the planning for change, and how she becomes identified not only with the successful change but also with the exciting and interesting change process.

A nurse practitioner is hired by a school system to work in a large city elementary school. In addition to the traditional school nurse functions—putting Band-Aids on scraped knees and treating nosebleeds—her duties include developing medical histories for each child in the school, making recommendations and referrals to care for medical and emotional needs, and working with the teachers to develop plans for managing children with special problems like seizure disorders.

Soon she is accepted as an important part of the school, and both faculty members and children seek her out for all kinds of problems. Mostly, however, she is used as the school nurse has usually been used, for minor medical problems that the teachers are happy to turn over to her. Though she has talked to the teachers and identified the children with special problems, the evidence she has is that teachers remember children with problems they identify as serious and usually forget which ones have lesser problems. When a crisis does occur in a classroom, the teachers rarely use the information given to them by the nurse; they merely send someone to fetch her so that she may deal with the crisis.

In addition to this state of affairs in the regular classrooms, something quite new is happening in the school. As a result of the passage of Public Law 94–142 (the Education for All Handicapped Children Act of 1975), children with various disabilities are being admitted to the school. Disabilities range from severe and profound retardation to specific learning disabilities, from mild locomotor disorders to inability to speak. The objective is optimum education for each child, to the limits of his ability.

Each morning, the "special" children are delivered by parents and bus drivers and congregate in the corridor outside the principal's office. While the size of the group increases, teachers and classroom aides also arrive, and stand or sit on the single bench, talking with each other and with some of the children.

When most of them have arrived, the adults take them to their classroom, which is three doors down from where they have been waiting. As the morning goes on, a lone child will wander in and remain in the corridor until an adult comes upon him and takes him to his classroom.

Though the objective of the law is to "mainstream" most of those children who have been kept separate or provided with no education at all, there is no attempt in this school to bring these children into classes with the so-called normal children. Those with severe disabilities are kept in one room all day, even eating their lunch at the same tables where they work. Those who get around and are able to communicate more easily go to the art and music teachers once a week, but as a group, having no contact with other children taking art and music. A few of the special children are allowed out alone at recess, where they may—if they can, and if they are accepted—interact with other children.

The nurse practitioner sees the whole matter of managing disabilities as a single problem, taking in the "normal" range as well as those considered "abnormal" or "special."

She begins to make some tentative connections between the ways in which teachers manage children with problems in their classrooms, and the way in which the "special" children are incorporated into the organization of the school. Can it be that both the administration and the faculty of the school are tacitly collaborating to ignore the mainstreaming mandate because they are reluctant to learn how to manage children with problems? Can it be that they feel incapable of such management, or is it just that they are unwilling to increase the amount of work they will have to do? Are there teachers in the school who are concerned with the problem, as she is? Will they be willing to discuss it with her?

She begins to think about a system for dealing with the problem:

STEP 1

Before she begins to get in touch with other people, she must be clearer in her own mind about what is happening, and also about what she wants to happen. This does not mean that she will rigidly maintain that her perceptions are completely accurate or lock in her objectives so they cannot be changed. Once the planning process gets under way, additional input may cause her to revise her original analysis.

However, if she wants to lead, she must have a general direction in mind, even if she subsequently discovers that the path is not linear, but filled with doglegs, detours, and backtracks.

She starts with a number of stated objectives of the education system that she believes are valid and attainable. One objective is to produce educated people, that is, people who function effectively in their lives. These are individuals who interact with others in productive and satisfying ways, are independent, earn their livings, participate in the operation of their communities, and generally feel good about themselves.

These objectives are consistent with the democratic ideals of our society and consistent with what we know about human growth and development. We believe in the worth of the individual and in his right to the opportunity for optimum development. Independence is one of our society's values. Democratic participation in the running of our communities and our country is also a value we hold.

From psychology, we learn that the individual grows and develops through the satisfaction of a hierarchy of needs—from basic biological needs for food and shelter, through the need for love and respect, to the highest need for self-actualization.

The nurse believes that the system as it operates in the school could contribute to the attainment of these objectives but is not doing so. She can identify practices that actually interfere with the attainment of those objectives. For example, children who are segregated into groups of so-called normals and specials have no opportunity to learn to interact effectively with each other, to accept each other as valuable, or to contribute to each other's growth and healthy development. Also, teachers who do not perceive their areas of concern as including children of all kinds do not have the opportunity to change their negative attitudes and behaviors. This limits their ability to teach children how to interact without prejudice and discrimination.

Knowing the ideal objectives of the education system in our society, the nurse-practitioner now looks at the real outcomes of the system in her school. She asks herself the question: What are the measurable objectives of the present system? She tries to cut through all those objectives that sound nice, that are articulated for public relations purposes, or that are dutifully repeated because those are the objectives the system is *supposed* to have. What she is looking for are the actual, measurable outcomes of the system as it currently functions.

In order to answer this question, she needs information. She needs to know what the children with disabilities feel about themselves. Though she has some information from individual children she has examined or treated, she knows that Teacher No. 1 has conducted a number of sessions with the children in her class dealing with self-concept. She will ask that teacher for information obtained from those sessions. She will also ask the special education teacher for information on her children's self-concepts.

She needs to know how normal children and special children interact. She already knows that most of the special children have no opportunity to interact with the normal children. Only a few, labeled learning-disabled, encounter them in the school yard at recess. She needs to be out in the school yard at recess time. Those children with problems who are in the regular classrooms should be observed in their classrooms as well as in halls and in the school yard before and after school and during recess.

For these observations she will need to be able to recognize the children with problems. She will also need a way to record her observations efficiently.

She can also obtain information about interactions in regular classrooms from some of the teachers.

She must refresh her memory about the data on the relationship between self-concept and learning and self-concept and success; and on the relationship between self concept, effective interaction, and life satisfaction.

She then lays out a tentative plan for starting the process. (In Figure 3-1 circles represent feedback. Diamond inserts represent decisions.)

In this case, further planning must involve a system for monitoring the measurable outcomes of the new organization for mainstreaming, and instituting changes as the need for them becomes apparent. The nurse-practitioner, who assumed leadership in this instance, motivated the teachers, principal, supervisor and parents to bring into closer harmony the ideal objectives of the teaching profession and the real outcomes of the children's school experience.

Components of the System

The interdisciplinary context and the informal organization

In addition to the leadership skills discussed elsewhere in this book, the nurse-practitioner needed some specific knowledge and skills associated with systems analysis and planning for change. She also needed certain sensitivities vital when working with systems containing human beings.

Probably one of the most significant skills is the ability to step outside the traditional constraints of a single discipline and approach problem-solving in an interdisciplinary context. A systems approach to thinking requires analysis of the flow of knowledge and material through a system. This flow is required to fulfill the objectives of the system and it cuts across the traditional disciplinary and departmental boundaries. ". . . Improvement

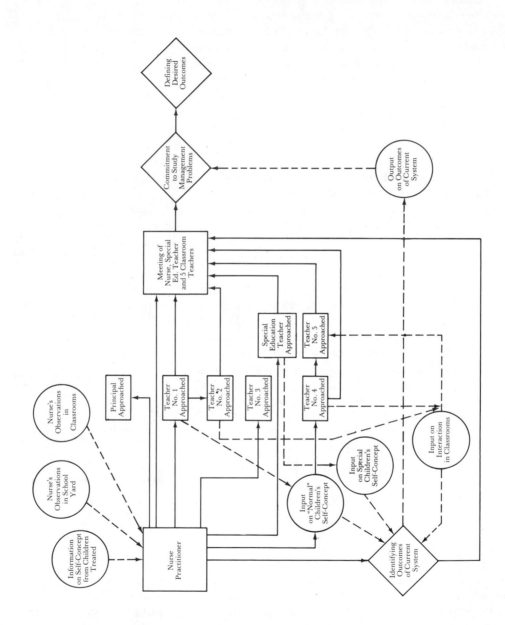

Figure 3-1. System Model for Initiating Process of Change.

in the enterprise as a whole requires the investigator to disregard formal boundaries, or to cross them at will."[3]

Thus, the nurse-practitioner in this case already embodied an interdisciplinary departure from the traditional school nurse functions. She had been certified as qualified to do extensive histories on the children, traditionally a physician's function; she had learned that an important part of her work was the continuing education of teachers in the management of children with medical and psychological problems; she had made a professional commitment to contribute directly to the optimum education of the children in her school. Though the school nurse historically was supposed to teach the children health and hygiene, the opportunities for doing so were sporadic and often unsatisfactorily limited. The need for teacher education was more often honored in the recognition of need than in the practice.

Armed with the knowledge that there is nothing sacred about professional "turf," the nurse leader took the initiative in managing the process of introducing change, a function usually seen as the principal's. (The principal, however, takes his cues from the next person in the administrative hierarchy of the school system.) Knowing this about public schools—that the principal is the manager of change—the nurse was careful to make the first approach to him, and bring him into the change process. Characteristically, he was willing to leave the management to her, as long as he was aware of what was going on and was formally asked for permission to make the necessary organizational changes. The identification of needs, however, and the actual decisions to change were appropriately made by those immediately affected, those who would have to operate professionally in the changed situation—the teachers. The nurse recognized that deciding upon and implementing the change could not be imposed from above, even though she might have been able to convince the principal of the desirability of such a change.

Here the effective nurse leader brings into play her philosophy of planned change, rooted in her knowledge of human development. She believes that the people most affected by the change have the right to make the decision to change. This right to control one's own life is an integral pa a democratic philosophy.

From the psychological point of view, a sense of control over closely related to how a person perceives himself. The greater *ive* control, the more worthwhile an individual feels. The more *ople* feels, the more able is he to accept others, to apply hi *nager* problem-solving with the expectation of success, and to *ve the rigidly* to control their own lives. In immediate, practical *teers, ways* imposes a change that has not been accepted by *ange. And* change, that change will probably never be impl authoritarian setting, where people feel com will be found to circumvent the orders through it all, the sense of powerlessness, the feelings of worthlessness will be exacerbated.

The intensity of her belief that both the special and the normal children would be better educated in the new organization made the nurse overlook an important body of data in her analysis of the system—the strong feelings of the parents. Though she was aware of and accepted the feelings of the children and saw the need for direct education in dealing with prejudices against the special children, she forgot that the children's feelings probably matched their parents. Reliance on feedback information that can be used at any point to change the system is integral to the systems approach. When she realized that an error had been made in proceeding without the participation of parents, she immediately made provisions to include them in the problem-solving process.

If she had been involved in the school for a longer period of time, her own professional education would soon have helped her to realize the importance of including families. Her clinical experience had helped her develop skills and sensitivities in drawing families into the process of bringing patients back into the mainstream of daily living. This school setting, however, generally excluded parents unless there was trouble with an individual child, and she had fallen into the trap of thinking that the parents had no real part in what happened in the school.

So sure was she that the special children would be better served in an integrated setting, she overlooked the real fears of their parents that the special children's needs would be ignored in the larger classes—fears that were realistically rooted in their experience with most teachers who taught subjects rather than children.

This nurse leader would not make that mistake again. The nurse is uniquely qualified, in utilizing systems analysis, to resist the mechanization and dehumanization of the system. There are those who become enamored of systems technology and the alluring possibilities of greater and greater "efficiency" in solving problems and providing services. For example, the vision of automated diagnosis of medical symptoms already has us talking to computers; systemic allocation of funds has resulted in closing community hospitals and emergency rooms; and designs for efficient traffic flow have virtu-ignored pedestrians and resulted in higher accident rates.

ipated consequences

s her model, things occur that she did not anticipate—partly limited experience working in schools, partly because of some al values, and partly because no system can anticipate all The events identified by asterisks indicate the unantici-

STEP 2

She asks the principal how he feels about having a meeting to talk about children with disabilities—not just special children, but also those in the regular classrooms. She tells him that she has been thinking about the effects of their disabilities on the childen's learning, as she is sure he and the faculty have, and she would like to have an opportunity to sit with other interested people and share information and concerns.

* The principal says he would like to come to such a meeting.
* He also expresses concern about teachers not invited to the meeting who may feel hurt.
* The nurse practitioner suggests that she post the invitation on the bulletin board. If it comes from her, no one who is not interested will feel obliged to attend. The principal agrees, albeit reluctantly.
* After speaking to the principal, she realizes that she has set no time and place for the meeting. She checks again with the principal on the availability of a room after school on the following Wednesday. He designates a room, but makes it clear that keeping the building open after school creates problems with the custodian. She must remember to find another place for the next meeting.

STEP 3

She makes a list of teachers who have remembered most of what she told them about children with problems in their classes. Two of these teachers had also taken the initiative in suggesting they plan for the management of these children, using all they knew of the medical and pedagogical data including the consequences of mismanagement.

She suggests to each of them that they meet to discuss the education of children with disabilities, and asks each one who agrees to meet to invite other teachers who might be interested. She makes a point of inviting the teacher of the special children, because—as she says to her—her particular information will be very useful.

STEP 4

At the first meeting she raises the question: What do we need to know about children with disabilities? She offers to list the needs as they are expressed, so they may then plan how best to fulfill them.

*So much time is taken by the teachers expressing needs to know and identifying problems that require solutions, that her decision to speak to them about the real outcomes of the current system must be postponed. They decide, instead to take one problem at a time and, pooling their information, try to solve it. They pick the target problem and set a time for the next meeting. The principal apparently changes his mind and offers to make the same room available.

*STEP 5

For six meetings, teachers gather and pool their increasing information about disabilities and the teaching/learning/management problems related to them. At each succeeding meeting they deal more with their own feelings about disabilities and children who have them. (The principal did not attend after the first meeting.)

At the end of the sixth meeting, the nurse-practitioner asks if she may take a part of the next meeting to present a summary of what they have accomplished. She says that the discussions have revealed important information about the results of the present way of dealing with disabled children, and she would like to try to pull together this information.

At this point, the nurse further develops her model of planned change (Figure 3–2).

She then resumes the implementation of her model. Here, again, she finds that she must alter her plan because of unanticipated contingencies. (These unexpected happenings are noted by asterisks.)

STEP 6

One of the teachers had previously asked the nurse to help her work out a problem in her classroom. The nurse requests permission to collaborate with her in presenting the problem to the group. The process of problem-solving is demonstrated to the group. In addition, they are shown a practical example of instituting change that supplants a system outcome with one of their own desired outcomes.

As a direct result of this presentation, several of the other teachers present problems for solving. The nursepractitioner makes herself available for consultation.

STEP 7

One teacher who solved a problem concerning a normal child is asked by the nurse to accept one of the special children in her class. This special child requires the same kind of management as the normal child.

The teacher agrees to take the child. The teacher and nursepractitioner clear the decision with the special teacher. Then all three get permission from the principal.

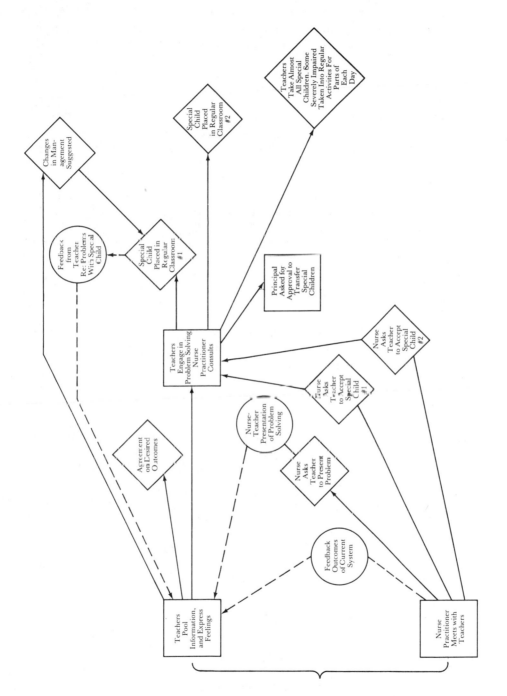

Figure 3-2. Continuation of the System Model for Change Process.

After several days, the teacher comes to a meeting with the information that the special child is not doing well in her classroom. The other teachers re-evaluate the problem and suggest some changes in management.

STEP 8

The nurse approaches another teacher and asks how she feels about accepting a special child into her class. The teacher agrees to do so.

*The day after the child enters, the principal gets a call from the child's parent. She wants her child to remain in the special class because she feels he gets more attention and more qualified help there.

*The principal tells the teacher to return the child to the special class. The teacher brings this information to the meeting, and asks for help in convincing the principal to rescind the order.

*The nurse-practitioner realizes that a serious error has been made: the model does not include parent involvement.

STEP 9

*The principal is asked to come to a special meeting of the group. He is prevailed upon to invite the protesting parent and several other of the more involved parents of both special and normal children.

STEP 10

At the next meeting, the teachers make a presentation to inform the parents of their objectives and the evidence they have to justify what they are doing. They also permit the parents to express their doubts and fears for their children.

*The parents are assured that they will be involved from now on and kept apprised of their children's progress. The parents, some very reluctantly, agree to the changes.

The principal assures the special education teacher that her class will not be broken up. She tells him that she is not worried about this, that even if all the special children are put into regular classes, she has a role in helping the classroom teachers to deal with crises as they arise and in continuous planning for optimum education of the children.

STEP 11

A third teacher requests a profoundly impaired child for his class. At a meeting he tells about his experience with his own brother, also profoundly impaired. The mother of one of these children offers her child for admission to the teacher's class.

*The district supervisor for special education visits the school and learns from the special education teacher what is happening. She tells the principal that she is opposed to any attempt to break up the class for special children. She says that it is run by someone trained to teach disabled children and she does not want untrained teachers to interfere.

At the next meeting, teachers, parents, and nurse agree that another error has been made: The district supervisor should have been included in the planning.

The parents express confidence that their involvement in the changes will carry the day, since PL 94-142 provides for final parental approval of any plan for the education of their special children.

Figure 3-3 shows a model of the way the plan finally worked out, including the unexpected events. The retrospective model serves as a guide to planning for future changes, and to avoiding the pitfalls encountered with the original plan.

Nursing, which is in its very essence a humanistic profession, can keep the humanizing factor forever in the forefront of systems analysis. If the welfare of the patient and his family is maintained as the primary referent for all decision-making, the objectives of hospitals, health centers, and other treatment facilities will not be subverted in the name of efficiency. Carol Taylor, in her book, *In Horizontal Orbit*, points out how nurses have, in assertive and creative ways, circumvented systems that dehumanize the people who are a part of them.[5] She describes a situation in a hospital system where the organization chart (see Figure 3-4) indicated that Mr. A, the administrator of a sixty-four bed unit, Dr. B, the physician in charge, and Miss C, the nurse in charge, were all on the same level in the hierarchy, and presumably functioned as peers.

Actually, all three felt that Mr. A could not function effectively "because his boss didn't understand, and sometimes couldn't care less about, the problems on the unit. Mr. A, Dr. B, and Miss C rearranged matters so that Mr. A stayed in the background, while Dr. B and Miss C worked together to change decisions made by Mr. A's boss when they felt that it was to the best interest of the unit to do so."[6] The *real* organization chart looked like Figure 3-5.

In hospitals as well as in other bureaucratic systems, the informal organization is usually used to circumvent bureaucratic systems that ignore the human factor. Nurses move from function to function across disciplinary and job lines to provide the best care for their patients. However, much is lost in both efficiency and money by masking the reality of the situation. Perhaps it is time for nurses to assume the leadership and point this out. A Mr. A who makes an administrator's salary and then spends his time running errands for the doctors ultimately contributes unnecessarily to the high

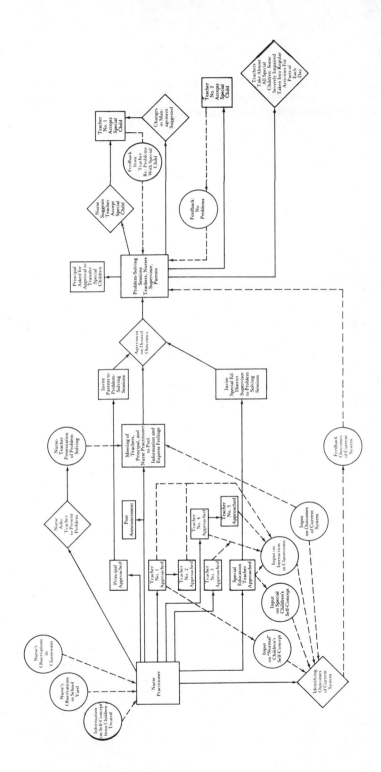

Figure 3-3. Retrospective Change Model Incorporating Unanticipated Outcomes.

cost of hospitalization. The fact that Mr. A doesn't seem to mind the arrangement is evidence that something is happening to his development toward self-actualization: He goes along with the prevalent view of himself as inadequate, apparently doing nothing to examine the consequences of his acquiescence to the organization and to his own sense of worth. A nurse who

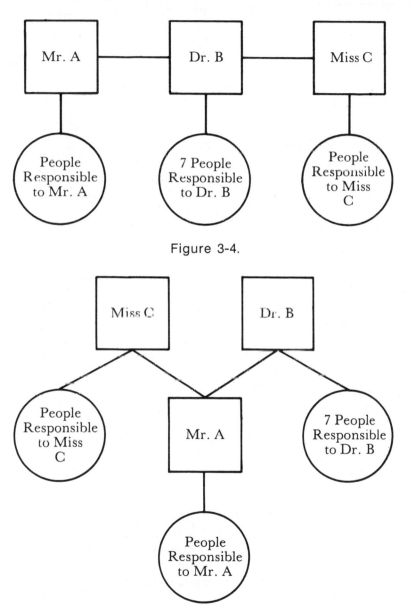

Figure 3-4.

Figure 3-5.

"periodically acts as if she were a pharmacist, a dietitian, a sterile-supply worker, a maid, and a storekeeper"[7] could better use her skills in direct patient care. A systems approach requires that the system ultimately be structured so that the results are consistent with the stated objectives. Unproductive bypasses in the structure are uneconomical of time, money, and human growth.

In summary, the nurse leader's essential goal is to identify needed change and to implement such change. For this she must have the knowledge and skills involved in approaching the change process systematically. The essential skills needed for a systems approach to problem-solving, in addition to the other problem-solving skills identified in this book, are information gathering, identifying measurable outcomes, mobilization.

Information gathering

The lifeblood of any system of thought, or plan for change is information. The flow of relevant information from element to element in the system gets a new system started in the right direction and helps identify errors in an old system. Feedback information provides a basis for continuous system correction and keeps the system moving toward its objectives.

Oddly enough, with all the years we spend in institutions for formal education, we do not become proficient in information gathering. Most of our teachers have doled out to us bits of information considered important for one reason or another, and our primary training has been in recalling these bits on examinations. The term papers we wrote also consisted of bits of information collected from a limited number of recommended sources and rarely synthesized into systems of thought or used in processes of problem-solving. It is this kind of experience that makes us vulnerable to the advice of experienced professionals to forget most of what we learned in school and relearn our professions on the job.

To understand a system, we must use several sources of information: theoretical and research data in the appropriate disciplines, people involved in the system, and our own observations of the interactions of the various elements in the system. Without the theoretical knowledge, our own observations will probably be defective, filtered through our own limited experiences and our own biases. For example, a nurse has been educated to believe that parents should not be permitted to spend more than a limited amount of time with their hospitalized children. Not only do they get in the way of hospital routine, but they encourage the children to cling to them, to make unreasonable demands for attention, and to resist treatment. When she looks at the system in her well-run pediatric unit, where parents' visits are strictly limited, she sees no reason to change this practice.

However, if she were familiar with the appropriate information in child development, in the studies of the reactions of children to the bombings of London in World War II, and in the initial school experiences of children, she would realize that separating parents and other familiar people from children during a time of crisis probably increases their anxiety and fear. The implications of this increased fear and anxiety are based on a knowledge of the relationship of fear and anxiety to learning. If the objective of returning the patient to optimal health is to be reached, the patient needs the opportunity to learn to accept treatment, follow medical instructions, and become independent. His ability to learn will be impeded by anxiety and fear. The direct relationship of the physiological concomitants of fear states to healing, though not as clearly defined, may also be deduced from knowledge in the field. If she has all this information, the nurse must begin to reconsider the usefulness of keeping parents off the pediatrics unit. It is clear, too, that the information is not drawn from a single discipline. To gather it, the nurse must become familiar with data in psychology, sociology, and education, as well as physiology and medicine.

In addition to the theoretical knowledge of various fields, it is important to search out empirical data on successes and failures in achieving similar objectives. We cannot identify achievable objectives if we do not have this information. There is no point is defining objectives shown by experience to be unrealistic. Nor is it useful to avoid setting goals that no one has ever tried to reach before. Given our knowledge of human behavior, we may detect reasons why people fail when success is possible, and reasons why people maintain the status quo when change would be beneficial. Our knowledge thus makes us surer and braver when analyzing systems, identifying objectives, and planning for change.

Information about the system itself involves an awareness of such things as, for example, the external constraints that affect nursing service in a hospital:

> Educational constraints and meliorants may include such things as lack of knowledge among personnel, the availability of specialized professional and technical education, the prevailing attitude toward education, and the extent to which education matches the requirements for skills and abilities. . . .
>
> Sociocultural constraints and meliorants include such things as the general attitude of other health professionals and society at large toward nursing administrators; the dominant views on authority and subordination; the extent of cooperation from professional organizations, unions, administration; and the prevailing view in the country toward health and the significance of its cost.
>
> Legal-political constraints and meliorants include such factors as political stability and the flexibility of laws and legal changes regarding health.
>
> Economic constraints and meliorants include such things as the basic economic status in the country, whether within the health care industry private or public ownership prevails, whether it is a competitive economy, and the extent to which the government controls economic and health care activities.[8]

Sometimes, newcomers to the systems concept are dismayed by the emphasis on information, and feel that there is too much to learn about information gathering. They forget that they have spent many years in gathering information and, in spite of the gaps in their education in this area, have developed useful skills with which to start their searches. The exercises at the end of this chapter will help refresh your memory, refine the skills you already have, and add additional necessary ones to your repertoire.

Defining objectives

No matter how much information we have, we cannot work effectively toward objectives if those objectives are not behaviorally or operationally defined. Unless we can see people behaving differently from the way they were behaving under the old system, there is no evidence of change. In planning for change, if we do not say how people will do things *as a result of* that change, we cannot be clear about what changes we want to effect. The relationship between the system and the outcomes of that system must not be obscure if we are to justify the system and continue to refine it as we measure the outcomes. If we know exactly what outcome we want, and we do not get that outcome, then we can continue to modify the system until we *do* get that outcome.

Anything less than clearly-defined, measurable objectives may lead to some questionable responses by professionals charged with such responsibilities as educating children and nursing people back to health. For example, teachers have blamed parents for children's failure to learn in school, when an analysis of the instructional system would make it clear that all available information is not being used and that system objectives are not defined in measurable, behavioral terms. The nurse who aims in a general way toward nursing her patient back to recovery often does not realize that he is fearful about being discharged from the hospital, that there are large gaps in his information about his condition, and that he needs skills for self-care that he has not learned. If her objectives for the patient were behaviorally defined, she would know whether or not she was achieving them.

In order to make sure that we are not forgetting that human beings are the most important elements of any system, we must ask ourselves some pointed questions: Do the objectives deal almost exclusively with skills, and overlook the fact that people have feelings and needs associated with those feelings? Does the system provide for objectives related to the humane development of the people involved, that is, with their growth toward self-actualization?

Though care deliverers very often provide for people with concern and sensitivity, the quest for efficiency may lead to absurd contradictions in our health care systems. Carol Taylor's observation that "The transactions in the Admission Office tend to erode [the patient's] sources of psychic support and

to increase his anxiety,"[9] is one example of a procedure that has great potential for depersonalizing the individual and reducing his ability to deal with
stress. Since, as she notes, unrelieved stress interferes with the person's ability
to respond to treatment, the admission practices run directly counter to the
stated objectives of hospital care.

Even such a respected part of the hospital system as the coronary care
unit, often a model of technical efficiency, may actually be effecting some seriously undesirable outcomes that can be traced to those very efficiency factors that set the CCU apart from other hospital facilities. The unrelenting
observation, the bright lights, the machinery, the scurrying, preoccupied
staff, the severe rationing of family visits, may all be contributing to psychological stress. Prolonged illness and even fatal arrhythmias may be resulting
from this stress.

The gathering of information and the clear defining of objectives becomes even more significant when we realize that short-term plans for solving immediate problems may in the long run exacerbate those problems. If
we do not stay alert to new data and maintain our flexibility in adapting the
system and changing our immediate objectives, we may even destroy ourselves. Our current concerns about energy sources provide one illustration of
this kind of danger:

> Some evidence on the trend of global temperature seems to show a very slow in-
> crease from the beginning of the industrial revolution to about 1940, and an
> alarmingly steep decline in global temperature thereafter. This pattern has
> been attributed to the burning of fossil fuels, which has two consequences—the
> liberation of carbon dioxide . . . into the atmosphere, and the simultaneous in-
> jection into the atmosphere of fine particles, from the incomplete burning of
> the fuel. The carbon dioxide heats the Earth; the fine particles [reflecting back
> the heat of the sun] cool it . . .
>
> [A]n increased burning of fossil fuels in a short-term attempt to stay warm
> can result in more rapid long-term cooling. We live on a planet in which agri-
> cultural technology is responsible for the food of more than a billion people.
> The crops have not been bred for hardiness against climatic variations.[10]

The implication is that we may be heating ourselves into global fam-
ine. Clearly, our basic survival system needs some changing.

For an example closer to our professional concerns, let us look at what
has happened in one area of health care delivery: Physicians have, over the
past few years, generally eliminated the practice of making house calls. The
short-range outcome has been the increased use of hospital emergency-room
facilities to deliver routine health care. But emergency-room operations have
long been identified as financially unfeasible, and many hospitals, unable to
get adequate government support for such services, have drastically curtailed
or eliminated them altogether. People are now often abandoned to trying to
find a way out of this dilemma: on the one hand having to make doctor's appointments long in advance, and on the other hand needing immediate treat-

ment for colds, bruises, and anxieties. Health care planners are not using these outcomes quickly enough as a basis for modifying the system. The long-term effect may very well be a whole new group of professionals who will make house calls on request and in other ways provide for the health care needs that are not being met. The evidence for this effect is already becoming apparent in the statistics on new types of practitioners providing primary care.

Mobilization

We cannot implement changes unless the people who will be affected by the changes are committed to them. Just as in community work the process of mobilization has as its objective the involvement of people in planning and implementing the changes that affect their lives, so any change agent must build into his system elements that provide for the identification and involvement of the people whom the change will affect. The flow of information must proceed to them as well as from them, and they must participate in defining the system objectives based on this knowledge.

Aside from the clear evidence that those who are left out of systems planning because they are considered less knowledgeable, less important, or less prestigious than those included can circumvent the system and prevent the achivement of objectives, there are more basic considerations involved. To prevent some people from participating in the decision-making that controls their lives is antihumanistic, a denial of the striving of human beings toward self-actualization. We must ask ourselves: How can patients achieve the goals of optimum health, when those who are charged with helping them achieve those goals are themselves prevented from achieving optimum health?

Insofar as continuing psychological growth and development is a function of health, individuals who feel powerless and out of touch with the forces running their lives are unhealthy. Such people cannot provide opportunities for growing for others. The traditional hierarchical bureaucracy, in which most people in a system are viewed as takers of orders and instruments of production, has no place in a system committed to health care.

Practicing Systems Skills

Gathering information

1. Identify a small change that you would like to see instituted in the organization of which you are a part: the class, the school, the hospital, or the community agency.

2. Use the following framework for identifying the areas of information you need before you can reasonably begin to organize to plan for the change:

DESCRIPTIVE INFORMATION

- What is the current situation?
- Exactly who is doing what?
- What institutional resources are involved?
- What are the current outcomes of the situation? (Exactly what is different as a result of what is being done?)
- How consistent is the situation with the stated policy of the institution?

Sources of descriptive information

Systematic observation and recording are necessary to obtain an accurate description of the situation.

Having more than one observer—all independently recording their observations—reduces the possibility for error when assessing the situation preparatory to planning.

Using a list of questions like the one here assures that the observational data of the different recorders will be comparable.

AFFECTIVE INFORMATION

- How do the people involved feel about the current situation?
- What are the feelings and related values of those in charge?
- What are the feelings and related values of those directly involved in doing the work?
- What are the feelings and related values of clients?
- What are the feelings and related values of others?
- What are the community feelings about the current situation?
- What are the related values in the local community?

Sources of affective information

There are three ways of identifying people's feelings and values. First, we can ask directly that people describe them. Second, we can observe people's behavior and deduce what their feelings and values must be to make them behave the way they do. A third way is not quite so direct as the question, but neither is it inferential. It is a strategy that involves helping the individual to identify his own feelings and clarify his own values. Often we make decisions and react to people and situations with a minimum of introspection, so that we are never quite clear about the affective and philosophical bases of our behavior. This is part of the reason that it is clear to objective observers that our behavior is inconsistent and unpredictable. The rationality on which we pride ourselves seems often to be more honored in the breach than in our behavior.

Below are two strategies for identifying a person's feelings and values. They serve to reveal those feelings and clarify those values even when the people themselves are not clear enough about them to answer a direct question.

You might, before you use them with other people, try them out yourself and see what you can discover about your own feelings and values.

Deducing feelings and values from behavior requires some knowledge of sociology and psychology, much of which you already have. For example, a person might say things like: "I think old people are really funny. I love working with them." Such a comment indicates feelings of condescension toward old people, a belief that they are somehow inferior, and a belief that they are all pretty much alike.[11]

Another example is the person who spends significantly less time with patients identified as dying than he does with people with a more positive prognosis. Such a person may also sometimes admit that, "I never know what to say to her," as a reason for his avoidance. We may deduce that such a person feels discomfort in the presence of a dying patient. Though we need more information to identify the specific nature of the discomfort, it is not unlikely that a large part of it is fear. It is also possible that the avoiding person believes it is desirable not to talk about dying to the terminally ill—perhaps not to talk about dying at all. It may follow that he thinks it better not to tell the terminally ill patient that he will soon die.[12]

When it comes to assessing community feelings and values, there is no substitute for going out into the community and speaking to the people. Speaking to storekeepers and customers while shopping, to school children and teachers, to people working in other agencies, even becoming involved in a community organization can help you tune into a community's values. Reading local newspapers (including back issue accounts of significant events) and listening to the people who come into your own agency are also ways of learning more about the community.

HISTORICAL INFORMATION

- How long has the current situation existed?
- Who instituted the current practice (practices)?

- Was it a matter of institutional policy or did it just seem to develop?
- Are the people who started it still working here?

Sources of historical information

Sources for such information may be found in early statements of policy, early interoffice memos in old file drawers, the memories of individuals who still work in the organization or who have retired, and in newspaper and other public accounts. Sometimes, workers in similar organizations may have data about this one because they once worked here or because they were in the area when this one was started and may have had a hand in its inception.

Depending on the organization, there may be no sources of historical data. It is important to search out whatever may be available because individuals often attribute to the original intentions of organizers and founders the reasons for perpetuating a situation. A study of the past may reveal no such intentions.

SCIENTIFIC INFORMATION

What scientific evidence do we have of the effects on people of such a situation?

What authoritative knowledge do we have about people that leads us to infer the effects of such a situation on their growth, development, health, and general well-being?

What scientific evidence do we have of the effects on organizations of such a situation?

Sources of scientific information

Most of us know how to search out this kind of information because our professional preparation has been in this area. We may be less knowledgeable about some disciplines than about others, but we know the method of searching for scientific data and we can collect them quite competently.

When we encounter a word or a concept with which we are not familiar, it is not difficult to locate a professional in another discipline, or a compendium of terms and concepts, to clarify the data for us.

Most of us, however, have not quite caught up with the many new data retrieval systems available for our use. Here is where the reference librarian can be of great assistance in our search for information. She can show us how to use not only the printed and filmed retrieval systems, like research abstracts and microfiche files, but also the computer terminals that are increasingly accessible in libraries.

CULTURAL INFORMATION

What comparative information do we have about human societies and cultures that we may apply to an understanding of the current situation?

What does our legal philosophy imply about the current situation? What does the statutory law include about the situation?

Sources of cultural information

Comparative anthropology helps us to see the universal similarities of human needs, human behaviors and human cultures. The hierarchical objectives of survival, love, and self-actualization are universally identified and targeted. The constraints on the processes for achieving them lie in the different physical or cultural environments in which human beings find themselves.

Such a systematic view refines our perception of differences among individuals and groups in our own culture. It enables us to cut through the traditional pattern of categorizing and stereotyping and to help free people to reach for their optimum levels of functioning.

The basic law embodies the essence of our cultural philosophy of life. As we grow toward a less flawed democracy, we change our Constitution to mirror our growth, and our statutes and practices to conform to our broad commitments as outlined in the Constitution.

Not infrequently, there are inconsistencies among our professed beliefs as stated, for example, in the Bill of Rights, and our current behaviors and statutes. In examining the efficacy of how we live our lives, we must ask some hard questions about the relationship between our professed principles and our behavior. We must also raise some questions about the principles we profess, even though we have been conditioned to view our Constitution as a sacred document.

Focusing on the systematic approach, identifying objectives that are consistent with what we know about human needs, and insisting that the means to those ends are also humanistic, can help us keep our law and culture in perspective and plan fearlessly for the futures we want.

Strategy for identifying feelings and values

VALUES

This strategy has a three-fold purpose: to help the individual clarify his own values; to enable him to make the connection between his values and his behavior; and to provide information to the information gatherer about the values of his subject population.

In order to construct a useful instrument that will help clarify the relevant values in a particular issue, the information gatherer must be familiar with every aspect of the issue. He needs to be careful that he states, as clearly as possible, every point of view, no matter what his own view happens to be. If he is able, he should submit the various points of view to individuals who hold them in order to provide a check on the accuracy of the statements.

On the Equality of Nurses and Physicians

Below are four points of view on this issue. Pick the one that comes most closely to your own point of view. Feel free to make any changes to more clearly express your point of view. If you prefer, you may write your own statement. If you think you would like to give this more thought before you make up your mind, that is acceptable.

In the column at the right, next to each statement, are the behaviors characteristically displayed by people who hold that point of view. In order to help you clarify your own point of view, check those things that you do and compare them to your point of view. (Do you find that you behave in ways that seem to reveal a point of view that you say you do not hold?)

When you have completed this exercise, write the statement of your point of view on a separate piece of paper and give it to the information gatherer. If you cannot decide on a point of view now, write that down.

Point of View	*Characteristic behavior of people holding this point of view*
1. Nurses don't know as much about medicine and healing as physicians do, and so it is entirely fitting that they take their orders and direction from physicians.	**1a.** The nurse does nothing for the patient without written orders from the physician.
2. The function and objectives of nursing are completely different from the function and objectives of doctoring, so nurses and physicians should practice their professions independently of each other, leaving it to the patient to consult one or the other as he feels the need for their services.	**2a.** The nurse provides care for the patient in those areas that have been specifically identified as nursing concerns. She does not consult the physician about what is needed or what she should do.
	2b. Though she dispenses medication and provides other medical care specifically ordered by the physician, she does so only because she has no choice at this time in history. Actually, she says that various aides and techni-

cians should be trained to follow these medical orders, and the physician should provide more of this kind of care.

2c. The nurse works to change the law and institutional policy so that her practice may have the same kind of independent status as the physician's.

3. Any plan for leading a patient to good health and helping him to maintain wellness requires the combined knowledge and skill of physicians and nurses. Unless the physician and nurse understand each other, appreciate each other's unique expertise, consult with each other, and work together on behalf of the patient, there can be no optimum health care delivery.

3a. The nurse meets with the physician to plan total care for the patient.

3b. The nurse provides information to the physician about all aspects of the patient's condition.

3c. The nurse tells the physician that she expects information from the perspective of his discipline about all aspects of the patient's condition.

3d. The nurse makes suggestions and recommendations to the physician based on her observation and knowledge of the patient.

3e. The nurse asks for suggestions and recommendations from the physician based on the physician's observation and knowledge of the patient.

3f. The nurse refuses to follow the physician's orders when they go counter to what, in her professional judgment, is for the good of the patient.

4. The nurse must follow the orders of the attending physician without question. However, there are some aspects of patient care that the nurse is specially qualified to provide, and she must use her own

4a. The nurse follows the written orders of the physician without questioning them.

4b. The nurse develops a nursing care plan that includes the physician's orders as well as nursing professional expertise and judgment in providing them—as long as the physician does not object.

care that, in her judgment, is needed.

4c. Where there are differences of opinion between what the physician orders and what the nurse decides is needed, the nurse defers to the judgment of the physician.

THE FEELINGS CONTINUUM

Ask the people who make up the population (or part of it) that will be affected by the change to gather for the purpose of exploring feelings about the relevant issue. Make two spots on the floor to indicate the opposite poles of the issue: Equality of nurses and physicians. Label one spot, "Nurses are properly the eyes and ears of the physician." Label the other spot, "The practice of nursing and the practice of medicine are separate and should be practiced independently of each other."

Now, direct the people, one at a time, to stand at some point between the two poles that best indicates their own point of view. As each person takes his place, let him articulate his point of view, trying to make clear why he is closer to one polar point than the other, what aspects of his point of view make it different from the extreme and so on.

When everyone is on the line, the range of views and values on this issue should be pretty clear. Not only has each person had an opportunity to clarify and communicate his values and feelings, but you—the one who is gearing up to plan for change—have additional information about the relevant population.

A Note to the prospective leader

This process of information gathering may seem like an inordinate amount of work for instituting some small change in an organization. However, it is well worth the investment of time and energy because a sound data base may mean the difference between success and failure:

1. Arguments against the change are easily countered with supporting data. People with strong emotional investments in resisting change will not be able to succeed in their opposition by implying that they know more than you do.
2. The more people who are involved in the data-gathering process, the more will be convinced of the desirability of the change, and the less resistance there will be to the change.

3. The more people are involved in the data-gathering, the more they will feel a part of the change process, and the more they will feel in control of their lives. Such people are more motivated to continue to learn and to grow, are more committed to behaving productively, are healthier. Providing a fertile milieu for achieving health is not only the essence of nursing, but also the basic process of leadership.

NOTES

[1] Louis Untermeyer, Ed., *The Pocket Book of Story Poems* (New York: Pocket Books, 1945), pp. 187–189.

[2] Carol Taylor, *In Horizontal Orbit* (New York: Holt, Rinehart and Winston, 1970), p. 14.

[3] Van Court Hare, Jr., *Systems Analysis: A Diagnostic Approach* (New York: Harcourt, Brace and World, 1967), pp. 2–3.

[4] Leila Sussman, *Tales Out of School* (Philadelphia: Temple University Press, 1977).

[5] Taylor, op. cit., pp. 7ff.

[6] Ibid., p. 11.

[7] Ibid., p. 10.

[8] *Role Expectations—Nurse Administrators, Governing Boards, Chief Executive Officers* (New York: National League for Nursing, Pub. No. 20-1693), pp. 38–39.

[9] Taylor, op cit., p. 91.

[10] Carl Sagan, *Broca's Brain: Reflections on the Romance of Science* (New York: Random House, 1979), p. 194.

[11] Charlotte Epstein, *Learning to Care for the Aged* (Reston, Va.: Reston Publishing, 1977).

[12] Charlotte Epstein, *Nursing the Dying Patient* (Reston, Va.: Reston Publishing, 1975).

chapter four

The Interdisciplinary Component of Leadership

Our whole approach to knowledge and learning tends to reinforce the idea that there are different "subjects" that require different specialists with separate and distinct areas of knowledge. Courses taken in school in fifty-minute blocks of time, in different departments of the high school, and later even in different colleges of the university, reinforce a fragmented rather than a unified concept of knowledge.

Training in this kind of fragmentation inevitably interferes with the concept of holism in human services delivery. People in need of care go from professional to professional, are referred to specialist after specialist, in a search for help with what may be perceived as several problems, to be addressed by a number of people who often have no contact with each other. If there are interlocking causes for and effects of the various conditions of the client, no one service deliverer has enough information to perceive these relationships. Grave questions thus arise concerning the success rates of the various professions, especially in cases of individuals with many problems.

The holistic approach to service delivery, including health care delivery, attempts to reverse the practice of professional fragmentation in problem-solving and thus to raise the quality of human service. More and more institutions of all kinds are requiring the close collaboration of various professionals to help people develop their resources for optimal living. Though at first, the difficulties of such collaboration seem almost insurmountable, given the differences in language, in interests, and in the traditional perceptions of the role and status of the various professions, closer examination reveals large areas of overlap and shared assumptions, values, knowledge, and skills. Perhaps it is because professionals are often unaware of how much they have in common that they become involved in conflict and are unable to work productively when trying to function together in teams.

One assumption that all the professions share is that the ministrations of its members are for the purpose of improving the quality of the client's life. On the face of it, such an assumption does not necessarily redound to the good of the client, for the concept of the good life probably varies with every individual. However, a shared assumption of caring is not a bad basis for improving communication among the professions, raising the level of interprofessional trust, and above all working to improve the general relationships between the public and professionals. Recognition of such a shared assumption may also provide something that all professions need: that is, the courage to evaluate systematically the effects of delivery of professional services. If, as professionals, we are reassured that our motives are pure, we may be able to admit that all of us, despite our integrity, often operate on the basis of limited knowledge, relying on faith to flesh out our reasoning. Once through that dangerous tunnel, we professionals can come out on the other side prepared to investigate how closely our limited knowledge and our faith actually bring us to improving the human condition.[1]

This is not to say that professionals have not contributed to the improvement of the quality of life. The reduction in the incidence of a number of communicable diseases is no small success, for example, though one wonders if this could have been accomplished in an age when there was almost universal illiteracy and no media. The enormous number of people who can read is at least partly due to the efforts of the teaching profession. The fact that so many more people today still have their natural teeth when they die may be a factor in improved nutrition, which is related to spread of disease. And this says something about the quality of dental care. This is part of the problem of evaluation; it is difficult to ascribe success totally to one or another profession, which brings us to the necessity for interprofessional collaboration if we are to improve the quality of life.

Though the fantastic proliferation of knowledge has reinforced the tendency to treat the human being as a collection of discrete parts, the ideology of all professions implies that no one part of a human being can be touched without affecting the rest of him. Though some professionals may be somewhat more faithful to this assumption in their practice, professionals generally do not seem able to pull their attention away from their special concern. Thus, though social work as a profession cares about the whole person, individual social workers tend to focus on one aspect of the client's problem. And, in the shuffle of referrals, the client himself may forget that he is a whole person.

Some areas of human services are more interdisciplinary in their data and philosophy than are other areas. But this appears to be so only because these special fields are emerging at a time when the movement for holistic approaches to treatment and prevention is getting stronger. Thus, specialists in the field of aging are studying not only the physiological and biological changes that accompany old age, but also social attitudes toward aging and the aged (including their own attitudes), the re-education of the aged to more realistic conceptions of themselves, and the communication problems involved in influencing social policy in regard to old people.

—This kind of interdisciplinary development helps to move us closer to the concept of holistic treatment of clients. A human being's problems are not arranged in terms of the different professional disciplines any more than knowledge is divided up into fifty-minute blocks called math or chemistry or literature. Just as all knowledge is interrelated, so solutions to a person's problems need the knowledge and skill of more than one profession. A person with cancer needs help, not only from the physician and nurse, but also from the psychologist, the sociologist, and the teacher. Part of the individual's problem may be caused by a cancerous growth, but a significant part is also caused by social attitudes about cancer, medical attitudes about dying, and individual attitudes about sickness and death. At least one group of writers in the field of health predicts that defining a profession in terms of a narrow, discrete body of knowledge will interfere with adequate service delivery in the near future. "Health professionals," they say, "will have to . . . begin to accept the idea that the hallmark of professionalism will be a commitment to broad social goals and not to a 'unique body of knowledge.'"[2]

I cannot think of a profession that does not assume that a high level of interpersonal skills is necessary for the effective professional. These skills include the ability to communicate with clients in a way that will increase the client's ability to function more adequately. For example, a physician must enable his patient to understand a diagnosis even though he does not share all the physician's knowledge; a social worker must help his client become aware of the quality of his own problem-solving skill, even though he may not share the worker's professional vocabulary; a teacher must convince his pupil that it is safe to ask questions and express skepticism, even though the child has learned to suppress curiosity and doubt. The life of client, patient, or pupil may often depend, not on the special knowledge of the profession, but on the ability of the professional to establish communication, with all it implies of mutual understanding and trust.

Most professionals also profit from knowledge of the dynamics of group interaction, not only so that they may achieve their professional goals in interaction with clients, but also so that they may function more effectively in interaction with colleagues in their own and other professions. There is no doubt that such knowledge helps in the establishment of trust between client and professional, between community groups and workers in the community. However, the evidence we have indicates that either there is lack of knowledge or that the acquired knowledge is not adequately used in interprofessional communication. In some instances knowledge may be available to the individuals involved, but affective components of the interprofessional relationship may interfere with communication.

—— At any rate, many professions seem to be moving toward more interprofessional functioning. Some are merely adding facets of other professions to their own roles, in which case they must learn more about those other professions. Others are working more closely with other professions to provide more complete care for their clients, in which case, also, they must learn more about those other professions.

Among other sensitivities shared by the professions are a profound awareness of the pain in the world and an equally profound belief in the improvability of the quality of life. In an age when the main thrust of efforts is for the accumulation of material goods, human services professionals struggle every day with the alleviation of pain that persists despite our national wealth. They see pain that might be reduced if we contributed more money and time to research; pain that might be prevented if we distributed our wealth more fairly; pain that might disappear forever if we thought more clearly and behaved more responsibly.

Skills based on knowledge of group dynamics and interpersonal communication are needed by all human services professionals. However, a common error in higher education, including professional education, is to equate knowledge *about* a subject with skill in the application of that knowledge. Consequently, many professionals have their education cut short at the knowledge level of group dynamics, without ever becoming adept at working in groups. They also know much about what constitutes effective communication, but are not proficient in their own interaction with others.

There is one basic skill that all of us are supposed to have learned in elementary and secondary school, a skill without which we cannot function effectively in our personal, much less in our professional, lives. That skill is the ability to identify and solve problems systematically and logically. All human services professions require a high level of skill in problem solving. The practitioner, once he has identified a problem, can proceed logically to hypothesize about causes and solutions, then go on to gather data with which to check out his hypotheses and come to some conclusion. And he will hold to those conclusions only if they test out during systematic application. There is no optimum human service delivery—or optimum living, for that matter—without skill in problem solving.

Without the skills that are required for increasing self-awareness, the human services practitioner is vulnerable to grave errors in his judgments and in his relationships with clients and colleagues. All human services professionals seem to be more or less cognizant of the connection between self-knowledge and effective human relationships, though, as with other skills deemed necessary, the skills for self-knowledge acquisition are not always systematically taught and practiced. Rather, knowledge *about* the connection is taught, and students are left to pick up the skills in the field. Social work and psychiatry are professions that do much to develop such skill; education flirts with it in the single required course in group processes.

It is recognized that the individual who believes he has not been affected by the pattern of group prejudice and discrimination in our society is liable to insult people without knowing it, discriminate unfairly against others without being aware of what he is doing, and have distorted perceptions of people and their needs without realizing it.

Based on our knowledge of human behavior, it is also generally accepted that authoritarian individuals tend to be inflexible, suspicious of the motives of others, and overbearing or submissive depending on the absence or presence of an authority figure. At the other end of the personality spectrum, the democratic individual deals better with ambiguity and change, accepts others, and permits them to maintain control over their own lives and behaviors.

The practitioner who is not aware that his attitudes and behaviors fall on the authoritarian end of the scale may give lip service to the client's right to independence while telling the client how to live his life. He may say that he agrees that changes are needed in an agency, a community, or the world, and yet act in a way that impedes change. He may say that he wants clients and coworkers to have as much knowledge as possible while keeping much of what he knows from them because he does not trust them to use the knowledge wisely.

Until he becomes more conscious of his conflicting values and behaviors and the differences between what he feels and what he says he believes, he will, in his professional activity, actually stand in the way of achieving his (professed) goals. Skill in the development of such awareness is a necessary part of professional education.

The demand of clients to be fully informed about procedures, risks, and all possible consequences of treatment is causing ethical problems for professionals. Whose life is to be prolonged with machinery, whose heart is to be replaced, whose blood is to be purified when there are not enough purification systems for all who suffer from kidney failure? Is the mother who wants to know whether or not her baby will be born healthy entitled to know all the risks of amniocentesis? Is the person who agrees to participate in the testing of an experimental drug entitled to know that he has been chosen to receive a placebo? Who has the right to decide which one hundred poor families will be chosen to receive a guaranteed annual income in the process of testing the feasibility of such a program? Do parents and children have a right to know the possible intellectual risks they face when they agree to participate in a new educational program?

No single professional, working alone with his patient or client, should be required to bear the total burden of decision-making in this time of transition and change. Each decision requires the knowledge and introspection of other professionals if the margin for error is to be substantially narrowed. And only a shared accountability can help us cope with the anxiety that attends professional decision-making. (The alternative seems to be professionals who refuse to deal with any but the simplest problems where the risk of action is very small. Succumbing to the threat of malpractice suits seems to be the alternative to shared assumption of responsibility.)

It is interesting to note that some researchers in the field see so much overlap between professions that talking about the need for links for communication of knowledge seems almost superfluous. However, the compulsion to maintain professional identity and to protect one's profession against the encroachments of the other professions, continues to interfere with effective interaction between the professions.

All professions are faced with the problem of absorbing and using the large amounts of new knowledge bombarding them. The growth of knowledge has led to specialization in the professions and the emergence of new professions while adding momentum to the movement for holistic approaches to treatment. Though computer technology may reduce somewhat the need for individuals to learn all there is to know in any profession, there is still the problem of synthesizing the knowledge of all professions for a unified approach to treatment. Improved communication among the professions probably constitutes a required first step to developing real understanding of the whole person.

Interdisciplinary Communication

The difficulties of interdisciplinary communication seem, superficially, to revolve around (a) differences in professional vocabularies, (b) uniqueness of professional concepts, and (c) differential levels of knowledge. However, if the expected outcomes of interdisciplinary functioning are discussed by the team members, these apparent difficulties may be resolved. The social worker on the team will admit that she does not expect or desire to learn the body of knowledge that the physician has learned. She is, on the contrary, willing to accept his judgment in matters related to his professional competencies. However, she realizes that identification with a profession does not make an individual the possessor of all the knowledge and skills identified with that profession. Nor is that person's individual level of knowledge and skill known merely by virtue of his being a member of the profession. In addition, one professional does not represent all the variations in philosophy, values, and attitudes to be found in that profession.

All of this may not completely allay the discomfort associated with the possibility that people outside one's area of professional competence will be evaluating one's behavior. However, expressing the feeling of discomfort and going on to negotiate the parameters of evaluation may make all team members more conscious of the universality of anxiety and the basis of defensiveness, no matter how prestigeful the position. Such consciousness of shared discomfort can contribute to the closeness of team members and create a desire to protect each other from destructive communication.

Within this perceptual framework, every member of the team—professional, paraprofessional, and nonprofessional—may become involved in an open pattern of communication, through which each learns from the others and, in turn, teaches the others. Professional vocabularies need not be abandoned; they need to be clarified and explained. Professional concepts need to be laid open to questioning, rational analysis, and additional information. How much of the knowledge of one field will be learned by members of other fields must be left to the decision of those members. As long as every person recognizes the limitations of his knowledge of other fields, the group's decision-making will maintain an optimum level of rationality.

A leader can articulate this approach to communication, openly abandoning the traditional pattern of according a mystical "respect" for one or another profession—or an equally prejudicial disrespect for other lines of work.

In one hospital, a nurse-physician advisory council was formed for purposes of collaborating to improve patient care. Participants in the council have observed that

> To assure successful interactions within the council, the nurse representatives should be chosen with care. Because physicians are usually perceived as being powerful, a counter-balancing force is needed to prevent physician-domination of the group. Thus, nurses appointed to the council should be perceived as being powerful either by virtue of their position in the hierarchy or by virtue of their expertise. Furthermore, an ability to communicate effectively is essential. The nurse members of the council must be articulate and knowledgeable regarding the practice of nursing . . ."[3]

We suggest that the nurse-leader, who may herself be articulate, knowledgeable, and powerful in the hierarchy, can give recognition to those members of the team who are having difficulty articulating what they know because they are intimidated by what they perceive as the superior knowledge or prestige of other team members. By revealing some of her own feelings of constraint and disclosing some of her own procedures for overcoming reluctance to speak she can move the group toward greater cohesiveness and productivity by helping the others to examine their own feelings and behaviors.

Providing opportunities

There are many settings in which the interdisciplinary team is already established. Mental hospitals and mental health centers very often have interdisciplinary teams of physicians, nurses, social workers, recovered patients, and even community people who have never received treatment. However, in most hospitals and other kinds of institutions, the interdisciplinary team is recognized as valuable more in the breach than in the practice.

There are several ways to establish the interdisciplinary team. For example, in a hospital organized for primary nursing, the presentation of cases at the regular nurses' meetings provides an ideal time for inviting physicians and other professionals to listen to the presentations and contribute insights to the nursing plans. Before physicians, aides, dietitians, pharmacists, social workers or other people who are not nurses are invited to hear a presentation, permission must be obtained from the presenter. Nobody should be expected to make a presentation to other professionals unless she has had the opportunity to decide if she wants to do so. This alone may not be sufficient. If the registered nurses, licensed vocational nurses, and nurse aides have been meeting regularly to present, the nurse leader should only bring up the idea of asking members of other disciplines to the meeting, and leave the final decision to consensus. She may offer what information she has on which to base such a decision, but others must be permitted to offer information, too.

The occasional invitation may set the tone for regular participation in meetings where nurses are presenting cases.

In a hospital with team nursing rather than primary nursing, other professionals might be invited to contribute knowledge and insights to a solution of some problems. If the goal is to form an interdisciplinary team that meets regularly to plan for the best kind of patient care, these occasional invitations to work on problems can continue until the value of interdisciplinary contributions has been established. Once this happens, the nurse leader may suggest a regular schedule for such meetings.

As time goes on, the nurse leader may take the initiative in presenting clearly the rules by which the interdisciplinary team will function. One rule might be that everyone who has patient contact may have a significant contribution to make to the understanding of the patient and his problem and to planning for optimum care. The attendant's contribution may be, at different points of the patient's stay in the hospital, almost as significant as the contribution of the physician who sees him for only a few minutes each day. The attendant who is there for hours every day and has the opportunity to check casually and to observe interactions between the patient and other patients, the patient and his family, the patient and other staff can often provide information that nobody else has, information without which any care plan would be deficient.

The nurse leader can make it clear that all contributions concerning the patient complement each other. There should be no attempt to evaluate the importance of the contributions. Everybody knows that the physician has, by virtue of his expertise, important things to say about the patient. But the nurse leader must make it clear that *everyone* has important things to say, that all information must be listened to with equal interest and respect.

The frame of reference of the discussions and contributions is always the optimum treatment of the patient. How old the contributor is, what his status is, what his profession or his job is—none of these factors are to weigh in the balance when evaluating the importance of the information and deciding if the information should be used. The information itself must always be checked for validity and significance.

It is important at some point to allow time for discussing the team's interaction. In spite of the "rules," often historical factors as well as personal/social/psychological factors may interfere with acceptance, may prevent individuals from saying what they really want to say, may cause some people to remain silent in the presence of those they consider to have more authority, or may cause some to respond with hostility and defensiveness because they think their contributions are not being given proper consideration.

It might be useful to examine which team member always speaks directly to which other team member, which team member tends to dominate all the discussions, which team members gradually fade away from the group and stop coming to team meetings. Are there cliques in the group? Do some individuals support only certain other individuals, and tend to denigrate the contributions of still others? Is there a detectable pattern to these reactions; for example, are the high-status people always supported and the low-status people always denigrated by some individuals? Who are the people who tend to cluster together and set up adversary relationships with other clusters? All of these questions relate to the dynamics of any small group and can interfere with achieving the objectives of the group. Only bringing them out into the open and examining them systematically and rationally, making a conscious effort to perceive the behaviors realistically and understand their causes can prevent detrimental effects on the group process and help a group function effectively.

All of this must be done, of course, in such a way as to minimize ego-threat to the group members. Focusing on describing behaviors rather than on who does what can be less threatening. The best techniques result in raising each group member's perceptions so that he recognizes his own behaviors and their effects on the other people and on the achievement of the group's objectives. Then he is equipped to make a conscious decision to change his behavior if that is indicated.

The nurse leader is, above all, aware of the pattern of interaction of the group and the dynamics of any small group. She takes the initiative of bringing the group together originally, and in the course of the meetings she acts to protect those who are traditionally vulnerable in the interdisciplinary set-

ting. She recognizes who is reluctant to speak and does what she can to encourage everyone to speak. She tries to maintain an atmosphere that is so accepting and nonthreatening that the most fearful may risk saying what they
have to say. She summarizes what has been accomplished at regular inter-
vals. She assumes responsibility for bringing people back on the track when
they wander off and forget their objectives. She may remind them of the objectives. She may start meetings by suggesting that objectives be defined, that
there be some framework for keeping the discussions on track.

One pitfall the nurse leader must avoid is meetings that occur so often
and for such long periods of time that people begin to resent the time they
spend at meetings and, eventually, stop attending them. Always, what is accomplished at interdisciplinary meetings must so obviously relate to the individual objectives of everyone who participates in the meetings that participants will be drawn to continue their attendance and participation in order
to do the job they have set themselves to do. One must not overlook the fact
that there are a great many personal considerations that keep people coming
to meetings.

Status and communication

If there is one thing that characterizes our culture, it is the value we place on
differential positions and roles and the status ascribed to those positions.
Though we have implicitly put the stamp of approval on this pattern of
functioning by describing it in the sociological literature as if it were somehow a sine qua non of social organization, actually it is not too different
from patterns observed in preliterate societies, where there is no sophisticated awareness of the destructive effects of differential status ascription.

We are forever jockeying to be considered more prestigious and consequently more acceptable in our own and others' eyes because of the nature of
our position. The high school teacher has more status than the elementary
school teacher. The university professor has more status than the high
school teacher. The Supreme Court judge has more status than anybody; and
the physician has an aura of status that is almost godlike. The nurse is usually a woman; consequently her status is tenuous. The hospital attendant
does manual labor and his status is not at all high. Among nurses, the four-
year graduate is more prestigeful than the two-year graduate. The graduate
of a clinical program has more status than the graduate of a community college program. The nurse with the master's degree has so much status that she
can no longer be a nurse in the essential sense; she must be a manager, an administrator. And the nurse with a Ph.D. talks only to God.

So concerned are we with maintaining our own status positions, that
we are wary of whom we speak to and how we speak to them. Sometimes it
seems that the patient has the least status of all; nobody asks for his contribution to his care plan.

One of the ways to overcome this jockeying for status, this wariness in interacting with each other, is to make every person feel worthwhile. The individual who appreciates himself as a human being and is obviously appreciated by the people around him is less likely to need the trappings of status to make others listen to him. The person who appreciates himself and is appreciated is less likely to feel the need to prove that his job is more important than the jobs of the people around him. People who feel good about themselves can afford to recognize that they share a common objective—the best care of the patient—and that whatever they have to contribute to that objective is worthwhile.

It is really paradoxical that we are so committed to team sports in our society and yet are often so reluctant to function on a team in other more significant pursuits. As a nation, we started out as a cooperative society, helping each other survive in a new land. But always the stronger belief in "rugged individualism" has set its stamp on the way we live. But the individualism of the pioneer, which was largely an egalitarian individualism, has rapidly given way to a competitive individualism that drives us to get ahead of the Joneses. The idiocy of social Darwinism persists in our attitudes and practices, and we look down on the poor, make the garbage collector the butt of jokes, and, with consistency in some convoluted way, fight against equality for women.

How can a society that preaches the importance of every player on a baseball team overlook the importance of every player on a health team? What is needed is some balance between the concept of the team as an ideal system with important objectives, and the team as a contemporary gimmick exemplified in the current institutional mania for working on committees. There may, indeed, be times when individual planning and decision-making are better, more efficient and more rational than working on a team, interdisciplinary or otherwise. However, when it comes to planning and working to improve the condition of a human being, nothing can exceed what the team has to offer. This conclusion is based on our knowledge of the nature of a human being and is consistent with the concept of holistic medicine that is often made explicit in statements of nursing's values and objectives.

Holistic medicine implies that a person is not a collection of mechanical parts. He thinks, he feels, he relates to others, he has values. Each of these characteristics implies a need for similar characteristics in the people who are trying to understand him wholly.

Who thinks most like the patient? Is it the physician? Does the nurse by virtue of her position and status as a professional think more like the patient than the attendant does? Maybe it is the patient in the next bed who can communicate important information that the patient has communicated to him. Maybe the doctor, the nurse, the nurse's aide, the dietitian, the social worker have no idea of the thoughts the patient has about his past, about his future, about his stay in the hospital, and about his ability to take up his responsibilities once he is discharged.

And who is most competent to empathize with the patient, who feels most like the way he feels? Who most nearly approaches in his own body the fears of the patient who is about to undergo surgery? The despair of the patient who is aware that he will soon die? The anxiety of the patient who knows that his family, his dependent children, can no longer depend on him? Empathy is not the prerogative of the high-status person, the expert in dietetics, or the social worker with a master's degree. Our professional education programs are notoriously lacking in courses for teaching empathy or other skills for effective human interaction. The person who most nearly feels what the patient feels may be the nurse's aide who has had a similar experience. It may be the nurse who has learned to view illness from the point of view of the patient.

And with whom can the patient best relate? With whom does he feel most comfortable? The doctor whom he perceives as too busy to spend too much time with him? The nurse whose white uniform reminds him of being in the hospital as a child? Perhaps it is the social worker who, with her ease of manner, her friendliness, makes contact with him and puts him at his ease so that he can tell her what he is thinking. And who, of all the people with whom he has contact in the hospital, shares his values, his belief in what is important, his faith, his perception of the world, of what has most value for him? And this human being who can learn—given the opportunity, the motivation—who can teach him? Who can help him know he can learn, manage to teach him, using the words and the approaches that fit his unique style of learning? Is it the physician, the nurse, the aide? Is it the social worker, the dietitian? The pharmacist who is able to teach him what he must not eat while he is taking certain medication?

The practice of holistic medicine, the planning of optimum treatment and care requires a holistic perception of the individual, and a holistic perception of the knowledge to be applied for the care of this individual. There is no medicine separate from psychology, no psychology apart from nutrition, no nutrition apart from nursing. There is no single aspect of knowledge, no single profession that can treat the whole person. But, together, they approach somewhat the understanding of the whole person. They cannot function all together by sending the person first to one specialist and then to another. At some point they must all get together and share what they know. Out of this sharing comes a comprehensive plan for the care of the patient. There simply is no other efficient way. A care system is an interdisciplinary system.

Inter-Role Interaction

Horwitz makes a nice distinction between a *coordinate* and an *integrative* team. The integrative team that exemplifies the conceptual framework is presented here.

The character of the collaborative process, we suggest, may be conceptualized as predominantly coordinate or predominantly integrative. In the former case, the autonomy of each worker within some defined practice area would be more jealously guarded, task performance by team members would in most cases be seriatim, or in parallel, and consultations would commonly be formally arranged . . . in essentially independent service processes. . . . [C]ollaboration of the integrated type would be characterized by conjoint therapies and a principled endeavor to blur the borders of private preserves. Further characteristics of the integrated process would be collegial initiative in offering uninvited suggestions and comments to a worker; continual and informal consultation; a tendency to plan the service process as essentially a group undertaking from start to finish, with no problem area as the exclusive concern of one member; and a general laissez-faire attitude toward the allocation of specific tasks to one rather than another discipline. . . . [T]he team's work might be regarded as organismic, different aspects being so intimately related to the whole as to be devoid of meaning if the integrating pattern were to be abstracted. Conversely, collaboration of the coordinate type might be conceptualized as a structure in which each brick is an independent decision made by one of the associated, but primarily autonomous, professionals. Action taken by the team as a unit, therefore, might more likely be the outcome of a voting process in the coordinated work style, and of informally achieved concensus where the integrated pattern prevails.[4]

Increasing interprofessional activity in team settings inevitably begins to blur the clear role definitions laid down in the descriptive literature of the various professions. Much of the negotiation that goes on in the team revolves around the attempts to clarify and productively change—traditional role expectations. Again, a humanistic orientation demands that such expectations are securely rooted in reality. An open, creative, problem-solving team does not ignore the reality that a physician's education provides him with more of the knowledge required to make appropriate *medical* decisions than a dietitian's education provides. However, it is also true that the dietitian has knowledge that most physicians have never learned, knowledge that may substantially contribute to achieving a health goal for a patient. The role negotiation here involves not so much who will sign the treatment orders, as who will insure that all available knowledge is utilized in developing a treatment plan.

The physician cannot insist on his traditional prerogative of having the final say if the team recognizes that he persistently omits from his consideration data that others on the team believe to be important. The team's discussion must, then, revolve around such questions as: What are the available research data? Is the reluctance on the part of the physician to use these data characteristic of the profession? What, if anything, does the medical profession say about this body of information? How does the physician in the team feel about being urged to consider this information? Is he willing to hear more about this information? Is he willing to incorporate it in an experimental way with one or two patients?

It is likely that until the physician is convinced of the significance of the nutrition data, he will probably, by force of tradition and practice in the institution that houses the team, have the power to omit the relevant data from the care plan. At this time, it is not likely that the physician role is so blurred that he can be overridden by the other team members. The blurring occurs in the team process that provides for continual challenge of traditional unquestioning acceptance of the physician's decision.

Role clarification

Ultimately, the blurring of traditional roles results in clarification of roles in terms of current needs. For example, a nurse must be able to make clear when a medical diagnosis and goal interferes with a nursing diagnosis and goal. Though, from a traditional perspective, the physician may believe that his role is being blurred, the nurse perceives hers as being clarified.

We must remember that much significant treatment has always been provided but never given open recognition. For example, nurse's aides have helped people to die peacefully after physicians have virtually abandoned them. The difference in the interdisciplinary team is that the value of such an aide's knowledge and skill is recognized by the team and openly used in developing diagnoses and treatments. It is not necessarily that we are proposing that everyone on the team is equal, with one vote in every decision. This kind of simplistic concept of democracy is not even feasible in political situations. Given the enormous proliferation of knowledge and technology, given the differences in areas of knowledge mastered by different professions, what we need are the skills to recognize what everyone has to offer, and the good sense and strength to decide when a particular offering is not useful in a particular situation.

Functioning

Perhaps the following model of interdisciplinary functioning can provide a framework for team planning. It is a simple system for team functioning, and includes the essential factors that make up any systems approach.

1. After a problem has been identified, each team member states the goal from the point of view of his own discipline. Almost inevitably, a professional point of view is colored by the experience and values of the individual who holds it, so no team can ever assume it knows where a team member stands without listening carefully to what he says and observing his behavior just as carefully. Thus, one physician may define the goal of a care plan: The patient is well enough to be discharged from the hospital, even though he needs someone to take care of him as he goes out of the hospital door. Another physician may define the goal of the plan: The patient is able

to resume his life without needing anyone to take care of him. One nurse may define a care plan objective in medical terms: The patient's wound is free from infection and almost healed. Another nurse may define the objective in nursing terms: The patient has defined the level of wellness he wishes to achieve, has collaborated on a procedure for achieving that level of wellness, and is ready to embark on that procedure.

2. The group must then try to arrive at a mutually acceptable group goal. This does not mean that the most prestigeful member of the group makes the decision, or that the one with the most formal education does, or even that there should be a vote with the majority decision carrying the day. Ideally, all goals become a part of the final goal as new knowledge is presented and new insights developed. Nor is it necessary for every group member to have the team use his total concept of the goal. It is sufficient for everyone in the team to conclude that he can work for the final group goal without compromising his professional or personal integrity.

3. As in any systemic approach to thinking, there must be opportunities for periodic feedback to the team on the quality of service and the extent of progress toward the goal. Information from people providing direct service, new data from researches in every field, input from patients or other service recipients, and information from strategically-located sensors may require changes in the plan before the goal is achieved. It is at this point that the team may find itself struggling again with role definitions, because the one who has the responsibility for monitoring the plan and evaluating the quality and progress of the service is not necessarily the supervisor.

Each system includes individuals who are particularly sensitive to certain aspects of the system and specific factors that inhibit or free the process. It is useful for the team to identify such persons for each plan that is implemented, and assign them to provide feedback to the team. Often, of course, a supervisor or administrator is one of these people, because his role definition permits him considerable mobility and provides him with the knowledge not only of his own subsystem but connecting subsystems. Conversely, however, his involvement in "the big picture" may interfere with his perception of parts of a subsystem that other team members may be more aware of.

Though the institution may hold the supervisor accountable for failures in his area of responsibility, the trust developed in the team allows the supervisor to use the feedback data of other team members. Slowly, by the way he reports to his superiors—noting the bases for his evaluations, pointing up the nature of the team process, crediting team members for sensing needs and initiating problem-solving—the supervisor may bring about changes in administration's expectations of supervisory roles. Ultimately, of course, the formal organizational plan of the institution must change to accommodate the team concept. (It is interesting to note that the usual administrative view is that, by changing the formal organizational plan of an institution, the way the institution functions will also change. However, though almost every new administrator's first—and sometimes only—objective is to change the organizations' plan, organizations remain remarkably the same in the way they function. This is partly because the formal organization is never an accurate picture of the real organization and partly because the people affected by the change are not involved in the change process.)

4. No process, no plan, no system is worthwhile unless very clear procedure is developed and implemented for evaluating outcomes. However, evaluation is generally vague and unsatisfactory because of the way objectives are initially stated. Unless the objectives are worded in behavioral terms so that evaluators can recognize gained objectives without question, any report of success or failure is specious. Anyone who has worked in a service organization and read an annual report that prides itself on "twenty thousand contacts with clients" knows how meaningless that evaluation is. Similarly, the total number of clinic patients treated and discharged gives no clue to possible community hostility against clinic personnel—hostility that may one day result in a demand for around-the-clock police protection in the clinic. The knowledge and experiences of the team member who lives in the community may be vitally important in defining objectives that detail what patients say and do when they come for treatment, and what clinic personnel say and do in the course of treating people from the community. Those behaviors must be checked in evaluating any change plan.

The nurse leader's clarity about the relationship between behavioral objectives and realistic evaluation helps her keep the team honest in the least painful way. She raises the question at the outset: "What will people do/say as a result of our plan?" When the team addresses itself to the answer, it can prevent the cynicism of observers who are becoming quite aware of the Madison Avenue approach to evaluation. They are no longer so easily convinced by high-flown phrases and unsubstantiated ascriptions of worth. This includes not only the general public, but the internal population of an organization and the elected officials who must provide support for many organizations.

Though the interdisciplinary team provides for shared responsibility, the process for deciding just what this means is not an easy one. What may be done for a patient and by whom without team consultation must be decided by the team. Just accepting traditional parameters for functioning no longer serves the best interests of the patient or satisfies professional role expectations. For example, a psychiatrist, a psychologist, a social worker, a nurse, and an indigenous paraprofessional may all provide therapy. The nature of the therapy is a function not only of the person's formal education, but also of his knowledge, skills, and values. Only a team familiar with the competencies and attitudes of its members can decide who will treat the patient and whether there will be more than one therapist.

In getting the job done, a process should be established for notifying the designated therapist or an alternate when another member of the team is the first to recognize a patient's need. A decision-making system must be developed for determining when any team member may minister to a patient's need without notifying the designated therapist. Other questions related to doing the job must also be answered by the team. Who is the first to see a patient or client? What is the system for gathering all relevant information on the patient? Can any member of the team approach the patient for any reason at all?

Some of these questions may be determined by the institution—by its intake procedure, for example, and by its policy concerning the make-up of its clientele. This does not mean, however, that the team may expeditiously omit such questions from its deliberations. If change in the institution is to occur as a consequence of team functioning, then suggestions for institutional change must come from the team's determination that current policy and practice are not efficacious.

The nurse, the patient, and the team

Strictly speaking, the nurse and the patient make up an interdisciplinary health team. When we add the physician, the nurse's aide, the pharmacist, and the dietitian, all with direct responsibilities in the formulation of a care plan, it seems inefficient, if not downright dangerous, not to make concerted attempts to establish optimum communication. If one person, such as the nurse, takes responsibility for asking for data from every other discipline, correlating those data, and formulating a care plan, there may be undesirable consequences. For example, the nurse may not ask for some information because she is not aware either of its existence or its importance; she may decide not to use information because of her own beliefs and values; she may misunderstand and misuse some information. All of this is not to suggest that the nurse is not competent. The information we receive is always filtered through our own perceptions and a certain amount of distortion inevitably occurs. One way to minimize such distortion is in face-to-face efforts to make the communication as clear as it can be.

Especially now, when knowledge proliferates so rapidly, complicated technology is a part of patient care, and we are becoming more aware of many factors in human relationships that have not always been considered by most professionals, it is too great a burden to put the major responsibility for planning on one person. The one who is most closely related physically and psychologically to the patient in terms of his care is most likely to appreciate the necessity for such interdisciplinary collaboration. Answers to questions about how to help someone who is dying, when to remove life supports or provide extraordinary measures for resuscitation, even when to keep a person hospitalized or advise him to return him, require the knowledge, sensitivity, and skill of more than a single discipline.

The nurse who has continuous, ongoing contact with the patient has, I believe, the most significant leadership functions on the interdisciplinary team. He is in the strategic position of putting into practice most of the team's recommendations for care because he, of all the team members, has the most direct contact with the patient, especially if he is a primary nurse. (Of course, if it is a nurse aide who has the most direct contact with the patient, the team had better face up to the reality that its decisions rise or fall on the commitment and skill of the aide. Keeping her from participating as an equal member of the interdisciplinary team will amost inevitably result in a reduction of the effectiveness of the team's decisions.)

Not only the final care decisions, but also the general implications of the team's deliberations that give a sense of the treatment philosophy must be implemented by the nurse; someone who is not privy to those deliberations can unwittingly sabotage the care process. For example, if the thrust of the team's view is that the patient should have an active part in his own recovery and health maintenance, what is said to him while treating the acute phase of his illness may mitigate against that objective. A nurse or aide who says things like "Men are so helpless when they're sick," may discourage the male patient from vigorous attempts to work his way back to independence. Similarly, someone who has not heard the argument during team meetings between the social worker and the physician cannot watch for significant clues and avoid potentially destructive comments and behaviors.

The social worker maintains that the patient's progress is being impeded rather than helped because he is institutionalized. He has such a profound repugnance for being out of his own home and in a setting where his privacy has no value that he cannot get well in a hospital.

The physician refuses to consider this seriously, maintaining that there simply is no suitable alternative treatment site. (Though there are probably not many people like Norman Cousins who can check into a hotel and, with a nurse in attendance, recover from what appears to be a fatal illness that did not respond to hospital treatment,[5] being present to hear a controversy over the relative merits of hospitalization may cause subtle alterations in care not explicitly spelled out in the care plan.)

Finally, how is the patient helped to establish a therapeutic relationship with the team? Does he see one team member at a time? Does he meet regularly with the team as an integral part of it? Does he make the final decision about who shall treat him? If he does, on what is the decision based? That is, does he have an opportunity to learn something about the concept of holism and interdisciplinary treatment, or does he decide on the basis of conventional role expectations? How are differences between the team's philosophy and objectives and the patient's philosophy and expectations reconciled?

Here, perhaps, is where the humanistic values and the educational competencies of the nurse can come into play. Her recognition of the right of the patient to exercise control over his own life can help her keep the team—in its zeal for achieving interdisciplinary integration—from forgetting the human rights of the patient. As we noted in our discussion of systems, the patient is never an object, no matter how ill he is, no matter how many operations (in the generic sense) are performed on him. Nor is he a slave or a captive, no matter how much he needs help.

It is not only the team who needs to be reminded of this. The patient, too, often needs to be educated to recognize his own right to autonomy. Many nurses have assumed the role of patient advocate, knowing as they do how often the rights of patients have been violated. Perhaps now it is time to go beyond advocacy to education, and help the patient to become his own advocate.

One very real consequence of having a truly interdisciplinary team is that its existence is not so dependent on the shifts in power and in goals of the institution where it functions. If one member of the team is perceived as its "leader," and that leader becomes unpopular with the administration or leaves the institution for one reason or another, the team, which derives its structure from the need addressed by teamwork, will survive. Leadership functions do not cease because one person leaves or loses power; the need for multidisciplinary information and skills does not vanish because the institution must economize; the satisfaction derived from mutual respect and support is not relinquished because administrators reorganize the institution's structure. If there is a real need for the team and if the members address themselves realistically to the fulfillment of that need, the team is not so vulnerable to the vagaries of institutions.

Interpersonal Interaction

There is a tendency in groups for most people to submit to the leadership strivings of an individual and become followers even if they are not convinced of the superior knowledge and skill of the individual who takes the lead. If they have really strong feelings against that individual's right to be the leader, they may become merely passive onlookers in the group's operation.

We might bear in mind an observation of Maslow's with reference to those who aggressively pursue leadership roles. He suggested that in ideal societies the leader would not seek leadership. Rather, he would be recognized by people as having the needed knowledge and skills in a situation, and he would be asked by them to lead them. And the designated leader, recognizing his own suitability for the job of leadership, would not shirk the responsibility.[6] On the face of it this idea may appear to be a contradiction of this book's theme, but let us look at it a little more closely. The leader who works within the conceptual framework of humanism, teaching, and interdisciplinary collaboration should be one whose self-concept and world-perception is so tuned into reality that she knows when she is the person suited to do a job and when someone else in the group would be better suited. She is not interested in power for its own sake, and she would not respond to a call to leadership by people who wanted only a charismatic leader to lead them wherever she pleased and to make them do whatever she wished. She is a person who helps others become aware of her knowledge and skills, and also works to help people learn what knowledge and skills are needed in a situation. If it becomes clear that what she knows and can do are needed, and people realize this, then she can accept the leadership role.

Assuming leadership

In an interdisciplinary team, the nurse who is well aware that she has the requisite insights and skills for leading the team to a solution has a right to help the rest of the team recognize this and thereby gain their acceptance of her leadership in this situation.

What she must resist is the attempt by someone without the requisite knowledge and skill to assume the leadership role by virtue of irrelevant factors. For example, on the health team, tradition may dictate that the physician be the leader, that he determine the parameters of input and discussion by other members, that he make the final decisions, and that he take action without the necessity for consulting other members of the team. The physician himself may make the assumption that his role was determined before the team was ever formed. If the nature of that role is never questioned by the team, there will be no real health team—only a physician and his assistants.

Similarly, the expectations and demands of an institution may lead the ranking administrator or supervisor on the team to assume that she is the leader, responsible for the final decision-making and accountable for the effectiveness of those decisions. This assumption comes into direct conflict with the concept of shared decision-making and shared accountability that is axiomatic in interdisciplinary functioning. Though each member of the team has a responsibility to contribute what he knows, the others have an equal responsibility to use that knowledge wisely. Final decisions are team decisions—even when the decision is to follow the lead of one or another member in a particular instance.

The nurse leader, sensitive to the social-psychological pressures to defer to the traditional role definitions of physicians and/or administrators, needs the courage and the skill to intervene and raise questions about the assumption that these role definitions are most useful in interdisciplinary problem-solving.

A good way to begin to raise such questions is to restate the basis for the establishment of the interdisciplinary team and to always refer to the interdisciplinary format as an information-pooling device, a mechanism for sharing increasingly complex responsibilities, a process of continuing learning, and a system for mutual support. One must perceive the interdisciplinary team as a setting in which there is ongoing arbitration for defining the roles of its members and reiterative attempts to reconcile expectations that various professions have of their practitioners with the goals and constraints of the institution and the demands of true interdisciplinary functioning. Anxiety generated by conflicting loyalties and contradictory expectations may make people want to withdraw, or may make them persist aggressively in inappropriate behaviors; these difficulties cannot be resolved without persistent efforts to keep the struggle open, to make the arbitration part of the business of the team rather than a covert process that is fed in exclusive cliques, in quasi-social meetings, and in the activities of the formal and informal institutional organization.

Each team member must take the initiative to make clear what he can contribute, and not be bound only by what tradition, common usage, or even prevailing principles of management prescribe. However, the nurse leader must be alert to the pressures on lower-status people to down-rate the value of their own knowledge and skill, to defer always to the others. Giving lip-service to interdisciplinary collaboration while in actual practice maintaining a system in which everyone knows that a contribution's value is determined by the status of the contributor, destroys the morale of lower-status people and has effects that go beyond just the team meetings to the actual implementation of the decisions that are made.

Above all, the interdisciplinary team must take its cue from Maslow's self-actualizing model in relating to reality. Some people on the team know more than other people, some are more skillful than others, some make much more money than others and have more prestigious professions. There is nothing to be gained from pretending that such differences do not exist and that all members of the team are "equal" in some Eden-like milieu before the fall from grace. The equality of an interdisciplinary team does not mean that all team members are equal in knowledge and competence. It means that all are different, and that their different contributions deserve an equal hearing and equally serious consideration in the problem-solving process. Consideration means just that—a respectful hearing, an objective evaluation, and a determination of how that contribution relates to the problem at hand.

Part of the ongoing process of arbitration concerning role-definition on the team involves the development of mutual agreement on the limitations of competence of all members, so that no one's contribution is ever accepted or rejected merely on the basis of his status as a professional or as a member of the institution's administration. While it is only realistic to recognize that a determination of malignancy is the province of the person trained to make such determinations, the determination of whether or not an old man should be tied to his bed might be better left to someone who has had superior education in empathy. Keeping the team focused on specific knowledges and skills can help downplay traditional hierarchies. Such focusing is a significant leadership function that can contribute to the maintenance and effectiveness of the interdisciplinary team.

From this realistic assessment of contributions based on knowledge and skill comes the realization that the interdisciplinary team cannot be a closed, static system. Inevitably, in its attempts to gather information pertinent to solving a particular problem, it may become apparent that no one on the team has the necessary information or can provide the relevant skill. Then the team must decide to add to its membership an individual who can provide that knowledge or skill. Whether he is added as a permanent member or is consulted only for a single problem is also a team decision.

At some point in the meetings of the interdisciplinary team, the nurse leader might suggest that the problems of team members are also legitimate material for discussion. She may articulate what other team members are probably aware of—that people who have unresolved problems and are unaware of behaviors affecting their treatment can interfere with the carrying out of optimum care plans.

Modeling behavior

The nurse leader can model behavior that contributes substantially to the satisfaction derived by each person from participation in the interdisciplinary team. She can stay alert to behaviors that interfere with communication.

One of the benefits arising out of a leader's example of working to understand what others are saying is the freedom among team members to ask for the meanings of words and the clarification of concepts specific to a profession. There can be no sharing of information or interdisciplinary decision-making if the team members are reluctant to admit that they do not understand what another person is saying. Nor should any team member assume that he is being understood, since people outside of a profession may use terminology and perceive concepts inaccurately.

If people are ignoring each other's feelings, the nurse leader can establish a new group norm of self-disclosure and of checking on what people are feeling. The first time she says, "I feel frustrated because I get no response to anything I say. I feel as if nobody is hearing me," people may be momentarily surprised at her candor and at the mention of something that is not strictly business. But others who have been suppressing feelings that are making them withdraw into apathy, attack vehemently the contributions of others, or form cliques to express themselves privately may be encouraged to confront openly what is happening to them and make the group deal with it. The chances are that some of them will jump at the chance to follow her lead and not only relieve themselves of the pressure of unexpressed feelings, but also help remove some of the hidden roadblocks to the team's functioning.

The nurse leader may introduce an issue that she knows people are talking about in the corridors and at lunch but are reluctant to introduce in the presence of other professionals and, perhaps, of a supervisor or administrator. While it may be true that the controversial nature of the issue will put her at some risk with those in authority who prefer to pretend that there is no issue, the risk is generally overestimated. This is true especially when it is apparent that not only are people eager to deal with the issue, but that it can be dealt with productively.

It is possible that the issue may cause considerable conflict among team members. What the nurse leader must bear in mind is that there is nothing intrinsically wrong with conflict. Differences of opinion that require negotiation and compromise, differences in values that require respect and accommodation, differences in needs that require empathy and contribution all make up the living process of the team. It is through the successful negotiation, through the expressions of respect and acceptance, through the giving of oneself so that others may feel good about themselves that the team develops cohesiveness and increasing skill in getting the best from all its members.

Not infrequently, a team or a powerful member of the team may succeed in getting rid of a troublesome team member or in keeping a problem off the agenda. Though these actions will have eliminated the conflict, they may also have deprived the team of innovative ideas, the opportunity to learn how to resolve conflict creatively, and a chance for its members to add to their own strength and self-esteem.

Though the literature exhorts prospective leaders not to be afraid of conflict, it is difficult to provide practical procedures for reducing such fear. One time-honored strategy is to systematically enlist the support of like-minded people. Before introducing potentially conflict-producing issues to the team, the leader might identify individuals who agree that the issue should be introduced. If one can get some level of commitment from them, for example to give verbal support to the introduction of the issue or to engage actively in the discussion of the issue, it becomes less frightening than if one seems to be standing alone facing a united opposition.

Being in possession of sound data relating to the issue can also help to reduce the fear of bringing it to the team. Verifiable information about the effects of a problem on patient care can influence most members of a health care team to deal with an issue, no matter how anxiety-producing it is. Research information from the professional literature about the effects of the problem situation on patient recovery or on quality of service provided can undergird the self-confidence of the person who wants to deal with the problem.

If the team has previously dealt constructively and successfully with conflict, the fear of once again confronting a difficult problem with candor is substantially less.

Increasing group cohesiveness is not without its dangers, however. It is easy to fall into the error of believing that, just because everyone in the group agrees on an issue or a decision, that decision is the best one. If the group is closed off from changing viewpoints, from isolated or alienated groups, and from current and widespread, though minority, points of view, it may be unaware of the gaps in its knowledge or the errors in its conclusions. A perceptive leader, though she has a firm foothold in the team, also has one foot in the outside world. By the questions she raises and the experiences she shares, she keeps the team apprised of the wider reality. Her proposals to obtain pertinent information by adding new members to the team either temporarily, for specific problems, or permanently, maintains the intellectual and affective vitality of the team.

The nurse leader must maintain the team's access, not only to community information, but also to the institution in which the team functions. This is often very difficult because of the usual constitution of governing boards and the hierarchical structure of organizations. When a governing board, made up of prestigeful people from the community, is permitted to limit the nature and amount of communication that comes to it, decisions may be made on the basis of old perceptions and inappropriate expectations. For example, a board of businessmen may be unaware of the revolution going on in nursing. If nurses are not represented on the board, or if the only nurse is unable to assume any leadership functions on the board, the board's policy decisions can interfere with the essential change processes of the institution. Management consultants may be willing to suggest that the board "permit" a nurse executive to sit on a committee or two, or invite her to give a report on her area of responsibility. The nurse leader must use such opportunities to point out the importance of permanent representation on the board of those "sensors" on the staff who are tuned in to identifying current needs as they become apparent. The institution's board of trustees is, in effect, just another "interdisciplinary" team on which the nurse leader must function.

One of the most vital leadership functions in any group is modeling behavior that overcomes a basic defect in human communication, that we often do not take the time to really understand what we are saying to each other. A leader takes the initiative of establishing a group norm of checking with speakers to make sure she is understanding them, of paraphrasing what someone has just said to help clarify it for herself and the rest of the group, of asking questions that do not imply disagreement or attack but rather are designed to elicit more information. Not only does such behavior help the members of a group to clarify their objectives and the processes for achieving those objectives, but it provides for such enormous personal satisfaction that it substantially increases the enthusiasm and cohesiveness of the group. People are less likely to form cliques to get the recognition they need. People who feel they are being listened to seriously are more apt to listen to other points of view and to collaborate on developing consensus in a group. They are less likely to come late to meetings or fall away from the group altogether. They feel so good about themselves and their contribution that they more readily commit themselves to implementing the group decisions. A group's real agenda, that is so often taken up *after* group meetings, in corridors and during breaks, is openly dealt with during regular meetings, because people feel safe in venturing opinions, expressing feelings, or offering information.

Those groups in which members feel comfortable about bringing up their feelings of frustration and dissatisfaction without fear of being ignored or attacked, and in which such feelings are considered seriously and attempts made to understand and reduce them, are generally groups that function more effectively. The nurse leader, while appreciating the need of task-oriented members to stick strictly to the problem at hand and deal only with "business," must help them see that "business" can be subverted and aborted by people who feel that they are not being listened to because of the traditional status of their roles in an institution, because of their sex or race, because they are not physicians or psychiatrists, because they are new to the team or the institution, or because they are old. If people have a hand in implementing a care plan, they had better not be made to feel that the plan is none of their doing!

Practicing Small-Group Skills

One of the most difficult skills for those with leadership positions in organizations is revealing feelings vis-à-vis those lower in the job hierarchy. There is a prevalent idea, held most strongly in rigidly stratified institutions like the army, that leaders in order to be effective must maintain psychological distance between themselves and those they lead. Such distance is maintained by not revealing feelings of self-doubt, for example. The rationale is often that, if followers learn of a leader's self-doubt, they lose respect for him and his capacity to lead. The error in this reasoning lies in two misconceptions: (a) People believe there are individuals who never have self-doubts; (b) Those who do not speak about their doubts never reveal them in other ways.

There are few individuals who are not aware that leaders, like other human beings, are not perfect, often do not see their way clear to their goals, or sometimes worry about their need for additional skills and knowledge. When someone tries to present himself as completely certain and perfectly self-confident, the response is at best a healthy skepticism about his seeming perfection, and at worst a malicious anticipation of his failure.

No matter how aloof an individual keeps himself from the people with whom he must work, he is never so far that when he misses the target the others cannot see what has happened. When it does happen, and he needs the empathy and support of his followers, he discovers that no groundwork has been laid for support, and he is left to recoup his losses as best he can.

If we look at the data in leadership studies, we see that leaders need to know a great deal about the needs of the people they lead. Without this knowledge, they cannot assess the level of agreement between themselves and the others on goals, on means for achieving those goals, on basic values. Without realistic assessment, the "leader" may be pulling people in one direction, while they pull just as hard in another direction; the results are personal dissatisfaction and low levels of achievement.

To know the people they are to lead, leaders need to provide opportunities for communication and they need to listen well. But communication, to be effective, cannot go only one way. Most people are not encouraged to reveal themselves unless they trust those who are listening. Trust will rarely develop if the listener never reveals anything about himself.

Self disclosure

Self-revelation itself is difficult for many people, because they have never been encouraged to communicate their feelings. Self-revelation is doubly difficult in the face of the belief that it betrays weakness and so lessens effectiveness in leadership.

The following exercises may help people in leadership positions to share themselves with those they lead. It may help those who aspire to positions of leadership to become skillful in contributing to trust in relationships through self-disclosure.

EXERCISE 1

It may be somewhat easier to begin by expressing feelings that we know are shared by most other people in our culture. Given the nature of our attitudes toward aging and the old and given the quality of care we provide for old people no longer able to care for themselves, most of us are afraid of the prospect of a helpless old age.

You may be doing this exercise in a class, as part of a course. Or you may be a supervisor or administrator in an organization, in which case you may do the exercise casually in the course of your working day, or you may introduce it at a staff meeting or a small group training session. Find someone with whom you feel reasonably comfortable, sit down with her for a few minutes, and talk about some of the problems you know old people are having—because you have just read an article about it in the newspaper, or because you have just admitted a patient, an old woman who has obviously been the victim of physical abuse, or because you've just read a book about the problems of aging.[7] Tell the other person how you feel about being old. Ask her how she feels about it.

Then, sit down with another person with whom you feel equally comfortable, and talk about the same thing with her.

Repeat the procedure with other people. As you go from one person to another, you will find that it becomes increasingly easier to reveal your fears and perhaps even your anger at the inevitability of old age. You may also find that you are beginning to talk about this with people to whom you might have been reluctant at first to disclose such personal sentiments. Part of the reason for this is that you have discovered how similar your feelings are to those of the other people. Perhaps as you gather more clear evidence of the universality of your feelings, you may find the nagging guilt that accompanies them to be slowly disappearing. You may even be able to admit that the fears are not a sign of weakness, but are a function of education, experience, and an awareness of the realities of life for old people in our country.

If you are part of a class, you may hasten the process by sharing the results of your paired discussions with the whole group. You might respond to these questions: What have you learned about feelings concerning old age? What have you learned about yourself?

As supervisor, administrator, or instructor of the class, you may find it very difficult—perhaps even impossible—to take the first step in the exercise in the group, because there is no one in the group with whom you feel comfortable enough to be so open about your feelings. (If it were easy, there would be no need for exercises like this!) Why don't you, when you are planning for this exercise, arrange to include in the class or meeting one or two people with whom you *do* feel intimate enough to start the process? Then both you and your guests can continue to interact with the others as the self-disclosure becomes less painful. Your guests will make it easier for you, as you will for them.

EXERCISE 2

Before you go on to Exercise 2, you may want to repeat Exercise 1, using other topics of universal concern with significant emotional components. For example, you might tell the other person how you feel about being sick. What are your anxieties about being helpless? Do you like or dislike being tended by others? How much of your autonomy do you insist upon maintaining in decision-making concerning your treatment and care? What is the level of your trust for health practitioners?

Exercise 2 involves practice in self-disclosure concerning areas of functioning where the specific need for maintaining distance between superior and inferior roles has been inculcated in us. We can start with a question about a very small part of that area and try to increase the significance of the questions as we continue to practice the skill.

Using the same procedure as in Exercise 1, start with someone you feel most comfortable with, probably because she is on the same level of the social/institutional hierarchy as you are. If you are a teacher, tell her the fear you have about some of your students leaving your class inadequately prepared for professional practice. Let her tell you how she feels about it if she is also a teacher, or how she feels about a comparable aspect of her profession.

If you are a supervisor or administrator, tell your partner how you feel about not being able to know about everything that is going on in your sphere of authority. If you are a student, tell her your fears about watching someone dying and being able to provide that person the professional care he needs.

As you go from your peer to people who are involved with you in hierarchical relationships or relationships that traditionally demand reserve and distance, discuss the same feelings and encourage them to express their feelings about situations in their own lives that are comparable. For example, a staff nurse paired with her supervisor may reveal that she worries that she does not always have adequate information about a patient's relationships with his family, a lack of knowledge that may lead to errors in her nursing care plan. Or a student may disclose to her teacher her self-doubts about becoming a competent professional.

Eventually, talking in this systematic way with people you lead and/or follow about feelings that go deeper and deeper, you may get to the point—not without discomfort—of telling a group of nurses you supervise how hurt and excluded you feel when they stop talking among themselves because they see you coming down the corridor. You may get to the point of telling your students that you sometimes worry about not always being able to communicate to them in the most helpful way. You may get to the point of telling a patient that you wish you knew more than you do about what people need.

Notes

[1] The discussion of knowledge and beliefs shared by professionals is adapted from Charlotte Epstein, *An Introduction to the Human Services* (Englewood Cliffs, N.J.: Prentice-Hall, 1981), Chapter 4.

[2] Mary F. Arnold, L. Vaughn Blankenship and John M. Hess, *Administering Health Systems* (Chicago: Aldine-Atherton, 1971), pp. 48–49.

[3] Nancy A. Bruner and Lillian E. Singer, "A Joint Practice Council in Action," *Journal of Nursing Administration*, 1979, Vol. 9, No. 2, pp. 16–20.

[4] John J. Horwitz, *Team Practice and the Specialist—An Introduction to Interdisciplinary Teamwork*, (Springfield, Ill.: Charles C. Thomas, 1970), p. 64.

[5] Norman Cousins, *Anatomy of an Illness as Perceived by the Patient* (New York: W.W. Norton Co., Inc., 1979).

[6] Abraham Maslow, *Eupsychian Management: A Journal* (Homewood, Ill.: Richard D. Irwin and Dorsey Press, 1965), pp. 125–126.

[7] Sharon R. Curtin, *Nobody Ever Died of Old Age* (Boston: Little, Brown, 1973); and Charlotte Epstein, *Learning to Care for the Aged* (Reston, Va.: Reston Publishing Co., 1977).

chapter five

The Independent Nurse Practitioner: A Leadership Route

One of the observations made at a recent nursing research conference was that "advanced clinical nursing practice will never exist unless the management and political elements of nursing lead the way."[1]

In other sections of this book we discuss the leadership openings available to nurses in management and to those who have become involved in political activities. Here, I would like to examine with you some leadership behaviors affecting the establishment of independent clinical nursing practices that nurses interested in establishing such practices can engage in.

Impeding Factors

The courage and perseverance of individual nurses, together with the external pressure of the need for primary care practitioners, have already resulted in the establishment of thousands of nursing practices at various levels of independence from physicians' practices. What we need to do, it seems, is to identify social factors that impede the progress of nurses into independent practice; factors that impel many nurses into successful independent practice; factors that keep others in the traditional role; and factors that cause still others to condemn those who are making the change.

Fear of change

Maddy Gerrish, a nurse who owns and directs her own mental health center gives a clue from her own experience to what the general atmosphere has been in relation to independent practice for nurses: "The education and training I had gained did much to improve my skills in individual, family and group therapy and also community consultation, but there was never a suggestion that a nurse could work for herself or manage her own practice and perhaps employ others. This kind of thinking was deemed radical and impossible."[2]

Maddy Gerrish tells of her experience with bookkeeping firms that actively interfered with her objectives because the people who ran them were presumptuous enough to act on their prejudices:

> "Indirectly the messages we received were these: (1) women don't know how to run a business; (2) we did not have the credentials for such a venture. While several of the firms had handled professional corporations, they had been organizations run by male physicians. We tried to select the firm that had the least negative attitude toward us. Even so, the year was full of difficulties. Finally at the end of our fiscal year we discovered why. They were so convinced that we would not be viable that they were reluctant to give us any time (i.e., advice with problems that came up); we were relegated to the least experienced and least knowledgeable employee, etc. We solved the problem by changing accounting firms, first having obtained the names of several women accountants in the area and interviewed them."[3]

It may be that this kind of attitude should be classified under fear of change, a kind of "future shock" described by Toffler. To see change inexorably occurring while being unable to understand or accept the new world that results can be terrifying. Unfortunately, few of us have ever been formally educated in dealing with change. As a matter of fact, the way we are taught in school leaves us with the very strong impression that the world we know is immutable. Though teachers may say that change is inevitable, they do not really know what that means, nor do they know how to help children understand the meaning and implications of change, or how to encourage them to become involved in making the changes they think are desirable. By fact and by implication, teachers teach children that established values are to be accepted without question, that authoritative prescriptions for behavior are to be obeyed, and that what one reads in textbooks is true. The amazing fact is that so many of us grow up with some flexibility, some skills in adapting to change, and even some creativity in our approach to solving problems. It is no wonder that so many of us are frightened when we are confronted with the suggestion that our familiar world needs changing!

Sexism

Another factor that might be considered is the whole matter of sexism in our society. The fact that nursing has been permitted to develop as a woman's profession has exacerbated the difficulty of separating nursing practice from the stereotype of women. Thus, if women are weak, unintellectual, overemotional, and dependent "by nature," it follows that they are not competent to engage in responsible pursuits where they are accountable for the soundness of their judgments in matters of great importance. Consequently, the suggestion that a nurse is qualified to practice her profession independently is viewed as an unresolvable paradox; it is impossible to take it seriously. Should some of the misguided persist in advancing the viability of independent nursing, then the merely laughable becomes "dangerous" and opponents may go to extreme lengths to prevent the institution of such practice.

Ignorance of nursing

A third factor to be considered is the sheer magnitude of ignorance concerning the knowledge and skills of the professional nurse. The peculiar collection of beliefs concerning the work and knowledge of the nurse has been fostered by that modern maker of myth, the cinema. That the "angel of mercy" is also a well-educated professional, with sophisticated intellectual and practical skills, is only dimly noted by most people, who encounter a nurse when they are under great stress and who respond essentially to the immediate relief of discomfort she provides. The stereotype blocks the questions that might be raised when the person is not in crisis: What can the nurse teach me, how can the nurse help me, what can the nurse do to keep me healthy? These are questions people seldom ask physicians, yet they ask such questions of authors of uplift books, of beauticians, of gym instructors. It is time they started asking them of nurses.

It may be noted in passing that nurse practitioners are almost universally accepted by patients—for the quality of care delivered and apparently for other, more subtle factors that contribute to a positive perception of the care. One of these factors may be that most nurse practitioners do not present a picture of someone who is so busy with "serious" problems that she has no time to sit down and listen to the small concerns of the patient or client. Another factor may be that her responses are designed to communicate, not to obfuscate; the nurse will never tell a patient or his family, "We'll do what has to be done; it's too complicated for you to understand." The nurse knows that the patient's confidence in the practitioner must be a function of openness in communication and that he needs information in order to participate in the decision-making concerning his health. Fostering patient dependence by keeping him ignorant and in awe of the practitioner is not the nurse's way, and apparently patients like the nurse's way.

Personal/Professional Factors

What moves some nurses into the pioneering efforts required to become independent practitioners? The motivating factors are probably as varied as there are individuals and as complex as each person is unique. The best we can do is look at some of the behaviors of those who took the step and hear some of the things they say. Out of all this may emerge a pattern of a kind of leadership behavior that is identifiable, and perhaps teachable.

Lucille Kinlein became an independent nurse practitioner because she was tired of trying to rationalize away not doing on the job what she had learned was right.

> For example: "We should make professional judgments in nursing," nurses would agree. Then, however, each would add qualifications to that statement, and rationalizations, weakening her stance. The discussion would then be dominated by sentences beginning, "But we shouldn't . . ." And, "We can't . . . ," until finally the nurses would arrive at a definition of judgment so distorted that it bore little resemblance to the real meaning of the word.
>
> In this confusing way the contradictions were compounded and hence, what was defined as a nursing judgment between the hours of 11 p.m. and 7 a.m. was redefined as a medical judgment between the hours of 7 a.m. and 3 p.m. and as eclectic from 3 p.m. to 11 p.m.—the definitions being based on the timing of physicians' rounds in the hospital. Such mental gyrations have led to a continuing failure to appreciate and discriminate among the real meanings of the words *health, illness, nursing* and *medicine.* "To nourish and sustain a person" cannot be identical with "to diagnose and treat an illness," nor can the episodic nature of medical care be identical with the continuing nature of helping one to stay healthy.[4]

She rejected the idea that nursing was an extension of medicine, and saw it instead as an extension of *the client.*[5] The purpose of the nurse-client relationship was not medical treatment of the patient but increasing the ability of the client to improve or maintain his state of health.[6] This self-care concept is implicit in humanistic philosophy as we present it here and constitutes, as Kinlein maintains, a framework for nursing that is distinct and separate from the medical philosophy.

In setting up her own office to practice nursing, she identified five criteria of any professional practice and made them the basis for her nursing practice:

> 1. *Availability:* knowledge by the public that there are offices out of which the professional service is dispensed
> 2. *Accessibility:* contact by phone or letter for appointment
> 3. *Accuracy:* members of the profession use the latest developments in the

field, learned through data collection, results of lab tests, precedent cases, experimental design, etc.

    4. *Accountability:* constant communication between client and professional until a terminus is reached

    5. *Autonomy:* initial direction determined by the professional; initial decision-making, sustained implementation of judgments, evaluation of results, termination, analysis of effectiveness[7]

Leadership qualities of practitioners

1. *They have learned the knowledges and skills of the profession and they want to use what they have learned.* The really well-educated professional feels great frustration when she is not permitted to make decisions and take actions on the basis of what she knows. The frustration often provides the impetus for finding a situation where she can utilize all her knowledge and skills. The alternative is to permit the erosion of skill and the atrophy of knowledge so that, ultimately, one offers limited service with some degree of comfort, because the limitation matches the limitation in ability. Practitioners' high levels of knowledge and skill have given them the confidence to resist the assumptions by other professionals that they are not qualified to practice. Kinlein found, for example, that some laboratories insisted she needed to have a physician order and interpret results of tests, when she knew her own competence in this area and refused to accept the limitation to her practice.[8]

2. *The need to be autonomous is greater than the fear of being independent.* Some people have developed to a level of self-actualization where autonomy is a facet of their personalities. When a person's sense of self has developed to a point where he has a certain sense of control over his life; when he has learned to appreciate himself, recognize his strengths and forgive his weaknesses; when he knows that he is respected and can afford to respect other people, then he requires and obtains autonomy in managing his life. He makes decisions, some of which entail some risk, but he is willing to accept responsibility for those decisions. He establishes relationships with others that are mutually satisfying, giving and getting freely, recognizing the interdependence of human beings. He assesses situations realistically and, though he may feel fear when the risks are great or the situation beyond his knowledge and experience, his persistent need for autonomy and independence overshadows the fear and helps him prevail. Though many people succumb to the fear of being independent in such instances, the autonomous individual—though he may seek out help and support—maintains his autonomy and, ultimately, makes his own decisions and achieves his own objectives.

3. *The desire to go it alone is not so great that the need for support is over-looked.* The really autonomous, self-actualizing individual is not afraid to ask for help when he needs it. Because he is reality-oriented and knows what he does not know, because he is in touch with himself and knows when he needs others, and because he is, above all, independent, he can accept the knowledge and support of others when he needs them in times of crisis. However, the knowledge and support are used only to help him through the crisis quickly and on to the path again toward his goal. When the opportunity arises, he is ready to provide support to others in stress.

One of the problems faced by many pioneers trying to "go it alone" in breaking new ground is the feeling that they are all alone. There seems to be no one to talk with about mutual experiences, no one who will really understand what they are going through because they have been through it, too.

When I first took a job as social scientist with the Philadelphia police department, I spent most of my time in the job teaching race relations to police officers. The resistance to what was being presented was so great, and the strategies available at the time were so limited, that I often felt discouraged and anxious that I was not achieving the goals that I had set for myself.

Finally, in desperation, I volunteered to work with ambulatory patients in a local psychiatric hospital, hoping that I could establish communication with the psychiatric staff and perhaps share with them some of the problems I was facing in my work. The idea I had was that there might be some exchange between professionals facing similar problems, a sharing of insights and information.

What a hope! Since I was not a psychiatrist, the assumption seemed to be that there was no basis for communication. The staff were quite willing to permit me to work with the patients, thinking that as a volunteer I would bring them some minor distractions. When the chief of staff finally got around to observing what I was doing, he expressed surprise that I was working on a professional level using interesting strategies to help patients maintain their psychological connection with life outside the hospital. But by then my patience was at an end, and I terminated my program. It was not until years later that I met other human relations strategists who were coming into the law enforcement field; I was able to share with them some of my experiences, and to learn from theirs.

The resistance to equal-status, interdisciplinary communication is so great that most of us are deprived of the opportunity to learn much of what older professions have already experienced. Each new human service seems to be required to invent the wheel all over again.

One nurse-practitioner, to reduce the "loneliness and alienation of solo practice,'' makes a point of discussing what she is experiencing with nurses she encounters in other settings.[9] She not only helps herself, but serves an important leadership function by spreading the word about new professional opportunities.

Many nurses have discovered that forming a partnership or a corporation for independent practice fulfills many of the needs created by going into a new form of practice. Such organizations provide opportunity for peer review, for talking about the work with someone who understands, and for sharing information. It is important to choose partners for such an association carefully, to make sure that goals and personalities are compatible.

4. *The anxiety of working without clear authoritative guidelines is not overwhelming.* These are people who, in the absence of clear legal or administrative guidelines, are able to define their own parameters for practice. "Nurse practitioners need to consider and decide in advance the rules or policies they will abide by strictly and the ones on which they will compromise."[10] Because they have a clear philosophy of life and of professional practice, practical guidelines for functioning that are consistent with that philosophy develop naturally. If these guidelines imply a new interpretation of policy or law, the nurse leader is able to demonstrate that the old interpretation was an error. If the guidelines imply that the law as written is wrong, the nurse leader is willing either to challenge or to try to change the law, so that it becomes consistent with the philosophy she holds.

We do not suggest that this process of changing practice or challenging law can be done without anxiety. What we do observe is that the clarity of the nurse leader's philosophy seems to provide the self-confidence needed to cope with the anxiety and not be overwhelmed by it.

5. *There is a strong desire to fill an unmet need.* Most nurses who go into private practice seem to have recognized a particular population with a serious unfilled need for health care. One is in a community without a physician; another sees a group such as old people or children that is at risk but has not found its way into the health care system, or a group such as women who are in need of the kind of knowledge and sensitivity that a male-oriented system does not seem able to provide. These nurses all feel strongly about the rights of a group to adequate health care, not infrequently because something in their own lives has influenced them to be particularly sensitive to the needs of that group. Perhaps an awareness of the existence of prejudice or a deprivation in their own lives has led to this sensitivity. Perhaps a warm and loving experience as a child, or with a grandparent, has led to empathy for all children or for old people.

But, in addition to identifying populations in need, most nurses who venture into private practice have been able to delineate an area of practice as unique to nursing—an area of health care for which no other profession has assumed responsibility.

Kinlein notes that: "The variety of needs expressed to me by clients during the five years of my practice has included: help with a worry, a fear, a concern about the state of health they are in or might be in; help with a marital problem; help with a child; help with pregnancy; help in making a decision about medical care."[11]

Though each one of these needs may be within the purview of some profession practicing today, a person would be hard put to make his way from professional to professional each time he felt such a need. The profession committed to holism and humanism and not circumscribed by the mystique of "busyness," crisis intervention, and obscurity in communication is uniquely qualified to facilitate the person's course through life.

Perhaps it is here that the profession continues to miss its greatest opportunity, to educate students and graduates to recognize that, though nursing and other health professions inevitably have large overlapping areas in knowledge and skills, nursing does have a body of skills, sensitivities, and objectives that no other profession has systematically developed and marked out for itself. This is in the general area of prevention of illness and maintenance of health care.

6. *Nurses who go into independent practice seem to have a strong desire for status and prestige.* This is not an insignificant concern in a culture like ours, where status is closely associated with the kind of work we do and with the income the work generates. The women's movement has raised consciousness of the relationship between the low status of women, the pay differential between "women's work" and traditional men's work, and the whole attitude toward women as the "second sex."

Of course, other minority people in our society have long known that equal access to education, desirable jobs, and high pay do much to ameliorate White Anglo perceptions of inferiority of other groups. This experience has not gone unnoted by women.

Resistance in nurses

Just as we can identify traits in nurses who go into independent practice, we may also be able to identify personality traits of professional nurses who choose to remain in traditional roles or who actively resist and interfere with the work of independent nurse practitioners.

There are many people who need to be told exactly what the limits are to their authority, to their competence, to their behavior. They look to the law, to the supervisor, to the administrator, to the offical policy, or to the printed word. Often, to them, what has never been done is synonymous with what "can't be done" or "should not be done." Such people do not challenge the status quo, and often actually believe that the law is immutable. They need help in understanding the nature of our legal system, which preserves its vitality not only from the universal nature of the basic law as embodied in the Constitution, but also from the fact that it provides processes for changing the law as need for change becomes apparent.

Such people also need to examine the rationale of different modes of management in institutions, to learn that there are both authoritarian and democratic management systems currently operating, and that it is possible to identify the consequences of each mode. They might also learn about how people have effected change from one mode to the other.

This kind of cognitive approach to authority may ease some of the anxiety generated in some people when a challenge to authority is contemplated. However, they also need to practice skills in communicating with authorities and in planning for change.

Aside from the obvious observation that factors distinguishing the pioneers are not generally found in the personalities of those who travel the well-marked trail, there are some attitudes and behaviors that may distinguish the active resisters from those who just accept the status quo.

Practitioners report that they may encounter active hostility from many nurses in hospitals where the nurse practitioner makes requests for information; they may be snubbed when they come on to a unit; other nurses make it clear that they disapprove of what the practitioner is doing. Some have indicated to physicians and other nurses that they believe the practitioner is overreaching her area of competency, and at least one nurse I have heard about answered a patient's questions by telling her the practitioner was playing at being a doctor.

Such behavior seems to be compounded of a combination of guilt and envy. These nurses may feel guilty because (a) they are aware of needs that are not being met and are doing nothing to address those needs (as, for example, the needs of dying patients who are avoided by the hospital staff); (b) they know they have skills beyond what they are permitted to use and they have some feeling that they are betraying themselves (like the nurse who performed an emergency tracheotomy at three o'clock one morning and saved a patient's life, and then was reprimanded two weeks later at one in the afternoon for loosening a bandage applied by a doctor because she thought it was too tight.); or (c) they know that the games they play that contribute to the pretense that they are the stereotype nurse are dishonest (as in the doctor-nurse game in which the nurse makes recommendations to the doctor in such a way as to permit him to follow the recommendations even while he is pretending that she did not make them.)[12]

The envy of the nurses who may even go so far as to sabotage a practitioner's work may come from a thwarted desire to do what practitioners are doing, to find fulfillment, and even to achieve prestige. If the desire is there and is thwarted by fears of inadequacy, it may be achieved by education and the kinds of communication and support that can be provided by nurse leaders.

Nurses in supervisory and administrative positions who take a similar position of hostility and resistance may be acting on the basis of a somewhat different factor. In the system as it currently operates, they have apparently achieved the success they want. They have a certain amount of autonomy and power that goes with their position and they have attained prestige in their institutions and the salary commensurate with that prestige. They may believe that they have nothing to gain from permitting the nurses they supervise to practice with more autonomy, or giving the outside nurse practitioner hospital privileges. On the contrary, they may see the increasing independence of nurses viewed as lower in status as a direct threat to their own self-concepts. After all, if other people can achieve independently what they have achieved by adhering to the traditional precepts of loyalty, service, obedience, and denial of self, then how much is their achievement worth? At all costs, they must prevent the devaluation of their own success!

The shortsightedness of this view must be apparent. The increasing prestige of a profession redounds to the prestige of every professional. As leaders move the profession forward, these resisters will also be able to function with increased autonomy. The view is also self-destructive as it limits the development of the self-actualizing spiral, fixating the supervisor or administrator at a level of interaction characterized by authoritarianism or, at best, despotic benevolence. Such a supervisor may never achieve the development in autonomy, mutually constructive interaction, and sheer joy of living that she is capable of.

In spite of all this, it should be remembered that most nurses probably feel no hostility toward practitioners; though they may do nothing to support them, neither do they interfere with what they are trying to do. Also, in institutional and political settings, there are nursing supervisors and administrators who act as leaders in trying to change the traditional perception of the nurse's role. (There are professionals in other fields who are concerned with making changes—even when they must "blow the whistle" on the institutions that employ them. Though whistle-blowing deals more with public disclosure of institutional violations of the law when attempts to effect changes from within have failed, public disclosure of archaic practices may very well be an equally useful instrument in the future for professionals in nursing.)

Practitioner Roles

There are a number of leadership functions associated with the whole nurse practitioner movement that lend themselves to gradation on the basis of the various levels of responsibility assumed by the nurse practitioner. On the very lowest level is the practitioner who takes a job with an onsite physician and acts, in effect, like the eyes and ears of the physician. She takes specific direction from him in seeing patients, either in his office or as in England, for example, in home visits. There she takes information about the condition of the patient and brings it directly to the physician who uses the information to make diagnoses and give further direction for treatment to the nurse. In this kind of situation, the nurse acts almost exactly like the traditional nurse, doing nothing without direct orders from the physician. She does not answer questions concerning the patient's condition unless she is sure the physician wants her to respond to questions. The treatment she gives is generally limited to dressings and injections specifically ordered by the onsite physician. The nurse makes no referrals, taking what information she has back to the physician so he can provide further treatment or make what referrals he thinks necessary.

The nurse practitioner in this case has a job with somewhat extended responsibility; however, though she does see patients on her own, the fact that she has her office hours at the same time as the physician makes it clear that the physician is in charge of the office and is to be constantly consulted. Whatever decisions she makes concerning care planning and treatment are the traditional kinds of decisions made by the registered nurse. In the literature, this kind of practitioner is seen as contributing to the reduction of the physician's work load rather than taking on new functions that the physician has had neither the time nor inclination to take on.

Sometimes the press of work is so great that the nurse who assumes the job originally as merely an extension of the eyes and ears of the physician works her way into a more independent position where she sees patients who need a certain level of treatment. They come to her for that treatment without first going to the physician. She may have a separate office and treatment room; as patients come in to the physician's suite, some go to the physician directly and some come to her.

Out in the community, she gradually begins to make contact with patients of her own and, although she uses the physician as a consultant, she may make diagnoses and give treatment without consultation, making the professional judgment that consultation is not necessary.

In many areas, where physicians do not make house calls, the nurse practitioner fills a real need in that she makes many house calls over a wide geographical area. Not only is this important for people without transportation facilities, but she fills a real need for housebound people, for very old people who are physically unable to make their way around, or for families where one child is ill and the mother cannot leave the house because she must care for a number of other children.

One of the biggest difficulties in the way of the nurse practitioner lies in the fact that there are still some states that do not permit her to practice without a physician on site and available for immediate consultation. However, even with this bar to her practice, the nurse practitioner, especially the one who gets out into the community, is able to identify needs that the physician has never identified and to fill those needs.

One practitioner conducts a women's clinic in addition to her regular practice and provides not only primary care for women's illnesses but also advice and help in family planning, a service that has never been provided before in that community.

Another nurse practitioner heads a student health service in a college, where she provides primary health care for students. In addition she offers a comprehensive program of health education that has been lauded by the faculty and students. Students say that not only does the nurse give good health care but that she seems genuinely interested in their health, and is always ready to take time to listen when they want to talk to her about their health and related concerns. She works with individuals and small groups in the health education program and it appears to be very successful.

Still another nurse practitioner has been appointed special education nurse in a public school where she is responsible for primary delivery to children who are identified as special. These are children who have physical, emotional, and learning difficulties. In addition to dealing directly with the children, she has developed a program of counseling for their parents.

Leadership functions

Three essential leadership functions focus on the work of the nurse practitioner:

1. Outreach into the community.
2. Identification and drawing in of neglected groups to the health care system.
3. Changing the nature of the practice of primary health care delivery vis-à-vis these neglected groups.

Outreach requires knowledge of and skill in the dynamics of human interaction, especially in communities that are not native to the practitioner. It also requires skill in gathering information about a strange community, and the ability to develop trust in the stranger who is the practitioner. It requires the kind of sensitivity illustrated by these writers:

> There's an additional factor in the resistance of some clients to having nurses visit their homes. It imposes on their right to privacy. I've been intrigued with how strongly this has been felt by the working-class population. I'm not talking about particular racial or ethnic groups. I'm talking about ordinary people who say, "Why should I let you into my home? I'll come to you."
>   In terms of unmet health care needs, how do we fit into the kind of nonsystem that often occurs in inner cities? How do you do health care when you are

only safe if you go in pairs or if you get the person on the corner to go with you? Can we afford this kind of service? What kinds of access do nurses have to urban populations, particularly those living in concentrated poverty areas in cities? Health professionals wall themselves up in agencies, but so much of what needs to be done is right in clients' homes. If we went door to door in large housing projects letting people know we are available and responding to situations presented to us, how would we overcome their suspicions of the public worker who comes around and investigates? Many of the mental health clinics are set up so that they are sitting right across the street from neighborhood housing projects. The workers are literally sitting in their offices watching people becoming more and more disturbed on their balconies across the street. The only time someone intervenes is when the police or firemen are called to go in and drag a person out. How can nurses intervene in this kind of dynamics?[13]

A focus on neglected groups requires a knowledge of different cultures and life-styles. It requires an ability to relate to people with whom the practitioner has not had much experience. It requires sensitivity to what has happened to neglected groups, awareness of the group's experience so that what is said does not offend.

Changing the nature of primary health care delivery requires the provision of aspects of health care that have not been considered a part of the medical practice and so have not been offered to those who needed it. The whole matter of hospitalization in our system seems to cry out for creative change. Some nurse practitioners talk about the necessity for and difficulty of obtaining hospital privileges. In most hospitals, it is easier for nurses to come in and work with patients if they are called in as consultants by physicians. However, some hospitals have permitted nurses to go through the regular procedure for being admitted to the staff, and they are then free to see patients' charts and write orders and progress notes.

Some thoughts occur to me concerning nurse practitioners and use of hospitals. In institutions of all kinds—hospitals, universities, corporations—the individual caught up in the bureaucratic machinery is generally at a great disadvantage. He often does not understand the system and has things done to him that he feels powerless to control.

Some time ago, I wrote a few words about the feelings of helplessness of patients in hospitals that relate to this point:

We may be surprised to discover that many patients are afraid of hospital personnel. I do not mean that they are frightened about being sick, or about the treatments they must undergo. This, too, is frightening, of course, and understandably so. What I am talking about here is the kind of fear people have of other people that is the essence of captivity and enslavement. Patients are often afraid that, if they complain about what is happening to them in the hospital, they will be badly treated (in vague, unexplainable ways) in retaliation for their complaints. Some feel that if they make too many requests of hospital personnel, no one will answer their call when they are in serious difficulty and need help immediately.

To say that these fears are unfounded is really beside the point. They are the kinds of fears that are generated by feelings of powerlessness—whether the person is in a hospital or in any ordinary political-social situation. The point is that he finds himself in a repressive society, at the mercy of the people in power. He feels that he must play a completely submissive role or suffer dire consequences.

This does not mean that, if he feels that the hospital staff is authoritarian and threatening, he will do everything they want him to do without question or complaint. Not at all! We have learned in the societies of men that the oppressed find all kinds of ways to get back at their oppressors. Of course, the ways that patients find to retaliate against oppression and to reduce somewhat their feelings of powerlessness, often interfere with their getting well. (The patient who does not get well may be viewed, and often is, as their failure by the people who are treating him.) The fact that the patient himself is hurt by his behavior is not so surprising. In all societies people have immolated themselves for similar reasons—from the Buddhist monks of Vietnam who burned themselves alive to protest an oppressive political regime, to the American slaves who often rebelled desperately and futilely against the superior numbers and arms of their owners.

All of this may sound far-fetched to some people. After all, comparing patients to slaves! Really!! But what we must keep in mind is not the *degree* of oppression or frustration but the processes involved in the interaction between authoritarian personnel and people who feel unable to escape from their authority. Even school children with authoritarian teachers respond in similar ways, and are labeled 'discipline problems' and 'incorrigible' before they are banished to the Siberias of special classes and special schools.[14]

The very fact that he is ill often reduces the ability of a person to protect himself from instances of plain inefficiency. I know of one case where an old man was hospitalized because he had fallen and hurt his head badly. The doctor wanted him on complete bed rest, but no one could make him understand that he was not to leave the bed to go to the toilet. The hospital practice in such cases was to use restraints. The man's daughter refused categorically to permit her father to be tied down. She sat with him all day to see that he didn't try to get out of bed, and she arranged for a private-duty vocational nurse to sit with him at night.

The day after his first night in the hospital, she came in very early and found the LVN sleeping in an easy chair beside the bed and the old man's hands tied to the bed rails where he had obviously been struggling and twisting for a long time until his wrists were bruised. Ordinarily he would have been articulately indignant and have demanded that this outrage be ended. But, sick as he was, he was unable to do more than struggle weakly.

I have no doubt that a nurse practitioner who works with a client in the hospital, develops care plans, helps him deal with stress, acts as a link with his family, and works with him to prepare for leaving the hospital, can be of inestimable value in leading the patient back to health. However, when nurses begin to talk about having hospital privileges so they can put clients in the hospital for treatment of a nursing problem, I believe they are falling into the trap of the medical model. The philosophy and thrust of nursing practice in the community is to provide nursing care *outside* of institutions. The objective is to work with the person so that he continues his life effectively in his own setting. When it becomes necessary for him to enter a hospital for treatment of disease, that is a medical function. Once in the hospital, professional nursing care is needed, of course. Nursing judgments must be made and nursing objectives defined. But institutionalizing a person for any reason should, I think, be a last resort; not because there is something intrinsically wrong with institutions but because we human beings have been unable to manage institutions for the benefit of the individual. In the process of achieving what appears to be desirable outcomes, we subject people to quite undesirable and even destructive stresses and trauma. Often, the articulated outcomes are never really achieved, and there are a great many outcomes that institutional managers prefer not to recognize.

A nurse practitioner may undertake to change the nature of health care delivery with those groups of people who have traditionally been discriminated against. She has an advantage as a practitioner in that she does not have to convince a physician to make changes in care planning and in professional and personal interactions with patients belonging to these groups, nor that they should be included as part of his patient load. Working independently, she can do what she feels is right. She provides primary health care to a great many people who have had little or no such care in the community. Potential nursing leaders can find, without much difficulty, populations that are in great need but are not being fully served by health care providers. Marian M. Havlovic, for example, tells of patients with metastatic cancer who received oncologic treatment, but needed "continuous, consistent high-quality medical, psychiatric, and other related supportive services" that no one was supplying.[15] She stepped into the breach, conducting regular clinics and consulting with the referring physicians concerning psychiatric management of the patients.

Women, as a group, are in the market for nursing care, clearly expressing a need for collaboration with knowledgeable health practitioners to understand their own bodies and rid themselves of the myths on which they were raised.

It is worthwhile to examine a significant leadership role that the nurse practitioner can undertake with regard to the treatment of children. It has been noted that problem recognition is one of the most neglected functions: "Problem recognition is one of the most poorly and most under-performed functions. Middle ear infections and lead poisoning are common, particularly among disadvantaged children, and their consequences can be severe.

Yet these problems often go unrecognized even among children who see medical care providers.''[16]

Children as a group need nurse/advocates who can detect health needs, teach them how to maintain their health, and intercede for them with the system and with adults who do not care about or who are unaware of their problems.

The nurse practitioner has been able to get out into the community and talk to parents, develop a knowledge of the child's surroundings in order to recognize children's problems, and then, when children have had contact with a medical care practitioner, follow up to see that care is maintained and that causes of the illnesses are removed—activities that primary care deliverers rarely engage in.

Teachers as a group can use the services of a practitioner whose clinical experience has been in schools. The stresses of teaching are enormous, and colleagues are notoriously reluctant or unwilling to provide the support needed in recurring crises. A nurse who recognizes the stresses of teaching and can provide knowledge, support, and therapy to maintain health could carve out a busy practice for herself.

Nurses as a group could profit from the ministrations of a colleague whose empathy for their work-related stresses will be great. In spite of the fact that the experience of many independent practitioners has been that nurses do not support them in their pioneering efforts, there are nurses who would be grateful for a nurse's help.

Dying patients desperately need professionals who can be honest with them, can relieve some of their physical suffering, and can help them to come to terms with the awareness of their imminent death. Most health professionals abandon the dying, we know. Some few have moved in to fill the need, but many more are needed.

Parents are forever in need of help in maintaining an optimum quality of life. Their relationships with their children—and with each other concerning their children, maintaining the family's health, dealing with relationships in the family raise questions that need answering, not in a medical context, but in a health maintenance context.

Old people need advocacy and help in adjusting productively to old age. Younger people need help in facing their own aging and in relating to the aged in their families. A desperately needed service, I think, is one that will permit old people to remain in their own homes instead of being institutionalized. We have so much evidence of the undesirability of institutionalization for the aged; yet the pressures are increasing on old people to leave their homes for "nursing" homes (usually nothing of the sort!), boarding homes, or even the homes of reluctant relatives. Institutions for old people are generally inadequately staffed so that people do not get the assistance they need in the activities of daily living, exercising, bathing, and dressing; the physical facilities are usually dreary and not very clean, leading to depression, deprivation of sensory stimulation, and even disease. It is not unusual to learn that old people are given inadequate or unbalanced diets and that they are arbitrarily regimented (e.g. lights out at 9 p.m.) for the convenience of the institution's managers.

Old people in certain communities also are afraid to walk alone. Perhaps the nurse practitioner can devise some way of influencing the municipal government to assess realistically the safety measures provided in poor areas of the community and do something more effective to provide a greater margin of safety.

There is something else, too, to be considered here, and that is the perception of the nurse vis-à-vis her own safety in poor neighborhoods, and in minority-group neighborhoods. It is not likely that anyone reared in our kind of society is free from the fearful expectations of certain groups of people—expectations that are a function of the beliefs we hold about people. If the individual sees only what he expects to see,

> then each experience of 'seeing' merely provides corroborative evidence that the stereotype [his belief] is not a lie at all. I expect Black men to commit crimes; I see a Black man; he looks suspicious to me; I run; I am sure that if I had not run he would have done something criminal to me. So I become my own agent for providing the evidence that convinces me that I was right all along! . . .
>
> Among policemen, for example, we see this process operating with tragic consequences. Many of them start out with the conviction that Black people are more inclined to criminality than are Whites. Consequently, they are more suspicious when they see a Black person than when they see a White person in the same situation. They actually 'see' a Black person trying to hide something, or trying to hide himself, or having a bulge in his pocket that means a weapon. Therefore Black people—especially Black men—are more often stopped for questioning or frisking. When this happens very often, they become angry at the injustice and begin to resist the questioning and frisking, and arguments and fights erupt between policemen and Black citizens. The result is that many Black men get police records for assault and battery on an officer and for resisting arrest. It is a rare magistrate who questions closely to determine what crime brought the policeman on the scene and resulted in the attempt to make an arrest. The 'crime' with which the person is charged occurs after the policeman arrives on the scene!

Just recently a public health nurse insisted that she had clear evidence that all Black men carried knives. The "evidence" she pointed out was the Black handle that protruded from the back pockets of many Black men. Can you imagine her chagrin when a Black man in the group took an afro pick out of his pocket and showed it to her?

But the really significant aspect of her response was the obvious anger that was mixed with her frustration. Anger at being embarrassed? Anger at being proved wrong? I worried that this anger might be directed against the same people she still feared, because now—in some convoluted way—they were responsible for her humilation. This kind of prejudice can interfere with the nurse's ability to assess accurately the nursing needs of minority people, and to assume responsibility for filling these needs.

As it becomes clear that adequate identification of health needs seems to be lacking in medical practice, nurse practitioners articulate their own sensitivity to this and suggest that they are prepared to step into the breach. However, "It appears that most nurses bypassed collecting baseline data, doing surveys, or even responding to surveys done by others in identifying health needs they would address. Relating to a population in need or at risk is greatly complicated by the nurse practitioner's expertise, needs, drives, disillusionment with the system, and freedom to move geographically. Medical acceptance or tolerance may have as much to do with the nurse practitioner's selected area of practice as does a population with a health need. In terms of distribution of health care, identification of health needs to be met by potential nurse practitioners may be the essense of success in the future."[18]

It would seem that, though rejecting institutional nursing and establishing independent practices constitute leadership functions for the profession, as with most human functions these are somewhat flawed. If one were to view the nurse practitioner movement from the perspective of our society's needs, and then approach the strengthening of the movement systematically, we would need to use more available information than we do at present. More systematic assessment of needs should be an integral part of the planning and decision-making of the individual nurse going into private practice.

One nurse who was approached by people in her community for help said, "I figured the last thing I wanted to do was fight with doctors, and if the clients took care of that it would handle the matter."[19] She consequently informed potential clients that she would not accept them unless they got agreement from a physician to work with her. Flawed indeed!

Planning for change

The following composite scenario is based on the experiences of many nurse practitioners as well as other nurses who have had to deal with physicians' resistance to their attempts to practice their profession more independently. It is annotated to identify the various phases through which such communication and conflict go; it is diagrammed to illustrate graphically the many pitfalls confronting the nurse leader.

You will note that the essence of more systematic planning for change requires an effort to anticipate all possible eventualities and provide for them. There is usually more that one route to the desired objective; however, some routes are less fraught with risks than are others. (See Figures 5-1).

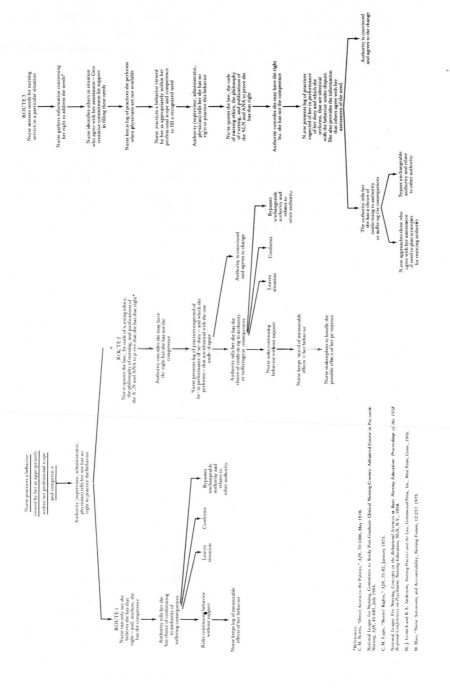

ROUTE 3

Nurse assesses needs for nursing service in a particular situation

Nurse gathers information concerning her right to address the needs*

Nurse identifies others in situation who agree with her assessment—Gets tentative commitment for support in filling these needs

Nurse practices a behavior viewed by her as it performs when physicians are not available

Nurse practices a behavior viewed by her as appropriately within her profes oral scope and competence to fill a recognized need

Authority (supervisor, administrator, physician) tells her she has no right to practice this behavior

Nurse quotes the law, the code of nursing ethics, the philosophy of nursing, and publications of the NLN and ANA to prove she has that right

Authority concedes she may have the right but she has not the competence

Nurse presents log of practices expected of her in performance of her duty and which she performs, that are identical with the behavior under dispute. She also provides the information that others agree with her assessment of the need.

Authority is convinced and agrees to the change

The authority tells her she has a choice of conforming to authority or suffering the consequences

Nurse approaches those who agree with her assessment of need to plan strategies for resisting authority*

Bypasses unchangeable authority and relate to other authority

Nurse practices a behavior viewed by her as appropriately within her professional scope and competence*

Authority (supervisor, administrator, physician) tells her she has no right to practice the behavior

ROUTE 2

Nurse quotes the law, the code of nursing ethics, the philosophy of nursing, and publications of the A N and ANA to prove that she has that right*

Authority concedes she may have the right but she has not the competence

Nurse presents log of practices expected of her in performance of her duty—and which she performs—that are identical with the one under dispute

Authority tells her she has the choice of conforming to authority or suffering the consequences

Nurse risks continuing behavior without support

Nurse keeps record of measurable effects in her behavior

Nurse makes plans to handle the possible effects of her persistence

Authority is convinced and agrees to change

Conforms

Leaves situation

Bypasses unchangeable authority and relates to other authority

ROUTE 1

Nurse can only say she believes she has that right—and, anyhow, she has the competence

Authority tells her she has choice of conforming to authority or suffering consequences

Risks continuing behavior without support

Nurse keeps log of measurable effects of her behavior

Conforms

Leaves situation

Bypasses unchangeable authority and relates to other authority

*References:
C. M. Norris, "Direct Access to the Patient," *AJN*, 70:1006, May 1970.

National League for Nursing, Committee to Study Post-Graduate Clinical Nursing Courses: Advanced Course in Psychiatric Nursing, *AJN*, 44:683, July 1944.

C. M. Fagin, "Nurses' Rights," *AJN*, 75:82, January 1975.

National League For Nursing, *Concepts in the Behavioral Sciences in Basic Nursing Education. Proceedings of the 1958 Regional Conferences on Psychiatric Nursing Education,* NLN, N.Y., 1958.

M. J. Lesnick and B. E. Anderson, *Nursing Practice and the Law,* Greenwood Press, Inc., West Point, Conn., 1926.

M. Mass, "Nurse Autonomy and Accountability, *Nursing Forum*, 12:237, 1973.

Figure 5-1.

Route 1 reveals little or no planning and consequently little or no anticipation of what may happen. The nurse must confront events as they occur, and she is usually not prepared with data or strategies to achieve the result she wants. She should be prepared with data before being confronted by authority, rather than collecting it after being reprimanded. She may never get the chance to use collected data in this situation.

What usually happens with those who choose Route 1 is that they remain in the unchanged situation while anger and frustration continue to build up. Finally, some small exacerbation of frustration causes them to quit the job.

It is possible that, in the particular situation in which the nurse finds herself, one that is not tightly organized into a hierarchical structure, she may be able to find another authority who is not so rigid and who will go along with her proposed change. This is the sort of alternative that employees of institutions or agencies generally do not have but which those who want to establish more or less independent practices in communities usually do have. If one physician won't accept the nurse's referrals, another may; if one laboratory will not do her tests, another may; and if one hospital will not accord her professional privileges, another one may.

Even in an institution like a hospital, it is sometimes possible to bypass the "chain of command" and reach someone in power who sees the validity of the proposed change and is willing to override the decision of the lower level authority. I know of one instance in which a nurse was forbidden by a physician to respond to questions about dying asked by a patient. The physician's response to those questions was either to change the subject or to leave because he was "so busy." Though the patient apparently was not ready to hear that he was suffering from a terminal illness, he was, in his own way, trying to prepare himself to face the fact of his imminent death by indicating that he wanted to talk about dying.

The nurse, herself a supervisor, went to the Director of Nursing Services, who, though she said she recognized the importance of responding to the obvious need of the patient, maintained that the final decision must be left up to the patient's physician.

Just by chance, the nurse met the hospital administrator at a social event and was able to talk to him about her quandary resulting from recognizing the patient's need and being forced to withhold addressing that need. The administrator expressed surprise that such an archaic response as the physician's was still being made, in the light of the progress we have made in freeing ourselves of taboos concerning death and dying. He volunteered to speak to the physician and in the meantime gave the nurse administrative approval to do her best for the patient. He assured her that he would support her in any confrontation with the physician. He offered to inform the Director of Nursing Service that he agreed with her point of view, too, thereby implying that the three of them were on the same side. (He intended to ignore the fact that the supervisor had refused to challenge the traditional pattern of control.)

This kind of process for effecting change may appear almost frivolous, but it should be evaluated in terms of the realities of our culture. We have long recognized that much of our leadership influence is exerted in social situations. At least one Supreme Court decision recognized, in outlawing discrimination against Black people, the importance to a businessman's career of being admitted to country club membership. It is not too far-fetched to suggest that certain skills in social interaction, such as establishing acceptance in social circles where it is possible to influence those with power, might be included in the repertory of leadership skills.

Looking at Route 2 in this effort to introduce nontraditional nursing behavior into a situation, we see that the nurse has prepared herself with some significant data that may bring her closer to her objective. When her behavior is challenged, she is ready to refute a position not based on the facts. Possession of all available factual and scientific data in support of a change can be the most important factor in strengthening conviction. Not only does the nurse taking this route know the law concerning nursing practice, but she knows the tenets put forth by her profession that, by implication, are accepted by other professions and by the public. Though all she is demanding is the right to practice within the law and within the defined professional parameters, to be able to quote the law and the codes can often forestall heated objections based on personal preferences for maintaining the status quo.

Added to this knowledge of what is permitted and prescribed in nursing practice is the clear evidence that the nurse is competent to undertake the challenged behavior. The nurse has, over a period of time, written down the instances where she has practiced this behavior with the full approval and sometimes commendation of the authorities in the situation. It is likely that any nurse who has worked at her profession for any length of time has had occasion to do everything that she is qualified to do at least once. She has done physical assessments, identified obscure symptoms leading to diagnoses, has treated physical trauma on emergency and nonemergency bases, and has used her judgment in a hundred ways when physicians were not present to issue orders or change orders made obsolete by changes in the patient's condition.

Physicians and other health care authorities—especially, perhaps, nurses in supervisory and administrative positions—usually agree tacitly to ignore this fact. An institutional or agency hierarchy can be maintained only by ignoring the fact that nurses sometimes perform duties that they would be reprimanded for at other times. If the real duties of the nurse were discussed in interdisciplinary meetings, in agency planning meetings, and even with patients, nurses could no longer be expected to function merely to assist physicians. In matters where there is disagreement between nurse and physician about treatment, it would no longer be possible to play games that make it seem as if the physician's opinion always prevails or is even always the right one. Physicians and nurses would then be perceived as colleagues, each with their own areas of expertise, and with inevitable overlap of their areas of concern. They would feel free to consult each other as colleagues.

Even in the wider social milieu, it is only by ignoring the reality of what the nurse does in a hospital or in many communities can the medical profession maintain its mystique and its superiority. Keeping forever in the public eye the real functions of nurses can help to break through the screen of selective perception that enables people to see and believe only what they wish to see and believe.

Upon presentation of knowledge of the professional parameters of nursing and the evidence that the nurse already performs a behavior at those times that the institution is willing to permit it, Route 1 may terminate in the capitulation of the authority. The first step in further change has been successful.

However, if the fears and anxieties of the authority relating to changes in the traditional status of nurses are very great, if his need to maintain the status quo is closely tied in with his own sense of self-worth, he may be unable to use the information presented. As a matter of fact, the more information he gets, the more "reasons" he will find to resist using it. Eventually, in the face of further argument, he may fall back on the power of his position: "You'll do as I say because I say you shall!" Estimating the discomfort of persevering in her behavior (or the risk of losing her position if this is the nature of her situation) the nurse may continue to do what she thinks is right. Depending upon how long she can continue, she may start collecting additional data to strengthen her position. For example, she may begin, systematically, to record the measurable effects of her behavior. Since there are generally other factors operating in our society to effect change, it is possible that eventually some of those factors will act on the resisting authority and force him to permit change; they may act on the institution as a whole and compel it to change; or the authority may be replaced with another, more flexible authority. When any one of these things happens, the nurse can use her additional data to establish a new definition of her role.

The nurse has the option of bypassing the resistor and establishing communication with another authority of equal or higher status than the one who rejected her change. There may be some risks associated with this, especially if the first authority is in a position to interfere seriously with her practice. But my experience suggests that the risk is generally overestimated, and bypassing an authority is not nearly as dangerous as most people believe. Often the bypassed one, in order to avoid any kind of confrontation or unpleasantness, will pretend there has been no change, and life will go on as before. If the other authority has some influence on him, he may permit the change, though not approving of it. (Eventually, when he becomes aware of the inevitable direction of the blowing wind, he may even begin to intimate that he always believed that the change was a good idea!)

On the other hand, there may be unpleasant recriminations and hostility toward the nurse, not only from the authority but also from colleagues who are intimidated by the opposition. The nurse leader must assess the risks realistically and decide how much trouble she is equipped to handle. Then she must systematically identify each possible result of her persistence, and devise a step-by-step plan for dealing with each result: The objectives of each plan should be the reduction or elimination of that particular trouble or the increase of her own tolerance to the frustration of the situation.

What the nurse must *not* do is just decide to "live with whatever happens." This approach often results in some kind of crisis, during which decisions are made in haste and feelings of powerlessness are exacerbated. If the nurse is unwilling to remain and continue her controversial behavior, she may leave the situation and find one more congenial to her perceptions of her role. As we have noted before, there are a great many opportunities these days for nurses.

Of course, the nurse may concede that the risks of staying are too great and the problems of finding a new place are too troublesome, and she may decide to conform to the authority's demands. This need not necessarily be the end of change for her. There are leadership functions that she may undertake even while she puts off making a change in the way she practices:

1. She may systematically begin to identify nurses and other professionals who agree with her. Even if she is never able to organize a group to institute widespread change, she will not only sow the seeds for someone else's leadership, but she will also have the satisfaction of intellectual support from others. Such support may very well provide the strength she needs to continue her efforts to effect change.

2. She may look for opportunities to teach about new facets of the nurse's role, and so prepare the way for future change. If she can teach in a nursing program, that is a good way to change the profession. But she should not overlook opportunities for teaching nonprofessionals and for increasing the community's level of acceptance of new roles for nurses. Civic groups, social clubs, and children's organizations all welcome speakers. A nurse has something important to say to them.

3. A nurse may turn her hand to writing. One kind of writing is accepted by the professional journals. Opportunities for publication in popular magazines and local newspapers should not be overlooked. Nurses have regular health columns in newspapers and write articles for health magazines. But there are publications that most nurses may not have thought of, such as college and school newspapers and inhouse newsletters published by many large businesses.

4. She may, as a good neighbor, volunteer some of her unique services to her neighborhood and let people begin to understand what she has to

offer. This is not the same as giving her professional services without charge; it is merely contributing to the community's life the way other people in the neighborhood do. Of necessity, any such contribution must be limited, but it can serve to initiate questions in the minds of people about why nurses are not more accessible to them to help in total health maintenance.

Route 3 provides for the initial assessment of needs for nursing service, gathering of data concerning the right of the nurse to address those needs, the identification of people in the situation who can be called on to work for the change, and the collection of experiential data that probably indicate that the change has already been partially effected. Thus prepared, the nurse is more likely to feel less vulnerable as she works for change, and to achieve the desired objective. She also sets the pattern for planning for other changes, with the nucleus of an organization committed to such planning, that is, if she does not decide to bypass the resisting authority in the interest of saving time. For relatively small changes this may be a preferable bypass. However, she should not overlook the value of having a strong working group to consider other necessary changes. A group that has been instrumental in making even a small change may use that success to undertake more ambitious projects. Also, we must bear in mind the importance of involving the affected individuals in any change process.

Leadership abroad

Just as we are often unaware of possibilities for professional functioning outside the parameters traditionally defined for use, we may be unaware of possibilities that lie outside the geographical area we are most familiar with and comfortable in. In spite of the fact that we are a jet-age society, and mobility supposedly characterizes our style of life, many of us still set our sights close to home. There are opportunities for the nurse leader in Europe, Asia, Africa, and Latin America as well as in the United States. Latin American nations, particularly, have been engaged in some interesting deliberations that nurses may profit from.

> One of the principle goals to which the Ministers of Health of the Americas have committed their peoples through the Ten-Year Health Plan adapted at Santiago in 1972 is the extension of health services in some form to every man, woman, and child in the hemisphere by the end of the decade. The nurse is in a unique position to contribute to the attainment of this objective. Recognizing the need to redefine the nurse's role in regard to the delivery of primary health care, PAHO/WHO, in collaboration with the government of Costa Rica and the College of Nurses in that country, recently sponsored a Seminar on New Dimensions of the Nurse's Role in the Delivery of Primary Health Care. Held

in San Jose from 27 October to 3 November 1976, this meeting brought together 19 professional nurses and 17 physicians from a total of 13 countries.[20]

The definition of primary health care agreed upon by this assembly
seems admirably suited to the objectives of the nursepractitioner function.

> Understood as the set of actions that are placed within the reach of the indi-
> vidual, the family, the community in order to meet their basic needs in regard
> both to the promotion and preservation of health and to the prevention and
> cure of disease, primary care functions as a part of the overall health services
> and generally serves as the user's portal of access to the more costly and com-
> plex levels of care.[21]

Though the representatives apparently agreed without question that
the primary care nurse needs supervision, presumably by physicians, this belief may be related to the quality of nursing education in some of the countries.[22] Nurse leaders from the United States may very well be the ones who
could provide such supervision, as well as provide educational leadership
through WHO or through institutions in individual countries. The need
for primary health care is so great that those who wish to take advantage of
the opportunities in Latin America will probably find few roadblocks in
their way.

Of immediate interest here is their identification of what has happened
to change the concept of the nurse's role:

- A new concept of integrated health care which recognizes that the health
of the individual and that of the population depend not only on the action of
the health sector but also on the efforts of the other sectors of society.
- Acceptance of the fact that participation of the individual and the community in the process of their own development is a right, and that it is a deci-
sive factor in the pursuit and maintenance of health.
- The notable shortage of physicians at the community level, which is ag-
gravated by the tendency toward specialization in clinical areas (where complex and costly equipment reflecting technological and scientific advances is
necessary).
- The rising cost of health care.
- Recognition of the fact that the nurse is underutilized and has the potential to assume more direct responsibilities in the delivery of primary care which
had heretofore been considered to fall within the purview of the physician.

Thus, the nurse is being called upon to contribute more directly and more
effectively in health care—to take over the following primary care activites:

- Diagnosis of the level of health of the individual and of the community as
a whole.
- Decision-making in situations that call for discernment and the application of pertinent solutions.
- Preparation of the individual and the community as a whole so that needs
can be identified and met.

• Evaluation, jointly with the users, of the effect of primary care actions on the health of the individual, the group, and the community.

The primary care nurse is a generalist* whose services and participation in integrated health care are felt directly by the individual, the family, and the community as a whole. This health worker has sufficient competence to take decisions and share responsibilities with the other members as they join efforts to raise the level of health of the population for which they are responsible. The polyvalent nature of the primary care nurse makes it possible for this professional to be used rationally and optimally in achieving effective coverage at low cost without increasing the time needed for basic training.

The work of the primary care nurse is carried out according to the norms contained in official health programs, which are geared to such priority areas as nutrition, maternal and child health, communicable disease control, and environmental sanitation.

Effective fulfillment of these tasks requires that the nurse be able to:

• Assess the overall health of the individual, the family, and the community and understand those mores, beliefs, and ways of life that bear on problems of health, involving the users in the diagnostic process and in discussions of how the problems should be approached.

• Give direct integrated health care to the individual, the family, other groups in the community, and the community itself.

• Initiate treatment or other measures within the nurse's sphere of competence or refer the patients to another level, make decisions in emergencies, and carry out health actions in accordance with program standards.

• Follow the health-disease process in persons with stabilized or long-standing conditions and implement an appropriate plan of care.

• Maintain epidemiologic surveillance in the community, take the necessary related measures, and report to the health system and to the community.

• Provide for and carry out appropriate primary care measures with a view to improving the nutritional status of the population.

• Educate and foster incorporation of the individual, the family nucleus, and the community so that they can identify and meet their own specific health needs.

• Train cadres of traditional health attendants and volunteers for their participation in community health programs.

• Work toward improving the environment and the health status of the population, of the community in general, and of the family nucleus in particular with the participation of the beneficiaries, coordinating this undertaking with the activities of workers in other development sectors at the local level.

• Incorporate the members of the community in the decision-making process in regard to the delivery and evaluation of primary health care services.

• Evaluate the results of primary care on a continuing basis with a view to generating informative feedback.[23]

---

*The term generalist is used in some parts of Latin America to mean the opposite of specialist. This latter concept, in turn, is used increasingly among nurses to refer to the colleague who has greater knowledge and more complex skills in a clinical specialty than the generalist, acquired through formal study.

The counselor or therapist, in working with clients, has usually become proficient in a number of skills designed to help the client work through his problems and arrive at some satisfactory way of continuing his life. What we may not realize is that the counselor's skills are generally useful for developing trust and gaining acceptance in a variety of interpersonal situations. An effective leader is one who is accepted by others as worthy of providing leadership in a particular situation, and one who is trusted to lead in ways that are mutually beneficial to goals shared by leader and followers. There is no reason to expect to receive such acceptance and trust before one has demonstrated behaviors that convince people that one has the knowledge required to explore a problem, and also has the ways of working with people that encourage them to bring their best to the problem-solving process.

At the outset, the nurse leader must realistically confront the facts about how different members of the team perceive a nurse, the stereotypes they hold, and the expectations they have of her appropriate role vis-à-vis the other members of the team. She can be instrumental in getting the team to allot some time to reaching agreement on the functions, not only of the nurse, but also of all the other members of the team. Unless these roles are made explicit, and there is some mutual acceptance of each team member's function, much of the problem-solving process will be subverted and aborted because members are rejecting the contributions of those who they think are overstepping the bounds of their traditional roles.

Defining the Nurse's role

To function in a group made up of people from other disciplines the nurse needs the ability to clearly define her own role and to identify the functions in which she is competent. Without such a clear definition, she cannot hope either to convince the others to accept her point of view or to begin the process of negotiation that may be required to arrive at a mutually acceptable and workable definition of her role and delimitation of her functions. Because writing helps clarify one's thinking by providing concrete feedback information on the results of thinking, this exercise requires that you write a definition of what you think your role would be in an interdisciplinary team.

When you are satisfied with your definition of the nurse's role in an interdisciplinary team and you have identified the nurse's functions in the team, you may wish to share your statements with the other nurses in your group. You will probably discover that many of the identified competencies are individual ones. That is, one person may know much about the community, may be a resident and an active member of community organizations, while another may come to the institution from outside the community and have little or no experience with the population served by the institution. Another nurse, as a result of the nature of her nursing practice, may have developed certain medical skills—such as postoperative neurological assessment of craniotomy patients—that other nurses may not have.

It is always necessary to adjust traditional role definitions to the competencies of the members of a working team. To omit this process of adjustment is to incur the risk of such great dissatisfaction that the team never achieves its fullest potential as a productive, interdisciplinary, problem-solving mechanism.

Any role definition should address itself to the following:

Knowledge and Skill Areas of Technical Competence.   This may include, not only those knowledges and skills that are usually accepted as the nurse's area of competence, but also those that have, by virtue of practice, become a part of the nurse's function, even though little or no public acknowledgement is made of that practice. This may also include areas that the most advance guard of the profession claims as its province. (It is in these areas that the most vigorous team negotiation will probably occur.)

Knowledge and Skill Areas of Competence in Related Fields.   This may include knowledge of various areas of sociology (like intergroup relations, psychology like the various schools of therapy), and knowledge of management and supervision. For nurses, it will also include medical knowledges and skills, whether or not the medical and nursing professions officially recognize them as competencies possessed by the nurse.

Knowledge and Skill Concerning the Immediate Setting.   If you are knowledgeable about the community in which the team functions and you have experience interacting productively with the people in the community, it is well to establish your competence in this area. If you are familiar with the real and informal structure and function of the organization, this can be a significant part of your role-foundation in the team.

Knowledge and Skill in Small-group Dynamics.   This includes matters of group maintenance and productivity, strategies for problem solving, and knowledge of concepts and functions of leadership. In this area we also have the knowledge and skills related to interacting effectively with individuals in different power and status positions.

It may be noted that identifying role competencies inevitably involves identification of values, though sometimes only implicitly. For example, in stating that a function of the nurse's role is interceding to support lower status people whose contributions are being ignored by a high-status member of the team, the implicit value is that it is important to accept the contributions of all team members and consider how they fit into the problem-solving process.

It is not necessary or advisable to read out the whole statement of role and function in a team meeting. There is too much material in such a statement to be dealt with all at once, and the work of the team may come to a halt for a long time while members try to grapple with all aspects of all roles. Rather, let first one aspect and then another aspect of the different roles become the focus of team discussion and negotiation, usually when some minor conflict occurs because of differing perceptions of roles and appropriate functions. At those times, it is important to be prepared with a clear idea of the target facet of the role, so that it may be put before the team for consideration.

Assessing a nontraditional competence

Pick a competence that you have included in your definition of your role on the interdisciplinary team. Be sure that it is one not generally expected to be part of a nurse's function. It may be a contribution of technical knowledge (for example, range of motion exercises for the neck for a postoperative patient); traditional medical knowledge (for example, the causes of hyperthyroidism); or a display of a group dynamics competence (for example, paraphrasing the contributions of team members to make sure they are being understood).

Write the competence down on a small piece of paper without letting anyone else see it, and tuck the paper away for future reference.

Now form a group of seven or eight people, sit in a small circle, and, for about twenty or thirty minutes, discuss the question, "Why is this patient taking longer than expected to recuperate?" (Pick any patient, even if all the people in the group do not know him. Part of the discussion will have to provide information for those who have not had contact with him.)

During the discussion, make every effort to demonstrate the competence that you described on the paper. Of course, you must do so with the welfare of the group in mind. That is, you must use your competence to address a particular group need or to move the group toward its goal.

After the discussion, let the group (a) try to identify the competency that each person was trying to demonstrate; (b) evaluate the effectiveness of the competency (Did the person accomplish what the competency is supposed to accomplish?); (c) evaluate the affective results (Did anyone in the group feel good about the display of the competency? Why? Did it clarify an objective, add to the group's knowledge, make someone feel better about himself? Did anyone in the group feel bad about the display of the competency? Why? Did it make someone feel incompetent, feel hurt, feel frustrated or angry? Was this primarily attributable to the person displaying the competency and the competency itself, or was it also an unresolved problem of the person who felt bad? For example, for some people, any contribution of information from someone else makes them anxious because they were not first to contribute that information; or angry because they think that a person of a certain status or profession is presumptuous in offering the information.)

If a competency is not identified, let the person who tried to demonstrate it tell what it was, and get the help of the group in discovering the factors that prevented identification. When some agreement has been reached on what the factors might be, the group may provide an opportunity in the near future for people to try again to demonstrate the competency more skillfully.

Encouraging consciousness-raising

Though it might appear that this exercise is more suitable for those who are not nurses, the inescapable fact is that nurses, too, hold many stereotypical beliefs of themselves and their profession. So do not hesitate to practice the skill with your colleagues even if you have access at this point only to other nurses.

If you would like to try it in a work setting where there are members of other professions in the group, suggest doing it when the time seems particularly appropriate. For example, someone has just made a blanket assumption about any group, like "That's the way men are"; "Everyone knows Latins are more emotional"; "Children don't know what's good for them"; or "Most of them are senile." The nurse leader can say, "It's unfair to say that about a whole group of people. Look what's happened to nurses because of that!"

Immediately, the nurse proceeds to suggest that the group look a little more closely at the factors that result in such statements and the consequences of believing them. If she suggests using nurses as the illustrative group, she may reassure those in the group who are not nurses that it is safe to express negative ideas; she is not afraid to bring them out in the open and she will not attack anyone else who does. She can thus establish a foundation for trust. Her courage may also spark courage in other nurses in the group, providing a basis for solidarity among them as victims who are, nevertheless, able to deal with the reality of prejudice and discrimination.

If there are others in the group who are made very uncomfortable by this exercise, we can only point out that it is, indeed, more comfortable—momentarily—to avoid confronting unpleasant reality. However, the obvious danger in pretending that we have no prejudices is that prejudice and discrimination persist; the victims continue to suffer and the perpetrators continue to believe that all's right with the world.

In the small group or the team, ask the question, "What do people who are not nurses generally believe a nurse is like?" Then, very quickly, write down on a chalkboard or posted newsprint the question and all the answers that come from the group. Some people may start with the "right" answers: Nurses are just like other people. Nurses are individuals, they're not all alike. Accept these answers and write them down and continue to urge the group to confront the prevailing attitude by asking "How do many people picture nurses?" "What are the characteristics that people expect of nurses?" The answers will begin to come quickly:

white

angels of mercy, caring, sensitive

tough, insensitive to pain and suffering

sexually promiscuous

carry out doctors' orders

women

know less than doctors without questioning them

Now encourage people to provide anecdotal illustrations for each of these traits.

For example, in one group a Black nurse told of answering a patient's call. When she came into the room and asked how she could help, the patient answered, "No. I want a real nurse. Please send in a real nurse." It took a few minutes to elicit the information that a "real" nurse was White. Only practical nurses and aides were Black.

Another group member described a conversation at the patient's bedside between her, the attending physician, and the patient. The patient was insisting that, he go home upon discharge, where he could complete his recuperation with his family's help. The doctor was recommending that he go to a nursing home, because he would need care that required time and energy, and he didn't think the patient should expect his family to provide it. "You can afford it," the physician kept insisting. "Why don't you wait until you're on your feet and able to care for yourself before you go home?"

"I can recover faster at home," the patient answered. "I'm more comfortable at home."

The physician turned to the nurse. "What do you think, Miss Walters? Don't you think it makes more sense for Mr. Jones to go to a nursing home?"

The physician had never discussed the matter with Miss Walters. Because he believed that nurses carry out the doctor's orders without question, he also apparently believed that Miss Walters would corroborate his point of view in this case. He was startled and angry, therefore, when she answered "Oh, I don't know, doctor. If Mr. Jones would feel more comfortable at home and his family is prepared to give him the minimal care he needs, I see no reason why he shouldn't go home to recuperate."

When the anecdotes about stereotyping nurses have all been told, ask the people in the group if they can recall any anecdotes illustrating the stereotyping of other groups. You might start the ball rolling by saying:

The prevailing stereotype of old people is that they are rather childlike and can most effectively be related to as if they had a child's limited ability to make sound judgments. An experience that shows this belief in practice is what happened to one eighty-year-old woman. She had had a spinal tap and was told to lie quietly and not try to sit up or get out of bed for a day.

"Do you understand what I'm telling you?" the nurse asked.

"Yes, of course," the patient answered. "Frankly, I don't feel much like sitting up. I've got a headache."

"Well," answered the nurse, almost cajolingly, "Just to make sure you follow orders, I'm going to tie a string around one wrist." And she proceeded to tie the patient's left hand to the bed rail, making sure the fastener was inaccessible to the patient's other hand.

"What are you doing?" asked the patient, obviously puzzled.

"Just making sure you don't hurt yourself." And the nurse patted her on the shoulder and left the room.

When the anecdotes about stereotyping other groups have been related, ask group members if they can come to any general conclusions about the consequences of believing the stereotype of any group. Write down the answers where everyone can see them. They may give such answers as:

> people have their feelings hurt
> people are deprived of their rights
> people are made to feel inferior
> people are made to feel useless
> people are made to feel they are not worthwhile
> people are prevented from doing what they are capable of
> people are discouraged from taking initiatives
> people get angry
> people get hostile
> people get violent

Reading needs messages

One way to get others to trust you is to give concrete evidence that you care about their welfare. However, unless you know what kind of evidence will convince people that you care about them, you may inadvertently be communicating that, indeed, you do *not* care.

There are ways of learning what kind of evidence people need before they will believe that you care about them. One way is to acquire knowledge about people generally, from psychological and sociological literature, from autobiographical and biographical accounts of people's lives, and even from good fiction based on a realistic knowledge of human beings. The knowledge based on such reading provides a solid basis for making quick decisions when they are needed. It also provides material that can be used as a check on your perceptions of individuals, to keep you from becoming too complacent about the accuracy of your perceptions. For example, if your observations of an individual reveal information that goes far afield from the general knowledge of people, it may very well be that your observations are quite accurate, and that the individual is unique. However, it may also be that your observations are colored by unrealistic expectations and are therefore inaccurate. Keeping in mind the cumulative data about people helps us to maintain a healthy skepticism about what we are personally experiencing.

However, general knowledge is not a sufficient basis for taking action when a particular individual is involved. (Even though, as we have noted, there are times when we have no choice, when immediate action is necessitated by the nature of the situation.) If we assume that we know what a person needs just because we know what "people" need, there is almost certain to be a large margin of error in our conclusions. Consequently, we must become skillful in identifying desires and needs revealed by behavior. We must also make sure that our own behavior is not preventing them from sending us even clearer messages concerning their needs. These kinds of behaviors constitute solid evidence to people that we care about them and what is happening to them.

In this exercise, you will have an opportunity to practice identifying needs cues and encouraging others to make their needs clear. You will also be able to practice checking the accuracy of your diagnoses of needs.

Form groups of six. Each of you should briefly describe a situation where you needed the care, the understanding, treatment, or response of another person. However, do not reveal what your needs were; just describe your behavior at the time. You may have been ill at home and had needs that your mother could fulfill. You may have been ill in the hospital and had needs that a nurse could fulfill. You may have been part of an interdisciplinary team and had needs a leader could fulfill. You may have been part of a discussion group and had needs another member of the group could fulfill. Without writing down what it was you felt you needed, write what you said, what you did, and what the other people said and did during one five- or six-minute period of the experience. Following is an example of one such account:

> I remember having a discussion with some of the other people in my class about how to decorate the gym for our graduation dance. We were on a committee that was supposed to come up with a plan. We had been talking for about half an hour, and I hadn't said one word. I realized I had a frown on my

face—my forehead was all wrinkled up, and I kept tapping my pencil on the table. The discussion was going on, with everyone talking at once sometimes, but I said nothing. Finally, I blurted out, "I think all this is a waste of time! They'll never let us decorate the way we want to. Your ideas are just silly!"

The others stopped talking for a few seconds, then began to defend their ideas vociferously—again sometimes talking all at once, but this time facing me. I began to shout back at them, saying they were acting like kids.

After you have written your account, indicate at the bottom your age at the time (if you were under 25 or over 70), your sex, your race, your nationality, and your profession or relevant social role (mother, sibling, etc.)

On a separate page, write down what your needs were in the situation and what others might have done to help you clarify and/or to fulfill those needs. Put this page away for later use.

Now put all the accounts together and shuffle them. Let one person in the group pick one account and read it aloud. Let the group:

1. Describe the specific verbal and non-verbal behaviors of the writer.
2. Attempt to identify the needs revealed by those behaviors. (Record these on the board.)
3. Suggest what someone else in the situation might have said to help the person say clearly what he needed and/or to fulfill his needs. (Record these on the board.)
4. Devise things someone else in the situation might have done to help the person say clearly what he needed and/or to fulfill his needs. (Record these on the board.)

Through all this, the person who wrote the account is to listen and say nothing. (She may act as recorder.)

At the end of about ten minutes of discussion, let the writer of the account read her description of her needs and of the behaviors she wished for to help her clarify and/or satisfy those needs.

The group can now check the accuracy of its diagnosis and the usefulness of its suggestions for encouraging the person to express her needs clearly or to fulfill them.

As you continue to meet, repeat the process with the other accounts, trying to identify needs and behaviors for helping people to reveal their needs more clearly and to find satisfaction for those needs.

Accepting negative feedback

One of the characteristics of leaders seems to be a willingness to take risks. One kind of risk-taking behavior is encouraging feedback—including negative feedback—concerning one's own behavior. Managers, supervisors, and administrators have generally insulated themselves from feedback generated by the people directly affected by their behavior. In school systems, for example, principals evaluate teachers, but teachers rarely evaluate principals formally. Similarly, in hospitals evaluation proceeds from the top down, with each succeeding stratum evaluating the one below; seldom is the process reversed. In a broader sense, we can see that communication patterns in institutions and organizations are usually from the top down, not from the bottom up. Though there are sometimes efforts to modify this pattern, for example with suggestion boxes or one-level meetings to which a supervisor or administrator comes to hear gripes and suggestions, such efforts are sporadic. The system rarely gets the benefit of the ideas and feelings of all the people in it.

This does not mean that people do not complain, generate ideas, or evaluate what is happening. But they do it mainly with people on their own level, so it becomes a kind of circular communication that goes neither up nor down. The effect is often the development of an informal system of organizational functioning within the formal system, in which people devise methods of working that they find more effective and satisfying. They circumvent the system often in ways that supervisors and administrators are not aware of. Usually the gross defects of the system remain intact, while there is much dissatisfaction and circular complaining at each level.

The democratic leader, recognizing that an effective, democratic system requires optimum input from all those who are a part of the system, institutes feedback loops so that she will know what the people in her unit are thinking and feeling. If she is neither an administrator or supervisor, she can make her thoughts known and encourage others to do the same.

EXERCISE 1

This exercise provides practice in encouraging feedback and responding to it in productive ways.

In a group of seven people, develop a plan for changing the system in which you are working so that it provides feedback on how it is functioning. (If you are students in a class, use that system; if you are nurses in a hospital unit, use that system.) After working on the plan for half an hour put it aside and let each member fill out the following form relating to the functioning of the group:

Check

1. One or more people monopolized the discussion. _____
2. One or more people interrupted others. _____
3. One or more people implied they knew it all. _____

4. One or more people disagreed in a hostile
   way.   _____

5. One or more people insulted others.   _____

6. One or more people wanted to run the show.   _____

7. One or more people took credit for others'
   ideas.   _____

8. One or more people were unwilling to listen
   to evaluation of their ideas.   _____

9. One or more people were unwilling to listen
   to evaluation of their behavior.   _____

10. One or more people were more accepting
    of the comments of people in certain jobs.   _____

Tally up the check marks and pick the item checked most often. As a group, try to describe that behavior so clearly that there is consensus on exactly what it is and what its effects are, but do not identify the person or persons who are supposed to have demonstrated the behavior. Also, do not use pejorative language to describe either the behavior or the person using it; rather, if the behavior makes people angry, say so, rather than saying that the behavior or the person is "mean." *Be sure to determine how the behavior affects the planning process and the achievement of objectives.*

When the group has agreed on the description of the behavior and how it affects people and the process, stop the discussion for 30 seconds. During this time let anyone who wants to ask, "Did I act that way?" If anyone recognizes his own behavior, he may say, "I know I did that."

If someone asks for information from the group, provide it, again without denigrating the individual. If someone wants to explain his behavior and *does not ask for responses from the group,* let him speak without interruption.

When you have finished with one item, go on to the next one. When you have dealt with all the items (this may be done over a period of time rather than in a single session) you might discuss the questions: "How do I feel about getting negative feedback? How do I use feedback to modify the system?"

EXERCISE 2

If you are the teacher of the class or a supervisor or administrator in a team, you can model behavior indicating that you expect feedback from the students or the people you supervise. One way is to present a picture of the system in which you are working and to point out the feedback loop that will provide material for changing that system as changes are deemed necessary by the participants.

For example, figure 5-2 is a model of a college course that was distributed to education students on the first day of class. They were helped by the instructor to understand the model, and special emphasis was put on the opportunities provided for them to evaluate what was happening and to change the system.

(Follow-up on the students indicates that they are attempting similar procedures with their students.)

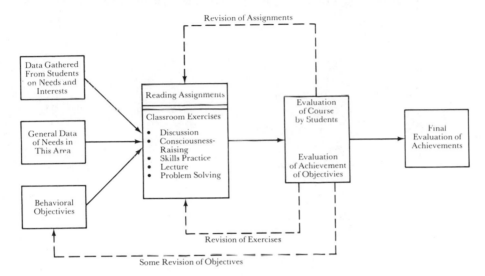

Figure 5-2.

NOTES

1   *American Journal of Nursing,* June 1979, p. 1048.

2   Maddy Gerrish, "Expansions: A Pioneering Experience," Paper delivered at 1975 meeting of the ANA's Council of Advanced Practitioners in Psychiatric Mental Health Nursing. In Ada K. Jacox and Catherine M. Norris, Eds., *Organizing for Independent Nursing Practice,* (New York: Apple-Century-Crofts, 1977).

3   Ibid., p. 57.

4   M. Lucille Kinlein, *Independent Nursing Practice with Clients* (Philadelphia: J.B. Lippincott, 1977), pp. vii-viii.

5   Ibid., p. xi.

6   Ibid., p. 8.

7   Ibid., p. 33.

8   Ibid., p. 37ff.

9   Jacox & Norris, op. cit., p. 42.

10   Ibid., p. 53.

11   Kinlein, op. cit., p. 98.

12   Leonard Stein, "The Doctor-Nurse Game," *Archives of General Psychiatry,* 1967, Vol. 16, pp. 699-703.

13   Jacox & Norris, op. cit., p. 45.

14   Charlotte Epstein, *Effective Interaction in Contemporary Nursing* (Englewood Cliffs, N.J.: Prentice-Hall, 1974), pp. 168-169.

[15]   Jacox & Norris, op. cit., p. 50.

[16]   *Toward a Primary Medical Care System Responsive to Children's Needs,* report of the Harvard Child Health Project Task Force (Cambridge, Mass.: Ballinger, 1977), p. 3.

[17]   Charlotte Epstein, *Affective Subjects in the Classroom,* (Scranton, Pa.: Intext, 1972), pp. 145–147.

[18]   Jacox & Norris, op. cit., p. 45.

[19]   Mary Gray, "Part Time Sole-Proprietor Private Practice," in Jacox & Norris, op. cit., p. 47.

[20]   *The Role of the Nurse in Primary Health Care,* (Washington, D.C.: Pan American Health Organization, World Health Organization, Scientific Publication No. 348, 1977), p. v.

[21]   Ibid., p. 2.

[22]   Ibid., pp. 9–10.

[23]   Ibid., pp. 4–6.

chapter six

Leadership in the Institutional Setting

The Dynamics of Changing Organizations

What causes an organization to change? What are ways of effecting change? What are some principles of planned change? What are the elements in the relationship between the change agent and the organization that is to be changed?

From psychologist Kurt Lewin's field theory,[1] we can derive some understanding of the nature of an organization as it relates to change. The idea is that within every system or subsystem there is a field of countervailing forces. The system remains the same as long as there is a balance between the forces for change and the forces resisting change. When the balance is upset, by an increase in the forces for change, for example, then the system changes. The system may go through a tumultuous adjustment period before the change is incorporated and stability regained.

When we speak of forces, we do not equate the term with people. Forces include all kinds of factors pushing for or against change. For example, in a community mental health agency there is a rapid turnover of clients, with relatively few people persisting in treatment until formally discharged. The agency's written mandate is to provide outpatient mental health service to a specified catchment area, in ways and at times that are useful to the people in the area. Also, the full-time core staff shares the commitment to providing optimum service to the community. These are forces for agency change, since the mandated goal is not being achieved and the paid workers perceive that there is indeed a problem.

Most of the treatment is provided by unpaid workers—physicians in the process of qualifying in psychiatry and their mentors who are full-time faculty members in teaching institutions. It is, therefore, not unusual for patients to be assigned to several different therapists in the course of their treatment, as students complete their term at the agency. Or they may be treated by students who do not have all the necessary competencies and are inadequately supervised because their teachers have other pressing duties besides supervision of students. There is not enough money in the budget to increase the paid professional staff. These factors are forces that stand against the necessary change.

> Systems theory suggests that when environmental factors that are important to the organization's functioning are stable, organizational programs and policies tend to persist over time. When environmental factors shift, the organization either adjusts to the external force, attempts to influence it, or both. Each interaction between an organization and its environment represents a real or potential internal change.[2]

When money is tight the funding for the agency may be reduced. This may necessitate cutting jobs, combining job functions, and reducing services. Similarly, when those in political power hold values inconsistent with the agency's practice, agency activities may be severly curtailed.

Change is inevitable in all human organizations, and there is a large body of literature that analyzes the processes involved in change and identifies the knowledge needed to understand those processes. With this information, we have entered upon a period in the development of organizations when we actively institute change processes in order to effect the kinds of changes we desire. Not that active intervention has not always been a part of human organizations, but today there is more to instituting change than a direct demand for change in an intolerable situation and the countervailing direct resistance by those who feel they will lose benefits by that change.

For one thing, change is planned even when there is no perceived crisis. For another, there are attempts to adhere systematically to principles of planned change. Third, most people at each level of participation in human service organizations are sophisticated enough to talk about and understand what is happening. Though managers are often charged with the responsibility for planning for change, they usually know they can accomplish little without the active involvement of all personnel.

Nevertheless, at least one type of change strategy involves the use of power to force compliance of the less powerful. This power may represent the legitimate use of the authority of law or agency policy, but there are times when the power is merely coercive, operating by intimidation and threat.

To condemn out of hand the use of legitimate power strategies like the force of law would be to censure tactics that can be rationally defended. For example, when teachers in a school make children conform by hitting them, a local law that puts hitting by teachers in the same category as assault by adults on each other can virtually eliminate a practice with questionable pedagogical validity. Such a law also raises children to the status of equal persons under the law. Though there is no such law in existence, similar administrative policies in some states have had the same effect.

The use of law to force change has been effective in other spheres of human behavior. For example, the practice of discriminating against Black people in public accommodations practically disappeared within a very short space of time as a result of the passage of law, even though the people who earlier enforced discriminatory practices probably have not completely changed their attitudes. It seems justifiable to use the force of law to see that principles to which society is committed are not violated in local practices.

Generally, those in control of economic and political forces can use them to exert power and authority to effect change. A state's threat to withhold money from a child care agency if it does not change its hiring practices, or a union membership's threat to strike if working conditions are not improved are examples of the use of power to effect change.

Floyd Hunter's study of decision-making in a city revealed the existence of an economic and political power élite that made most of the decisions.[3] Today such elites find it difficult to work secretly and groups wishing to influence them or nullify their power develop counterstrategies in the use of power.

There are other kinds of strategies for change that rely more on other factors than political and economic power. One kind involves the spread of knowledge, so that people may use enlightened reason to make beneficial changes. Another involves a problem-solving approach to change, utilizing available knowledge and inventing new technologies and patterns of action to solve identified problems.

Principles of Change

Six principles of change have been identified by Kenneth D. Benne and Max Birnbaum:

1. "To change a subsystem or any part of a subsystem, relevant aspects of the environment must also be changed." For example, if it were proposed that psychiatric aides in a mental health facility no longer be permitted to function relatively independently in therapeutic situations, that every therapeutic session have a credentialed psychologist, psychiatrist or psychiatric social worker present, there might be a number of resisting forces operating to prevent acceptance of this proposal: aides would resent the implied loss of status; workloads for the other people would undoubtedly be increased.

To get acceptance of the proposal, it would have to be seen as an attempt to increase the available skills in any therapeutic situation, with no loss of status for paraprofessionals; additional staff would have to be hired to balance the work load. These other changes would have to be made in addition to the target change.

2. "To change behavior on any one level of a hierarchical organization, it is necessary to achieve complementary and reinforcing changes in organization levels above and below that level." This need became apparent some time ago in the police department of a large city. The police commissioner decided to revise the traditional belief that training should be a function of command, and to bring in behavioral scientists to teach human relations and other subjects associated with law enforcement as an integral part of preservice and inservice education.

Some of the new instructors, in an effort to learn more about the police operation so that they could teach more effectively, began to ask questions about various police practices. In the course of conversations, they expressed doubts about the efficacy of some of these practices.

The students, who were patrolman, sergeants, and ranking officers, experienced increasing discomfort in their relationships with the instructors. Responding to questions about operations from "civilians" ran counter to the traditional practice of referring all such questions to the upper echelons of police. Some of the doubts so freely expressed by the instructors matched their own doubts, which they were afraid to express, and hearing real or implied criticism of the police from civilians called forth the defensiveness so close to the surface of most police-citizen interaction. Police supervisors saw this observation and questioning by the instructors as threatening to the order and discipline of their men.

If the commissioner had planned according to this principle, he would have not only brought in the scientists, but provided for the reeducation of all personnel, changing the strict hierarchical communication to a more democratic pattern of mutually responsive interaction between ranks.

3. "The place to begin change is at those points in the system where some stress and strain exist. Stress may give rise to dissatisfaction with the status quo and thus become a motivating factor for change in the system."

A dentist who insisted on checking each patient for the results of his dental assistant's prophylactic treatment refused to consider the idea that his assistant was competent to assume responsibility for her own professional work. When the dentist found himself working excessively long hours and even having to turn new patients away, he was ready to allow his assistant a certain amount of autonomy. As his practice continued to expand, she extended the parameters of her responsibility until she had what almost amounted to an independent practice in one part of his suite of offices.

4. "In diagnosing the possibility of change in a given institution, it is always necessary to assess the degree of stress and strain at points where change is sought. One should ordinarily avoid beginning change at the point of greatest stress."

A large number of teachers were transferred from positions where they had been for years in order to achieve racial balance in a particular school. They were angry and anxious about being in a new school, in a neighborhood they did not know. Most of them were teaching lower-class children for the first time in their professional lives.

Just prior to the transfer, a committee of teachers, classroom aides, and the principal had completed a plan for introducing the teaching of race relations to all the children. The new teachers, most of them White Anglos, faced with the necessity for talking about race with Black and Puerto Rican children, became so agitated that they refused point-blank to teach this subject.

It might have been more productive of change to adjust the new teaching plan at the outset. Children could have been exposed to race relations education by the established teachers who were not feeling vulnerable. Eventually, after a period of adjustment, the new teachers could have been drawn into the activity.

5. "Both the formal and the informal organization of an institution must be considered in planning any process of change."

A new director of a county welfare agency found it impossible to gain acceptance of any change he suggested to increase the effectiveness of the service and the accountability of the agency to the community it served. It was a long time before he came aware of the informal organization in the agency that was impeding his efforts at change. This group was made up of people who had been hired a number of years previously by a personnel supervisor who had expected to become the next director.

The new director had been brought in from a university, and had been highly touted by the agency board as a scientist and researcher. The old supervisor's clique quietly resisted everything he suggested, expressing doubts that the suggested changes would work, and implying that they knew the clients and the community and how they would respond, whereas he did not.

The new director finally left and the old supervisor became director, successfully instituting a number of changes quite similar to the ones suggested by the man who had left.

6. "The effectiveness of a planned change is often directly related to the degree to which members at all levels of an institutional hierarchy take

part in the fact-finding and the diagnosing of needed changes and in the formulating and reality-testing of goals and programs of change."[4]

I would extend this principle—as I would all the others—to include the institution's clients in the system to be changed. They are strategically placed to feel the effects of the status quo and of any changes that are instituted, so they can provide data and insights that agency workers may not have. Also, they can very effectively impede changes that they have neither identified as needed or that they see as being harmful to themselves.

Conflict and cooperation

In any attempt to make change, the whole matter of the constructive management of conflict must be considered. When there is widespread dissent in an organization or a group, fears of conflict may actually serve to keep hidden the real nature of the dissenting points of view. Without permitting the conflict to develop to the point where the different values, beliefs, and feelings can be openly confronted and examined, no basis for cooperation will be found.

Of course, there are times when the differences are so fundamental that there can be no basis for accommodation. As we have noted before in the use of the power of the law, it may be necessary sometimes to identify with overarching humanistic principles in establishing standards of appropriate behavior. For example, insistence by American Nazis that they have a right to make public statements advocating genocide and then to protect themselves against possible attack in the public streets by arming themselves seems to be an example of sociopathology that cannot be dealt with by means of collaborative conflict resolution. Perhaps we come to this conclusion only because our knowledge of how to deal with this kind of pathology is, at present, so limited.

Instituting change

Taking an unpopular public stand on a controversial issue is not an easy thing to do. However, it is a significant step toward becoming involved in making the world more like the way you want it to be. The reality is that the way you want it to be is not necessarily the way others want it to be. In an agency, you may find yourself in disagreement with a policy, a practice, or a point of view that others are committed to. Therefore, in planning for changes you must realistically assess the opposition and work to neutralize it.

Following are some general suggestions for proceeding to plan for change:

1. *Decide exactly what you want to change.* For example, if you believe that patients should have more opportunity for active participation in the development of their own care plans, do you want to work directly on this issue? Or would you rather work on another facet of the issue? Perhaps you would like to obtain recognition of the need for a nurse to sit for a certain amount of time each day at each patient's bedside, to establish productive communication with him? The point is, be sure just what behavior you want changed.

2. *Learn as much as you can about the target behavior.* Sometimes, one individual is responsible for the policy and the practice, and that same individual has the power to make the change. At other times, the problem is just one of getting people to utilize available resources—like using a conference room that stands empty most of the day for team meetings, instead of meeting in the nurses' station. At still other times, a decision to make a change is in the hands of a board, as in the case of the hospital that decided to close its emergency treatment room, and left a community without adequate medical care.

    The change agent should also know as much as possible about the causes of the target behavior and the effects of that behavior, so that he may be clear about why he is seeking to make the change. For example, should someone ask the question, "What's so terrible about the practice?" the change agent should have data at hand that document the harmful effects. Or, should anyone say, "There's nothing we can do about this; it's provided for in the will of a benefactor," one should know about the legal decisions against the rule of people no longer living.

    Not infrequently, it is helpful to realize that a particular practice is actually inconsistent with a stated policy or a cultural ideal. Pointing this out can help people in power understand the implications of the practice and may move them to consider changing it. For example, the written policy of a community hospital states or implies that one of its objectives is to contribute to the health maintenance of the population. However, nowhere in the hospital's practices, in the functional definition of staff roles, or in the daily assignments is there any indication that time is allotted for health maintenance functions: education, outreach into the community, or action research.

3. *Learn as much as you can about the opposing points of view.* Not infrequently, people hold to a point of view only because it is the only point of view they know. It is possible that the information that the opposition has may throw new light on your own stand; it may even cause you to relinquish that stand and begin to see the value in another point of view.

    At any rate, it is important to know all the arguments on the other side, to consider the validity of their data, and if possible to search out countering data that will make your argument stronger.

4. *Assess the risks of trying to make a change.* It is useful to realistically assess the risks in undertaking to work for change. In some professions, the tendency is to assess the risks too high, with the result that workers will rarely publicly express an opposing point of view, much less work for change. Teachers, for example, even when they are tenured and it is clear that no teacher has been fired in fifty years, are afraid to suggest that a mandated reading program is not suitable for their pupils. This attitude is so pervasive in the schools that even student teachers become fearful of protesting a practice that they have learned is counterproductive. When it is pointed out to them that (a) they cannot be fired; (b) the school system is not hiring so they will probably not even have to ask for a job; and (c) only their university supervisor is responsible for grading them, and the supervisor agrees with their opinion of the practice, they are still worried about saying what they think.

   Something similar occurs among nurses. In many situations, the worse that can happen is that people who disagree with you will not be friendly or cooperative. It is, however, extremely rare to find no one at all who agrees with your point of view or at least sees some validity in your stand. Identifying these individuals and establishing communication with them can help reduce the effects of personal unpleasantness from the opposition.

5. *Check to see if there is already a group working to make your change.* There is no point in inventing the wheel all over again. If there is a group that has taken some steps to effect a particular change, then they already know about some things that do not work, about some people who represent particular roadblocks. They probably also have a body of information that may be available to you, so that you do not have to begin your search from scratch. Allying yourself with the group may take you all closer to your goal.

   If there is no group, there may be individuals who have been affected adversely by a practice and who are fighting individually to effect a change. Allying yourself with them may be the beginning of an organization for change.

6. *Decide with whom you will communicate first.* It seems fairest, usually, to go first to the individual most directly involved with the practice you want to change. Aside from the fact that you may find an unexpected ally in this individual, you will probably learn more about the situation and the reasons why people feel obliged to perpetuate the practice. It is also fair to let that individual know if you intend to pursue the matter further. Though there are those who feel that one should keep everything secret from the opposition, it is clear, even on an international level, that secrets are never well kept, and that rumors exacerbate suspicions and antagonisms and interfere with the free flow of ideas. Sometimes, just letting the opposition know that you intend

to use all available resources can precipitate a change as a way of avoiding "trouble."

Once you have decided whom to approach, equip yourself with specific questions you intend to ask, and clear information for responding to questions asked of you. A good way to prepare, not only for questions but for expressions of antagonism or attempts to change your mind, is to role play the interview, having someone else take the part of the person you are to see, and using everything he has learned to date to defuse your commitment.

7. *Reassess your information and plan further strategy.* Depending on the conclusions you draw from your initial interview, you may want to see other people higher in the line of authority, you may feel that public attention should be drawn to the matter through the newspapers or the distribution of flyers, or you may realize that all these things have already been done without effecting change and that the only step left is direct protest action. Just be sure that every action on your part gives the opposition some time and opportunity to make the change, and that an action does not become an end in itself. Keep your eye on the specific change you have as your goal; at this point, it is probably not useful to engage in fantasies of effecting the establishment of an ideal society.

If you ever undertake to try to institute a change, it is at this point that you might consider some general observations about this whole business of commitment to and involvement in change. What are some of the things you have discovered?

- Does even the smallest change often need more time than you thought?
- Do people often get angry and frightened at the suggestion that change is needed?
- Do people often reject an idea before they have really heard it and before they clearly understand it?
- Are people in positions of power and authority often interested in new ideas and open to change?
- In reality, how great is the risk of becoming involved in achieving change?
- How prepared were you to deal with people in authority, articulate opponents, peers, the target population? What are some of the skills you wished you had? What are some of the things you wished you had done before confronting any of these?
- At this point, are you still committed to achieving the change? What are you going to do next?

Leadership in Bedside Nursing: A Care Plan Based on Special Knowledge

Intergroup relations

It is not easy for the nurse leader to model professional behavior that is above the norm in a particular institution. There is a certain amount of risk involved. Colleagues may resent the implication that their behavior is being criticized. Even supervisors may feel threatened, if they have not tried to raise or have not been successful in raising the institution's level of professional functioning. However, again, the nurse-leader is willing to assume some risk in her attempts to influence the people around her.

One way in which she can begin to show there are better ways to function is in the quality of the care plan she prepares for her patients. Not only does she incorporate the orders of the physician into her care plans, and not only does she provide routine nursing care, but she tries to learn something about the unique background and experience of the patient to determine his state of readiness to learn what he needs to know in order to help himself back to optimum health.

One area of knowledge that has been almost totally neglected in the education of most professionals, including medical professionals, is intergroup relations. *Intergroup relations* is a technical term that refers specifically to racial, religious, and nationality groups, and the content material subsumed under the term deals with prejudice and discrimination directed against these groups. (Recently, similarities have been perceived in the nature of the prejudice and discrimination against these groups and against women, the aged, and children.) Just as all kinds of errors are made in other professions in dealing with minority groups, errors are made in health care delivery. Sophistication in intergroup relations can significantly raise the level of nursing care quality, though it may sometimes raise eyebrows among colleagues and supervisors.

For example, a nursing plan expanded to incorporate knowledge not usually used in such planning resulted not only in successful treatment, but brought forth some interesting responses from team members.

The problem

The patient, a forty-year-old Vietnamese man, has been diagnosed as having a peptic ulcer. Though he presents obvious physical evidence of stress, he is unable to identify specific situations in his life that may be causing the stress and precipitating his symptoms.

Actually, the patient denies that anything is bothering him. He says that, when he first came to the United States four years earlier, he had much difficulty. He had been a practicing attorney in Hanoi, and he had fled the country with his wife and two children, leaving behind all his belongings. Once in the United States, he had to accept charity, until he could complete academic work and qualify to practice law here. But now everything was marvelous: he had a job with a prestigious law firm, a new house, and he and his family were very happy. Nothing was happening to cause the kind of tension that would result in a peptic ulcer.

General information

The nurse responsible for the care of this patient has made a special effort to become familiar with general data that may be helpful in developing a nursing care plan.

- The local newspapers have been carrying stories about the number of Vietnamese who have recently come to the area. They are repeatedly referred to as "boat people" and described as terrified and destitute refugees, with little education and very few of the saleable skills needed in an urban economy.
- In listening to friends and acquaintances, the nurse became aware of considerable hostility directed against these people. The feeling seemed to be that the government had no business letting them come here in numbers that constituted a drain on our resources. Americans were losing their jobs and even being deprived of enough to eat in some cases, while these foreigners were being given money to set them up in businesses. Special teachers were needed for the children, and additional personnel had to be hired in government agencies and other institutions to provide services to them. Most of them didn't even expend the effort to learn English, and probably thought Americans should provide services in their language.
- The nurse could find no evidence that these feelings of hostility were based on accurate information about the Vietnamese people as a group. Most of those who expressed resentment and hostility had little or no sustained contact with Vietnamese people.
- The nurse remembered some of her reading in history courses about the treatment of other Oriental people who had come to the United States in the past. She recalled that the Chinese were accepted as long as they were needed to build the railroads, and the change in attitudes and behavior of Americans when the railroads were finished and the competition for jobs increased. Before the recession the Chinese were perceived as industrious, frugal, and quiet; during hard times they were seen as uncommunicative, unassimilable, and loyal to the country of their

birth. She remembered the distrust fostered against Orientals by war propaganda (The Yellow Peril!) and how this distrust had been reinforced by the movies and other mass media. (The Saturday morning children's shows are still filled with Oriental villains being vanquished by Caucasian heroes!)

- The nurse knew, from her knowledge of intergroup behavior in the United States, that depressed economic conditions frequently precipitated open conflict between racial, religious, and nationality groups.

- The nurse was familiar with the studies of group attitudes and behavior that revealed an ingrained pattern of prejudice and discrimination. She was aware that this pattern was not always clearly apparent in some situations; that is, members of minority groups might be subjected to subtle snubs and denigration that only the victims could recognize. Minority group people might be excluded from economic and social situations, and the reasons given were clever rationalizations that masked the real reasons.

- The nurse knew that there was evidence that victims of prejudice and discrimination often suffered from stress, anxiety, and self-concept damage.

- She knew that there are very difficult adjustments to make when people come from one culture to another very different one; these adjustments are often accompanied by tension and anxiety.

Acquiring specific information

The nurse was well aware that this general information about intergroup relations, even if it were made more specific by a knowledge of Vietnamese people, would still be insufficient to understand the situation of this particular Vietnamese person—her patient. Consequently, part of the nursing plan involved getting information from the patient to help assess his situation and his readiness to help identify nursing care objectives.

Simply asking questions in order to elicit information about experiences and feelings is generally not the most effective way to establish a productive nurse-patient relationship. For one thing, it sets up a pattern of interaction similar to the traditional physician-patient pattern, where the physician takes the initiative by asking questions, the patient passively answers them, and then as passively waits for the physician to tell him what the problem is and what he should do about it. If the nurse wants to establish a more democratic relationship that allows the patient to participate in his recovery and health maintenance, then other strategies must be used to supply information for the planning system.

Consequently, the nurse planned to find some way of encouraging the patient to volunteer information about himself. She decided that a person is more likely initially to speak freely in an area where he has some expertise and in which there is no great emotional investment. Since he was a lawyer, and had been watching television programs that morning that dealt with the law, she commented on the content of a program. "I never thought that the law said a parent couldn't punish his child!" she laughed.

"I don't think the law goes quite so far," he answered. "But the direction that new interpretations are taking indicate that children have a right to the same protection against arbitrary and cruel punishment as adults do."

"I heard that in Sweden, teachers and even parents are not allowed to hit a child, or even to scold him in certain ways."

"It is not necessary to hit children or shame them. There are better ways."

"I've heard teachers in school really insult children. I imagine your children have trouble dealing with that when they're accustomed to being talked to quietly and with consideration."

He shook his head sadly. "That's not the biggest problem my children have to face."

Moving toward readiness to plan

Slowly, he began to describe experiences his children had been having in school. At first, when they were the only Vietnamese children in the school, they had been welcomed and fussed over. But since the arrival of large numbers of refugees, they had been subjected to the same name-calling and even violence as the new children. His bitterness was apparent.

The nurse listened and commiserated with him, and talked about the need for education of all children in learning how to live with each other.

"And," she added, "it isn't only children who could use that kind of education. They're no worse than adults, who express their prejudice only a little more subtly."

This evidence of her understanding of the problem of discrimination encouraged the patient to begin to talk about the things that were being said and done to him. Though he had experienced some of this in the early days of his arrival, he thought that was all behind him. Now with the advent of the new immigrants, he was again experiencing, in exacerbated form, what had happened to him earlier. Further anxiety was being caused by his fear of being thought ungrateful by Americans who had helped him when he needed it.

It was not difficult, at different times during their discussions, for the nurse to make the connection between what he was feeling and his illness. One day in the course of one of their conversations, he made the connection himself. Now they could, together, begin to develop a plan to help him deal with the victimization in ways that did not cause further damage to himself.

Consequences

In writing her nursing care plan, the nurse included the general information she had gathered about Vietnamese immigrants and the special intergroup information about the patient obtained from her assessment procedure. When she presented the care plan at the team meeting, it evoked varied responses: Two of the R.N.'s—one a nurse clinician—went right to the heart of the matter. They almost literally applauded the fact that the man was able to recognize the stress-precipitating situations after he had so carefully denied that anything was wrong. An aide told about a similar experience she had had in her own life and bemoaned the fact that she had not had such a nurse to help her through a very painful time. A pharmacist muttered under his breath about too much time being spent on one person—they'd never be able to finish a day's work. A physician asked if the nurse weren't taking over the psychiatrist's job.

The case came to the attention of the director of nursing education over the hospital grapevine. The nurse was asked to present the case to a number of different groups: nursing students, an inservice nursing seminar, and even to the staff of the psychiatric unit. Though there are no hard data on the permanent changes in practice or in education that occurred because of one nurse leader's action, it is salutary to contemplate the probable ripple effect in the thinking of personnel throughout the institution.

Leadership in a Nurse-Patient Relationship

Behavioral objectives

The overall nursing purpose in this relationship was to work collaboratively with the patient to establish an effective health maintenance plan.

The specific behavioral objectives were:

1. The patient will demonstrate knowledge of his disease and knowledge of how it is best managed.
2. The patient will make a commitment to assume responsibility for managing his disease.
3. The patient will demonstrate initial skills in management.
4. The patient will maintain his health without repeated hospitalization.

General knowledge and communication skills

The nurse in this situation demonstrated knowledge of a specific disease, knowledge of human behavior, skills in teaching and skills in communication—especially in those related to establishing trust: self-disclosure, expressing empathy, listening.

Establishing trust

*Ellen Baker came to the bedside of Beatrice Kaufman, and introduced herself:
"I'll be your nurse while you're here, Ms. Kaufman. I'm Ellen Baker." She
smiled and waited for the patient to respond.*

Ms. Kaufman's lips tightened slightly and she moved her head a quarter of an inch in a nod of acknowledgement.

*Ms. Baker's smile faded a little and she made a small move of mild self-
derision. "I always feel a little uncomfortable when I meet someone new,"
she said. "It's hard for me to be myself."*

Ms. Kaufman's eyebrows went up in surprise, and her mouth relaxed.

When Ellen Baker approached Ms. Kaufman, she already knew the patient's history. She realized that she knew a great deal about this person and
that Ms. Kaufman knew nothing about her. She could understand that a person might feel at a disadvantage in such a situation and respond with wariness and even resentment. Just having to speak to someone who was standing while lying flat on one's back might easily reinforce these feelings.

In an attempt to equalize the situation somewhat and also to begin to
establish trust, Ellen Baker admitted that she had feelings that belied any
perception of her as omnipotent, omniscient, and aloof. Ms. Kaufman communicated nonverbally that she probably had had a misperception of the
nurse, and that she now felt somewhat less resistant to her overtures.

Patient input

*"Is there anything you'd like to ask me?" Ellen Baker posed the question
quietly. While she waited for an answer, she walked slowly to the side of the
bed and sat in the visitor's chair. She had a small, tentative smile on her face,
and her eyes, with eyebrows slightly raised, stayed on Beatrice Kaufman's
face.*

Ellen Baker, like all the nurses on this busy medical-surgical unit, had a
full patient load and pressing supervisory responsibilities. She was a very efficient, competent professional with high standards of productivity for herself and her supervisees. However, she made it clear, by the tone of her voice,
her slow movement, and her apparent willingness to wait for an answer, that
her question had not been an idle one—that she really wanted to know the
answer. Even more, she was prepared to give answers to whatever questions
Ms. Kaufman was prepared to ask. (This first conversation, and most of the
subsequent ones, took no more than five minutes.)

Above all, Ms. Baker did not fill the waiting time after asking the question with words. To do so would have been to distract Ms. Kaufman from efforts to formulate her questions; might have served to change the focus of the
communication to whatever content the words had and so contradicted the

interest implied by the question; or served as a vehicle for the nurse's self-expression. This would not have been consistent with the purpose of the communication, which was to establish a collaborative relationship with the patient.

Listening

After a few seconds, during which Ms. Kaufman's hands on top of the bed sheet slowly unclenched, Ms. Baker continued to look expectantly at her, without any body movements to indicate a need for speeding up the communication. Finally, the patient heaved a profound sigh. "God, I hate being here!" she said with great feeling. "They can't do anything for me! What's the use of carrying me here every time I can't catch my breath?" She stopped and looked expectantly at the nurse sitting there.

"You didn't want to be brought to the hospital?" Ellen asked.

"No, I didn't! It's my mother. She panics every time! See, I'm all right now! There was no reason for all the fuss."

"You certainly seem fine now. You have no pain?"

"No, I never have pain," she answered, almost defiantly.

The young woman continued to open herself to communication, as evidenced by her body language. Ms. Baker let it happen. The explosion seemed to be partly an attack on the nurse (she seemed surprised when Ellen didn't rush to defend the ability of the hospital staff to help her), partly an expression of very strong feeling, and partly a willingness for self-disclosure that may have been encouraged by Ellen Baker's openness about her own feelings.

Understanding

"That's great. Now if we can control the other symptoms, you should be able to get along just fine."

"They're nothing much. I don't see why I should be treated like an invalid all the time. I'd get along better if people would just let me alone!"

"You hate people always telling you what to do and what not to do, don't you?"

Beatrice looked a little surprised. "Yeah," she said, almost grudgingly. "That's exactly right. I wish they wouldn't treat me as if I had no sense of my own!"

Beatrice Kaufman was a young Black woman who suffered from sickle-cell anemia. As a child, she had had a very mild form of the disease, controlled by her family's strict adherence to their physician's prescription: careful diet, no overexertion, no stress. Now, at the age of eighteen, she had been hospitalized three times in the past year.

Ellen Baker thought that she was denying her illness, denying that it was necessary to keep in mind all the time that she was not like other people. And she resented the feeling that she was not being permitted to live her life as an independent adult.

The patient seemed surprised that the nurse really seemed to understand her anger and frustration. No one else ever did.

Assessing the situation

"Just what would you do if people didn't bug you all the time?"

This kind of question serves two purposes: It opens up the process of thinking ahead, beginning to explore possibilities for changing the situation and it helps nurse and patient to assess the level of knowledge and awareness concerning the illness. How much does the patient know about the causes of crises, the prevention of discomfort? How aware is she of the seriousness of the disease and the importance of controlling it? Without this information, no teaching plan is useful, since every attempt to teach must start with where the learner is. Failing to assess the learner's level of knowledge and awareness results in the common plaint of teachers when their pupils do not achieve: "But I *taught* that for a *whole week*, and they act as if they never heard of fractions!"

"Well, I certainly wouldn't get so upset that I'd run up the stairs and start choking!"

Ellen Baker smiled and nodded. "Well, you certainly know what not to do!"

Beatrice seemed delighted at this evidence of approval. "I told you I do!" she laughed. "No one ever believes me!"

This conversation, as well as subsequent ones, revealed that Beatrice had an excellent grasp of many of the facts concerning her disease and a knowledge of the cause and effect relationships between activities, diet, and onset of uncomfortable symptoms.

It was also clear that Beatrice Kaufman needed to be told that she was competent to manage the illness and her life. Apparently, the communication she got from her family was that they could not rely on her to take care of herself. (Any teaching strategy that serves to convince the learner that he cannot learn is obviously counterproductive! People, if they are to learn, must believe that they can learn, and must believe, also, that they are worth teaching. Anyone who is convinced that he is unreliable and incompetent will not feel very worthwhile.)

Feedback

Once, during a conversation about the food on the lunch tray, Beatrice asked Ellen, "Why is folic acid so important in controlling sickle-cell anemia?"

Ellen explained the relationship between folic acid and red blood cell formation. Then she observed, "Before you leave here you'll know as much about sickle-cell anemia as any doctor or nurse."

Every learner needs feedback on his learning progress. If he is learning, such feedback encourages him to greater efforts. If there are gaps in his learning, feedback makes it clear that he is not "dumb," or "lazy," but that, if he will focus on this area, or that area, together teacher and learner can fill in the gaps. Those gaps may very well have been caused because the teacher didn't explain clearly or didn't ask appropriate questions.

Looking at causes

"Now I've got to get my mother to believe that," Beatrice said.

"Doesn't your mother think you know much about this ailment?" Ellen asked.

"We-e-ll, I don't know. I guess she must know I know about it. She's told me enough, and there are plenty of pamphlets around the house. And I've heard the doctors talk."

"Then why do you think she keeps such close tabs on you?"

"I don't know . . . maybe she doesn't believe I care about myself." She stopped speaking and seemed to go inward, examining what she had just heard herself say.

This is the kind of natural opportunity that can move one to the next step in a teaching plan, helping the learner look at causes and refine the problem, so that she can begin to see appropriate solutions.

Independence

Some time later, Ellen raised the question, "What do you think would convince your mother that you're ready to take on the responsibility for maintaining your own health?" Ellen asked her.

"First, maybe I'd better just tell her seriously that I am ready. I think maybe she never would listen because I acted like a kid throwing a tantrum."

"Do you think that will do it?"

"It's a start. Maybe when she sees me doing all the right things without being nagged, that will really prove to her that I can live my own life."

"You said 'maybe.'"

"I don't really expect her to change overnight. But, somehow, I don't think it will bother me as much as it used to."

Planning the next step can often be left to the learner. If the evidence up until now is that she has developed some self-insight and also is convinced of the importance of solving the problem, the initial question will help her pick up the planning process. Additional, rather noncommittal, questions can provide the learner the security of having a receptive listener as a sounding board as she clarifies her thinking and makes her plans.

Evaluation

"Beatrice," her mother's voice could be heard in the corridor, "You shouldn't be getting out of bed."

Ellen looked into the room and saw the young woman put her arms around her mother and hug her. "It's all right, Mother," she was saying. "I know what I have to do. Trust me."

The mother said nothing.

Beatrice was knowledgeable about the disease and she had made a commitment to manage it properly. Apparently she was managing also not to respond with anger to her mother's behavior, while she reassured the older woman that her child was in control.

Follow-up

Part of the nurse's leadership function will be to arrange for follow-up of Beatrice Kaufman, to determine if she continues to maintain her health. One way is to arrange for a systematic check on her future admissions to the hospital. Another is to arrange to meet her informally outside the hospital. A third is to encourage her to come back and visit sometimes, just to keep in touch and "Let me know how you are doing." Referral to a community agency for follow-up is probably not appropriate in this case because it suggests that the patient needs authoritative checking-up—something she had been rebelling against and that had precipitated her problem.

Obviously, these follow-up activities are not, traditionally, accepted as part of the function of the clinical or staff nurse. However, they are undoubtedly appropriate in terms of holistic care, prevention, and health maintenance. Insofar as hospital nurses are rarely afforded the opportunity by institutions to practice nursing in this way, taking the initiative to do so demonstrates leadership.

Leadership in Nurse Unit Manager Relationship

Lee Mercer works in a medical-surgical unit administered for primary nursing care. The unit has a very competent unit manager, Janet Mans, who leaves the nursing staff free to do nursing instead of being taken up with the many details of management.

One of Lee Mercer's patients has had a stroke resulting from cerebral hemorrhage. He has had a rapid recovery from feelings of dizziness and weakness and numbness in his limbs, but he is still suffering from both expressive and receptive aphasia, apparently caused by involvement of the middle cerebral artery.

When Lee returned to work after Sunday, she found that the empty bed in her patient's room now had a new admission. This new patient was not assigned to her.

Asking for a change

Lee Mercer: *(Sitting down in chair beside Janet Mans's desk) : Do you have a minute, Jan? I've got a problem.*
Janet Mans: *(Smiling) Sure, Lee. Why should you be any different? (A resident came up to the desk and asked for a file. Janet pulled one from the bottom of the pile on her desk and handed it to him.)*
Lee: *Bad Monday?*
Janet: *No, not really. Just hectic. What can I do for you?*
Lee: *It's about that new patient in 430.*
Janet: *(Laughing) Isn't he a killer? I never heard such yelling and complaining. You'd think he was the only one who ever had a pain.*
Lee: *I really haven't had a chance to find out much about him, but I get the feeling that that's the way he's going to be behaving for a while.*
Janet: *He's here for observation. It will be a few days.*
Lee: *I'm worried about my patient. He really needs to be in a quiet room.*
Janet: *Sorry, friend. That's it. There's no other place. And I figured better to put him in with someone who doesn't know what's going on than disturb another person who's feeling very sick.*
(At this point, the phone rang and Janet answered it with a promise to "get right on it."

Lee could have gone to the unit supervisor, who could be relied upon to appreciate the needs of an aphasic patient and to issue an order to change the room. However, she preferred not to rely on authoritarian methods for achieving professional goals when working with patients, people she supervised, or people who worked with her in non-nursing positions.

Assessing the other's knowledge level

Lee: Why do you think Mr. Warren doesn't know what's going on?

Janet: It's pretty obvious, isn't it? He can't speak and he doesn't understand when anyone speaks to him.

Lee: Oh, I see. I can understand that it seems as if he is not aware, but I assure you he can hear and he can feel, and that kind of noise can interfere with his progress.

Janet: Well, that's really too bad. But I don't know any patient who would feel good with that noise. We'll just have to try to calm that guy down and keep him quiet.

Lee: I can see you've got a million things on your hands, now. Do you think we could have lunch together and talk about it some more?

Lee asked a question that would provide information to help her assess the ward manager's level of knowledge, then she made a tentative attempt to offer a small amount of information to ascertain how it would be received. The answer to the question helped her recognize that she had reached the limit of Janet's knowledge of the situation, and knew that any voluntary change in room assignment would have to be based on further information about the patient's illness and his needs. Perhaps additional information would increase Janet's level of empathy for what Lee was feeling as well as for her patient's needs.

It was clear, too, that Janet was very busy, with many urgent demands being made on her. An attempt to inform someone who is distracted by other matters she considers more important is generally unsuccessful.

Lee thought that, perhaps, in a more relaxed setting she could bring up the matter again and try to make Janet understand.

Planning for leadership

Janet: I'd love to have lunch. But there's nothing I can do about this.

Lee: I'll see you at 12, then. Is that OK?

Janet: (Already bent over the pile of papers on her desk) Fine. I'll see you then.

Lee, having made a decision to take up the matter at lunch, let it drop for now, even though Janet reaffirmed her resistance to making a change.

In the meantime, as she went about her work, Lee gathered additional information about the new patient and about the availability of bed space. She also tried to identify some items of philosophical, intellectual, and professional thinking on which she and Janet agreed strongly.

Establishing communication

Lee: (After she and Janet had picked up their lunch trays and found a table
in the cafeteria.) It's good to take a breather. You were right; things
were certainly hectic today.

Janet: I'm glad it was Monday, and not Friday.

Lee: Yeah—you and I agree on that, don't we? Somehow I can always do
more on Mondays.

Janet: Not like most people, who take half a week to get back on track after
the weekend!

Lee: I think maybe the frustrations haven't had a chance to build up all over
again. So things seem a little easier.

Janet: That's right. I can take more guff without getting so uptight.

Lee: (Laughing) So I picked a good day to give you some guff!

Janet: (Joining in the laughter) First thing in the morning!

Lee: (Sobering) I really appreciate your willingness to listen. I think you
understand about nursing and you care as much as I do.

Janet: You're right, I do. I see what a difference good nursing care makes in
people's lives.

Lee: Can I tell you something about what I'm trying to do with Mr. Warren?
So you can judge for yourself.

Janet: I didn't think that anything much could be done for him. My Grandmother was never the same after her stroke. She went downhill
fast.

Lee: It's terrible to see someone you love deteriorate that way.

Janet: (Nods her head)

(They are both quiet for a moment)

Lee reveals, by what she says and what she does, that she and Janet have
some personal affinity and basis for understanding each other. Leaders who
are personally liked are generally more successful than those who have only
skill and knowledge to recommend them. She also shows empathy for Janet,
appreciating her feelings about the working situation as well as about her
personal life. She takes the time to communicate this empathy, by words and
by silence.

Maintaining ego safety

Lee: We're learning more about the management of stroke all the time. So
many people suffer from it and we're beginning to make greater
efforts to understand it and overcome the effects of different kinds of
strokes.

Janet: What can you do for someone who's had so much brain damage that

> *he can't speak or understand what people say to him? It seems*
> *hopeless.*

Lee: Actually, the prognosis for Mr. Warren isn't all that bad. I've seen peo-
ple start to speak again even after a year. That is, if they get the
right kind of help.

Janet: Really? What can you do?

At no time does she say or do anything to indicate that she thinks Janet
doesn't need to know about nursing, or that she is not competent to learn
what the nurse knows about this case. As a consequence, Janet does not feel
ego-threatened, and has no need to defend her lack of knowledge and so
solidify her resistance to learning more.

Achieving collaboration

Lee: I would like to begin to bring back his facilities by actually teaching
him. He may need more help with rehabilitation when he leaves
the hospital, but I think I can give him a good start on recovery.

Janet: You want to teach him in the middle of that craziness?! I have trouble
concentrating with a radio on!

Lee: (Quietly) You're right. It would be impossible.

Janet: I've seen you teach patients. Some of them get well faster and go
home sooner because of your teaching.

Lee: (Smiling) I'm not forgetting your teaching with Mrs. Wilson. Without
you to help me understand about the neighborhood she lived in
and to encourage her, that would not have been one of our suc-
cessful cases!

Lee has brought to present consciousness a mutuality of concern and interest
and a sense of success shared. These are no longer two people with conflicting goals and demands, but two colleagues working for the same objectives.

Janet: But how do you teach someone who can't speak or understand?

Lee: Well, first he needs quiet and no interruptions. Then we can begin
slowly to show him things he is interested in, and let him touch
them, while we say the words for them, over and over again.

Janet: You need a lot of patience for that kind of teaching.

Lee: (Nodding her head) If it works, it's worth it.

Janet: Let me see what I can do about another bed, will you?

Lee: I knew you'd understand! You're great!

Janet: I'm not promising anything. All I can do is try.

Lee: And I appreciate your trying! Incidentally, did you know that the
man in room 410 knows the new patient? They went to school
together.

Janet: I'd hate to inflict him again on someone who was once saddled with him!

(They both laugh)

Lee: Actually, when the man in 410 mentioned him, he seemed happy to know he was there. Said something about his having a big mouth but being OK underneath.

Leadership in the Nursing Team

The team meeting

This is the medical/surgical floor of a large general hospital. There are two nursing teams on the floor, each with a team leader. The head nurse is responsible for both teams. One team works on the east side of the floor, the other on the west side.

It is the end of the day shift and one team is meeting, as it does every day, with the head nurse to bring her up to date on the progress of the patients under the team's care, and to point out any special areas of concern that should be communicated to the next shift. The meeting is taking place in a small room off the nurses' station, from which the ringing of the phone and the patients' buzzers can be heard.

The people sitting around the table include the team leader, the other three registered nurses on the team, and the licensed practical nurse. The head nurse sits at one of the short ends of the rectangular table. As soon as everyone is seated, she starts the meeting:

Head nurse: What have you got, Janofsky?

Janofsky (team leader): 312 is still having trouble. He passed out again while voiding.

Head nurse: Did he get out of bed again?

Janofsky: He refuses to use the urinal. He says he . . .

Head nurse: Never mind what he says. Keep him in bed. Graham, has 314 been prepared for transfer?

Graham: Do you think that's a good idea? He's still pretty sick, and the nursing home can't give him the care he needs.

Head nurse: His doctor wants him transferred. Apparently, he thinks the patient is ready to leave the hospital.

Graham: Can't we . . . ?

Head nurse: We're over capacity now. We need the space. If his doctor thinks he'll get the care he needs in the convalescent home, it's out of our hands. Wilson, what was going on in 318 before? I couldn't get over there, but it sounded like a riot.

Wilson: Oh, nothing.

Head nurse: Something was going on! I heard yelling.

Wilson: Oh, she told her husband that nobody ever answers when she calls. She began to cry and he got a little loud about it. We handled it.

Head nurse: It sounded bad. Dr. Johnson was on the floor, and he looked at me when the noise started.

Wilson: It didn't last very long. He just got a little excited. He and his wife are both pretty scared about . . .

Head nurse: See that her buzzer is answered promptly. We don't want any more of that kind of thing. Now, are your notes all completed?

Janofsky: Dr. Walker forgot to reorder valium for 322.

Head nurse: Are you sure he wants it continued?

Janofsky: The patient is still agitated. He never said he wanted it discontinued. I think he just forgot. He always . . .

Head nurse: I'll get him on the phone.

Wilson: I wondered if any progress had been made on getting another nurse.

Head nurse: The request was approved. It's just a question now of getting the right person.

Wilson: I know someone who . . .

Head nurse: There's someone here in the hospital who's thinking of changing floors. She is highly recommended.

Wilson: This person I know is . . .

Head nurse: Why don't you give me her name and address and we'll see.

Wilson: It's a man.

Head nurse: Oh. Well . . . uh . . . give me his name and address.

Wilson: Would you like me to tell him to get in touch with you?

Head nurse: Uh . . . No, that won't be necessary. I'll take care of it.

Wilson: He's very good.

Head nurse: Oh, I'm sure he is.

(Ms. Wilson looks at her supervisor for a minute, then looks away. The head nurse, checking the points on her agenda, seems unaware that Ms. Wilson was looking at her.)

(A man stops at the open door and looks around at the people seated there. He speaks to the group in general.)

Man: Do you have Mrs. Tenner's chart?

Head nurse: Oh! Dr. Nosson! I'm so sorry. We were just working on the charts.

(She gets up quickly, goes to her desk, finds the chart and hands it to Dr. Nosson.)

Can we do something for you?

Dr. Nosson: No, it's all right. Go on with your meeting. I'll just look in on Mrs. Tenner for a minute.

Head nurse: It's no trouble, Doctor. The meeting will wait.

Dr. Nosson: *No. I'll be fine.*

Head nurse: *Thank you, Doctor.*

(She returns to the table and sits down. Everyone waits for her to resume the meeting.)

Head nurse: *(checking her notes) I think that covers everything. (Some of the people start to get up.)*

LPN: *Someone should do something about the cleaner!*

Head nurse: *Why? What happened?*

LPN: *Twice today I had to mop my spills because he was "too busy" to take care of it.*

Head nurse: *What was he doing?*

LPN: *Oh, swishing the mop around outside one of the rooms.*

Head nurse: *I'll remind him of what his job is. Thank you for telling me. (The LPN smiles in response)*

Wilson: *Can we talk for a few minutes about Mrs. Fisher?*

Head nurse: *The car accident? What about her?*

Wilson: *She seems really depressed. She just lies there. She has no visitors. She got some beautiful flowers yesterday, but she told me to give them to someone else. She won't answer her phone or watch TV or anything.*

Head nurse: *Her leg is healing. Dr. Winters told me he was beginning to think plastic surgery wouldn't be necessary.*

Wilson: *But she'll probably have to be in bed for weeks longer. She really is unhappy, and I can't seem to break through to her. I thought maybe you had some ideas about what we could do for her.*

Head nurse: *Do you know why she won't answer her phone?*

Wilson: *Not really. She just says she doesn't want to be bothered.*

Head nurse: *She's not very sick. Maybe she's just happy to be out of whatever she does—and she really just doesn't want to be bothered.*

LPN: *I saw her crying yesterday.*

Wilson: *You did?! I've never seen her show any emotion!*

LPN: *I was walking past the door and I thought I heard her calling. When I looked in, she turned away. She said she was all right, that she didn't want anything. But she was crying, all right.*

Graham: *Maybe one of us can spend a little time with her—just a few minutes sitting and visiting.*

Head nurse: *We don't have time for visiting! We're short-staffed as it is!*

Wilson: *What if she feels so bad she decides to leave before she should? She's very strongwilled.*

Graham: *(to Wilson) I'll get Mr. Johnson ready for the night, Jean. That should give you a few minutes with her.*

Head nurse: *Oh, I don't . . .*

Wilson: *That's great! It may be all she needs.*

(The head nurse's mouth tightens, but she says nothing.)

Wilson: *(to head nurse) I'll let you know what happens.*
Head nurse: *(somewhat mollified) All right, then, if there's nothing more. (The team leaves quickly, but Jean Wilson and Anne Graham stop in the corridor to speak to each other. As the L.P.N. passes the, Jean puts her hand on the L.P.N.'s arm.)*
Jean Wilson: *Thanks, Ms. Evans. That was important information about the patient.*
Ms. Evans: *(Smiles) I know. I'm glad I happened to see it.*

Group goals

Writers in the field recognize that team nursing is analogous to any group approach to problem solving, and, as a concept, has its roots in the ideas that (a) those who do the actual care delivery should be involved in the planning for that care if they are to function on the basis of a commitment to the plan and (b) the varied contributions of the team members reduce the margin for error caused by individual gaps in knowledge and misperceptions.

> Team nursing is a philosophy, not simply a methodology. There is nothing new about the idea of assembling a cluster of people to work toward the solution of specific problems. The philosophy of team nursing subscribes to . . . functioning of members as coequals with minimal emphasis of hierarchical lines of authority between the leader and the led . . . [5]

A number of factors must be present in the functioning of any problem-solving group if it is to work effectively.[6]

Self-Fulfillment

The dynamics of interaction on a nursing team are not different from the pattern in any small problem-solving group. People in a group or on a team, if they are not to remove themselves physically or psychologically from the other people, need to find in the group a measure of self-fulfillment. More importantly, however, when the needs of clients require the services of workers with different kinds of skills, efforts must increase among the workers to refine their skills in communicating with each other, so that all their skills are meshed in a smooth program of service delivery. Teamwork for the benefit of the client depends on all members of the team sharing information with each other—not only about their specialties, but also about themselves.

When there is honesty, openness and acceptance among the team members, these conditions extend beyond purely professional matters to more personal concerns. Team members feel free to bring to team meetings problems that, if left unsolved, contribute to ineffectiveness on the job. A supervisor who plays favorites, a physician who breaks the rules of sterility, a clique that creates disharmony with its exclusiveness and gossip, an aide who is so beset with family problems that she cannot speak civilly to anyone—these matters are also brought to the meetings, and all the team members contribute their skills and sensitivities to solving them. For human service workers, just like clients, are whole persons and must be related to as such.

What do people expect when they commit themselves to work on a team? Some expect acceptance from the other members. They feel confident that what they have to say will be appreciated and used. Their feeling of safety in the group makes them free to make their contributions openly, not holding back because they are afraid of being rejected.

Other people come into a group with trepidation. They expect to be rejected or having what they say ridiculed or ignored. They are afraid to say what they really think and feel, and so the group is deprived of most of their knowledge and skill.

Some people expect self-fulfillment from their group participation. They see themselves as contributing creatively to the achievement of the group's goals, and feeling successful when the goals have been reached. They are usually task oriented, concentrating on getting the job done quickly and well.

Some people's self-fulfillment comes from asserting their status and power in the group. By force of his position or personality, a team member may subdue others, compelling them to side with him—even against their own better judgment. In the process, he neutralizes the potential contributions. Still others get their self-fulfillment from being protective and nurturing of those group members who seem to need such nurturing.

The feelings of group members reflect their expectations and what they actually do get in the group. Some people feel important and powerful, others sad, frightened, vulnerable and rejected. The fearful ones may say and do things primarily for the purpose of allying themselves with the powerful ones, or getting under the protective wing of the nurturing ones. In either instance, they do not make an optimal contribution to the group goal.

Leadership Functions

The sensitive team member who is aware of these expectations, feelings and behaviors in the group, can take on the leadership function of identifying behaviors that seem to interfere with the participants' needs and with the group goals.

For example, when someone is interrupted in the middle of a sentence, how does she respond? Do her lips tighten in what looks like annoyance? Does she partially turn away from the group? Does she say nothing more for a period of time? Does she disagree with the interrupter the next time she speaks? The person alert to such behavioral cues may intercede on behalf of the one who is always being interrupted, may ask directly for a comment from the one whose comments seem always to be ignored, may compliment a generally submissive person on the originality of the idea he barely whispered. No matter who is the leader of record on the team, no matter who wields the most influence in the institution, the team member who can address herself to the feelings of the team members is fulfilling an important function on the team. There is evidence that, in the small group that spends some of its time dealing with the feelings and needs of its members and developing skills in interpersonal communication, there is increased participation, and greater efficiency in doing the job.[7]

The nursing team, in addition, has goals unique to its function. "Team nursing is one of the more common nursing care delivery systems and involves a group of people sharing responsibility for a number of patients."[8] In line with this general purpose, the members of the nursing team meet to share information about the progress of patients, to check with each other on the validity of nursing care plans, and to solve nursing care problems that seem to require collaborative effort. It is during these meetings, too, that assignments are made and new members initiated into the system.

Ambivalence and Confusion

In common with many work situations where the team structure is used, the nursing team generally departs somewhat from its philosophical underpinnings in its functions. In the same literature that defines optimal team functioning as essentially democratic, we find the team leader identified as what appears to be an absolute controller. "Under the team method the professional nurse acts as a manager to facilitate the work of a group of health personnel to meet the health needs of patients in a unit. This approach considers the concept of accomplishing group responsibilities through a team process whereby the nurse team leader plans, organizes, directs, and controls the care provided by the team."[9] Though the reference here is to a team that includes various medical technicians and specialists, the team goal, on the all-nurse team, is effective nursing care delivery. Presumably, the democratic philosophy of team nursing is also the basis of the formation of this kind of nursing team.

In what appears to be similar ambivalence, we find the following description that starts out as democratic functioning, veers off into authoritarian leadership and returns again to cooperative involvement:

> The *team system* is a mode for providing care developed in the 1950s in which a professional nurse facilitates the efforts of a group of diversified health care personnel to provide for the health needs of an individual or a group of

people in either a hospital or a community setting. In team nursing the leader's primary responsibility is to see that every activity is characterized by mutual sharing of work based on an interest and concern for the individuals served. All efforts are directed toward accomplishing group tasks with as much efficiency and expediency as possible. The thrust of every activity is directed toward delivery of individualized health care. Through the team process the nurse leader/manager plans, participates in, coordinates, interprets, supervises, and evaluates the care given. Consistent and continuous high-quality care is made possible through written nursing care plans developed by the nurse-leader and co-workers, with evaluation and revision of care plans as new insights are gained.[10]

This kind of confusion in philosophy and method can have serious consequences for a group's goal achievement. On the one hand, the leader is expected to encourage "mutual sharing." Presumably, as a facilitator, the leader must have the ability to free people from fears and other constraints that interfere with their saying what they know and feel. At the same time, the leader and the team have "efficiency and expediency" of task accomplishment as their goal. However, if the "leader," as this statement implies, does all the interpreting and evaluating, it seems that the mutual sharing would be reduced to a minimum, and the emphasis would fall on expediency. Though one would not deny that a balance must be maintained between the need for democratic functioning and the need for getting the job done, there is no evidence to substantiate the belief that less democracy results in a higher quality of care given. On the contrary, if care-givers feel that their own contributions to the care plans are not valued, and that they as individuals are not valued, how can they be fully committed to the implementation of those plans? Often the group's and the leader's lack of concern with the needs of the team members may cause personal goals to interfere with professional goals.

In the nursing team situation presented earlier, a functional division on the team's goal is revealed. Though it is probably true that all the team members would, if asked, say that the goal was optimum patient care, the behavior of the team members indicates that they actually have different ideas of the actual goal. The head nurse sees the carrying out of the physician's orders as a goal. She also aims to be informed about everything that goes on in her unit, apparently for the purpose of making all the decisions herself. Her goal is also to present to physicians (and to administrators?) a picture of an efficiently-run nursing team.

Ms. Wilson, one of the R.N.'s on the team, apparently sees the exploration and solution of problems seen as interfering with the patients' health and well-being as a goal. Ms. Graham, also an R.N., cooperates eagerly with her, leading the observer to believe that she shares Ms. Wilson's goal. The other R.N., Ms. Janofsky, sees the goal as feeding information to the team leader or head nurse. Both Ms. Janofsky and Ms. Evans, the L.P.N., make attempts to expand the team function to encompass the others' goal, but only Ms. Evans is able to do so at this time.

The goal as perceived by Ms. Wilson is rooted in the concept of professional accountability rather than in the idea of technical accountability. That is, she recognizes that, no matter what level of technical training a team member has, a significant part of her function must be to contribute what she knows and feels about the patient and his needs. Though the validity of technical contributions is limited by the parameters of the individual's technical training and competence, a large body of data exists about a patient that is not necessarily related to technical training. But such information becomes a vital part of the material used for problem-solving, and must be included in the assumption of professional accountability. No matter who has gathered this information, the team has a responsibility to consider it in its decision making.

Most of the team members are so oriented to the concept that leadership is a function of supervision that they seem unable to contribute fully to the team's discussion of a particular idea until the head nurse demonstrates interest in pursuing that idea. Once she becomes involved in pursuing Ms. Wilson's concern, the others are able to work on the problem. They become so caught up in their interest and enthusiasm once they feel somewhat freer to participate, that they plan collaboratively in solving a problem in spite of the head nurse's attempts to maintain control over the decision making. Nothing is quite so heady as the experience of working together and finding a solution to a troubling situation!)

Ms. Wilson provides the necessary leadership skill by risking breaking into the head nurse's agenda and so encouraging others to do the same. She also demonstrates the leader's sensitivity and concern when she makes a point of expressing appreciation to Ms. Evans for her contribution— not as a superior commending an inferior, but as one colleague to another who shares a common goal.

Leadership in Primary Nursing

Probably one of the most serious difficulties in providing optimum patient-centered care with functional and team nursing organizations is that there is no orderly communication system for the flow of information. As a result, the care becomes fragmented. We can attribute most of the errors made in patient care to this condition of fragmentation.

Primary nurses are responsible for the total care of patients assigned to them. They develop the care plans and, when they are not on duty, other nurses follow these plans and report to the primary nurse any unforseen consequences that may occur, so that she may revise those plans if necessary.

Primary nursing does not obviate the need for nurse leaders. On the contrary, with the nurse accepting accountability for total patient care, it becomes necessary for her to assume leadership in bringing others up to date on the needs of the patients with whom they all come in contact. Leadership skills are necessary to optimize the behaviors of people with such diverse backgrounds and motivations as family members, nursing aides, physicians, and inhalation therapists, to name only a few.

The process of coordinating care among the various care givers, the patient's family, and the patient himself requires all the skills of communication implicit in our operational framework. In addition, the primary nurse must have the ability to assume authority and act autonomously. The inveterate follower, looking always to others for authority and leadership, generally does not offer to become a primary nurse. Often the primary nurse must act without assigned authority to command compliance with her wishes. Thus all those whose behaviors affect the patient, and the patient himself, must accept the nurse as their leader in most aspects of patient care.

The whole issue of accountability, so hotly debated in the teaching profession and in other areas, comes to a head in primary nursing. There appears to be no other rational conclusion: *Accountability requires autonomy.* If the professional is to be held accountable for the quality of patient care and the consequences of that care, then she must be free to make professional decisions. She must also be able to communicate effectively to others the basis for those decisions and engage them in a system for participating in decision making. At no point in the process of nursing care delivery can she be permitted to justify an error of omission or commission with the excuse, "I was following orders," or "It was not my job to keep track of that."

Examples abound of what can happen when no one accepts responsibility. Almost a liter of blood is taken from a patient, 5 cc's at a time, for various tests over a period of 24 hours so that the patient, who is 74 years old, becomes anemic. A patient in an ICU is tubed because there are not enough nurses to provide proper lung care. A patient suffers from decubiti because aides refuse to accept the responsibility for turning him in bed. All such situations become the responsibility of the primary nurse, and that responsibility requires that she become engaged in various leadership activities, from inservice education to providing input at policy and budget meetings.

Staff development and supervision

Consistent with a belief in humanism and self-actualization, nursing recognizes that the "Personal and professional development of the staff is an outgrowth of the nursing care modality of the unit."[11] Consequently, the teaching skills of the primary nurse are brought into play to encourage that development, and to free other staff members to function autonomously within the parameters of their own expertise.

In one hospital, a primary nurse identified a behavioral objective based on a pressing need in the unit: Aides felt that turning patients periodically to prevent bed sores was more than they should be expected to do. The registered nurses maintained that they were so busy providing other aspects of physical care that they often had no time left to give nursing care. So, though her care plans included repositioning for patients who needed it, too often this part of the plan was not implemented.

There were a number of ways to approach the solution of this problem.

1. She could petition for a smaller patient care load. However, she knew that omitting aspects of nursing care was not necessarily a function of time. That is, even when nurses had fewer patients, they did not necessarily provide optimal nursing care. Sometimes it was because of the way they planned their work. At other times it was because they did not value certain aspects of care, did not think they were important for the patient's health. Still other procedures were intrinsically distasteful to some individuals, and they preferred to leave them for others to do.

2. She could berate the associate nurses who did not implement her care plan and threaten them with dire consequences. Realistically, however, she knew that she had no authority to impose sanctions on anyone. Staff personnel were hired and fired by the director of nursing service; and complaints to the director about individual staff members were received politely and that was the last time the complainant heard about them. Presumably they were acted on in some way, but just how remained a mystery. There was even some suspicion among the primary nurses that anyone who complained was somehow viewed as deficient in her ability to manage her staff.

3. She could approach this rationally, as a problem that needed solving, and use what leadership skills she had to achieve the desired objective. She saw the matter partly as an educational problem; the process of resolving it would provide educational development for the staff.

First, she held meetings with the associate nurses (who implemented her plans when she was not on the floor), the L.P.N., and the aides on the teams. (A separate meeting was held on each shift, in order to involve everyone in the process.)

At the initial meeting of one group, she first presented data on the length of hospital stay—significantly reduced, she believed, by the higher quality of nursing care provided since the reorganization to primary nursing. Her evident delight at being able to tell them this encouraged team members to openly congratulate themselves and each other. In one of the groups, individuals began spontaneously to point out special skills and strengths of others, offering each other the kinds of recognition and support that would probably continue to raise the level of functioning. One R.N. told of how she had taught a young woman to care for her colostomy herself—a woman who had been convinced that she would never again look at her body, and who insisted that she would have a nurse do what was necessary for the rest of her life. Another R.N. praised an aide for being observant and noticing a defective IV clamp.

Finally, one thoughtful L.P.N. brought up the problem that was on the mind of the primary nurse. "It seems to me," she said slowly, "that we could do even better if we didn't get so many people with bed sores." The interesting thing about this phenomenon is that people who feel good about themselves, who feel that they are worthwhile and recognized as such, and who expect and receive support from significant people in their lives can afford to admit the existence of flaws in themselves. They can also permit themselves to become engaged in correcting those flaws. This is quite different from the commonly held perception that one must forever point out what is wrong with the other person or he will never know what he needs to change in himself. Parents feel that they do this for the child's own good, supervisors do it in the name of increased production, teachers do it to raise the level of the child's achievement. However, what all of them generally succeed in doing is, at the worst, creating profound self-doubts that impede achievement for a lifetime, or, at the best, causing temporary or sporadic changes accompanied by resentment. Between these two extreme responses are many that affect the individual and the institution and people with whom he comes into contact in a variety of destructive ways.

When the L.P.N. raised the matter, some of the others nodded their heads. The primary nurse was ready with the data on the incidence and severity of decubiti in the unit, and several people expressed shock at the numbers.

One person, in spite of the positive support in the group, started to respond defensively: "We work very hard! Especially when two or three admissions come in at one time and we have all that initial procedure to do! We just don't have the time to keep turning patients."

Another picked up on the theme of defense against implied criticism, though no one had blamed anyone. (Apparently, they blamed themselves.) "It's not just the turning, you know. You can't walk in and just flip someone over; you've got to prepare him, and convince him it should be done even though it hurts."

The others nodded in agreement. The primary nurse nodded more in approval: "That's what's so great about the kind of nursing care we give. It's really nursing care, not just following medical orders. Treating people like human beings *is* important; caring about how they feel is what nursing is all about. And that takes time."

There was a long silence. Finally, one of the aides said: "I don't know how to turn a person. It frightens me that I may hurt him too much. Especially when the patient is very big and heavy."

An R.N. answered: "There are tricks to it. I can show you, so that it will not only be easier on the patient, but also easier on your back."

The aide laughed. "Maybe if two people did it, it would be easier."

Another R.N. suggested: "If we had a regular turning schedule for each patient, we could arrange for two of us to be free at those times. And if one person forgot, the other could come and get her."

The L.P.N. had an idea for posting the schedule and checking it each time a patient was turned so they would be sure to remember.

They all set to work to develop a system for achieving an objective that they had defined for themselves. Who was the leader of the group? Or, more accurately, who were the *leaders*?

Nurse-physician communication

In another hospital, the primary nurse was aware that she needed to establish communication with the patient's physician as well as with the other professionals participating in the patient's care. At the outset, however, there seemed no way that she could break through to one particular physician. When he came on to the floor, he nodded in a vague way to the people in the general area, picked up the chart and went to the patient's room. He stopped to talk only when he met another physician. His communication with nursing personnel was almost nonexistent as far as professional matters were concerned. When he had finished visiting his patients he often singled out one nurse (usually not one who was caring for his patients) and laughed and joked with her in a very personal and social way. If the nurse managed to be with the patient when he came into the room, he did not even acknowledge her presence. He certainly never asked her for her evaluation of the patient or for any information that she might have to offer. He accepted what she volunteered without comment.

Health team meetings were not scheduled, so no formal opportunity existed to establish professional communication across disciplinary lines. The nurse managed to meet on an individual basis with other health personnel; sometimes she asked one or another of them to come to a nursing team meeting to discuss a problem that needed their special input. However, this physician refused to attend the one time he was invited to a meeting, saying that whatever he had to say he wrote on the patient's chart, and it was just a matter of carrying out his orders.

The nurse decided that she would use a direct approach with this man. She identified several other nurses who felt the way she did and together they actually planned a program of education for him that would include:

1. What nursing is; what is included in nursing education; what competencies and areas of concern and expertise these particular nurses had.
2. What the women's movement is all about; women's rights to equal consideration and respect for knowledge.

3. What communication is all about; how people communicate without words; bars to effective communication.

They wrote nurse's notes that included references to these points; they stopped the physician when he came and went and engaged him in brief conversations about these matters; they periodically asked for ten-minute appointments to discuss a problem that involved the relationship between medicine and nursing.

One interesting spin-off of all this was that the physician and the nurses established a very friendly relationship, based on a growing respect for each other's professional ability. It finally led to the scheduling of regular health-team meetings, with the physician actively participating.

Preservice education

The primary nurse is in a strategic position to provide leadership in the education of new nurses. Often, there is a serious gap between the preservice education process and optimum professional practice.

In professional curricula, experiences are generally identified as didactic or clinical. Didactic experiences include lectures and laboratories; clinical experiences involve practicing professionally on real clients or patients. The idea is that knowledge is gained in the classroom and then applied in real life, under supervision. In the course of application, the student supposedly practices the necessary skills until he becomes sufficiently adept to qualify as a professional.

Unfortunately, a number of factors intervene to prevent reaching this goal:

1. The clinical situations in which students are placed rarely provide the systematic, sequential opportunities for practice needed for optimum skill development. What usually happens, in schools, hospitals, social agencies, and in law offices, is that students get an opportunity to try out a variety of procedures when the need for them happens to arise. There may be many procedures that he never gets the chance to practice, and others that he does over and over again. Not infrequently, he will spend most of his time at a variety of duties that relieve the regular staff of the simple, routine things.

   On the other hand, the repetition of certain procedures necessary for skill development may be avoided by students, who prefer to have experience in the broad spectrum of professional activities. Though they may get a variety of experiences, they never develop even the minimal level of skill needed to function effectively.

2. Rarely is adequate time provided after each experience to analyze it for component factors (like cause and effect relationships). The rush of

providing service, the urgent needs of clients, the rush to get the day's work accomplished all make the field setting an inadequate classroom. The need for recapping the day's events and for evaluation of the day's accomplishments in leisurely introspection is left to each student on his own. Without the assistance of information from more experienced workers, his examination of his own judgments and behaviors is colored by limited knowledge and lack of objectivity, so that he easily falls into repeating the same errors.

3. The student/supervisor ratio is rarely high enough for adequate supervision. If a particular procedure is not monitored by a supervisor, the student may get no feedback on his accuracy or level of skill. Even if he makes no serious error, he may very well be doing the work indifferently and ineffectively; however, he will never learn where he is falling short of optimum functioning.

An intermediate stage between classroom instruction and supervised field experience can provide for many of the deficiencies of the classroom-to-field model of preparation. Individual education instructors have tried this in the preparation of teachers, and it has been tried sporadically in the training of other professionals. For example, before the student is permitted to work in a classroom with children, or in an agency with clients, he participates in a series of simulation experiences in order to reach a level of skill more appropriate for field work than the level attained in course work. In a sheltered setting, with students, instructors, and others drawn in to play the roles of clients, children, and workers, students practice the relevant professional behaviors in systematic sequence and with the repetition they need to develop a high level of skill.

Sometimes these simulated experiences may be provided in conjunction with course work. Or the student may be recalled from the field periodically to engage in them for a short period of time. This is an opportunity to reflect calmly on the experiences he has been having under pressure and perhaps to test out some behaviors that he wishes he had thought of at the time.

The primary nurse can draw the student nurses assigned to her unit into the total learning process that is going on. The agenda of team meetings need not be limited to current problems. They may also include systematic examination of hypothetical problems so that the staff can be prepared for whatever contingencies may arise. In this way, students learn about professional matters that do not happen to come up during their clinical experience.

Students can also be oriented to a new world of supervision, in which people no longer take orders and follow directions without question. As they learn that job satisfaction is closely connected to feeling important, to participating in work-related decision making, and to having control over what happens to one, they may become skillful in recognizing their potential for leading others into such active participation.

Analyzing small-group dynamics

A group's pattern of interaction provides clues to the reasons for productivity or lack of it in the tasks undertaken by the group. The more aware group members are of this pattern of interaction, the more data they will have at their disposal for increasing the group's effectiveness. A working team may use the following exercises to practice the skills needed for identifying patterns of group interaction.

During one of your team sessions, let four people seat themselves at four points outside the perimeter of the group, but close enough to hear the discussion and observe facial expressions and body movements. They should position themselves so that, among the four of them, all members of the discussion group will be clearly seen.

Each observer should have a copy of the chart below; it may be easier for each observer to concentrate on only one column of the chart.

As the discussion proceeds, observers will make a check in the Count column of the chart each time a behavior is observed. At the end of the discussion, the observers tell the group the number of times each behavior was observed. Everyone in the group should realize that the observers will not record names of individuals or mention names in their feedback.

It is often helpful to have the completed observation charts given to the group so that they may read and discuss them without the presence of the observers. This reduces somewhat the tendency on the part of the group members to defend their behaviors. They may, in the course of their discussion, call in one of the observers to ask for clarification of a recorded observation. However, the group must make its own decision about how to use the data in the observation.

As the group works together over a period of time in problem-solving sessions, whatever commitments they make to change the behaviors observed can be implemented. They may decide to remind each other each time a group member acts in a way that hinders optimum interaction or they may decide to practice specific skills, like limiting the amount of time each person has to speak, or reflecting accurately what a previous speaker has said before making one's own contribution.[12]

Vicarious experiences for increasing understanding and acceptance of others

This exercise provides an opportunity to live for a while, relatively safely, in the shoes of another person. This kind of exercise must be done by people

Observing Small-Group Interaction

Behaviors related to Self-Fulfillment	Count	Behaviors related to Acceptance	Count	Behaviors related to Influence	Count	Behaviors related to Goal Achievement	Count
People showed signs of impatience at the length of speeches.		People interrupted others in mid-sentence.		One person was most dominant in the group: (He has a job that carries prestige.) (He's older than the other group members.) (He's the only man in the group.) (He did most of the speaking.) (He spoke with great assurance.) (He gave credit and attention to others.) (He called on people to make contributions.) (He made the final decision and announced that the problem was solved.)		People summarized what was said.	
People never spoke at all.		People tried to understand different points of view. They said things like: "Do you mean . . .?" "I don't quite understand . . ." "Can you give an example . . .?"				People noted what progress had been made.	
People directed their eyes and/or bodies outside the circle.						People reminded the group of the goal.	
People walked out.		People did not respond to others' point of view.				People suggested the group had moved off the track.	
People expressed feelings about their treatment in the group.		People said things totally unrelated to what was just said.				People identified a number of possible solutions.	
People said they didn't care about the problem or its solution.		People spoke defensively. They said things like: "I wouldn't say this if I didn't know . . ." "Everyone knows . . ." "When you're my age		People directed their comments to the dominant person. Two people competed for dominance:		People identified different points of view in the group and attempted to find areas of agreement in them.	
						People examined the consequences of different solutions.	

Observing Small-Group Interaction

Behaviors related to Self-Fulfillment	Count	Behaviors related to Acceptance	Count	Behaviors related to Influence	Count	Behaviors related to Goal Achievement	Count
		you'll know . . ." "I've had more experience than you . . .", People attacked others' points of view with such words as stupid, unimportant, ridiculous.		(They disagreed with each other.) (They belittled each other.) (They ignored each other.) (They interrupted each other.)			
		People accepted others' contributions. They said things like: "I never thought of that . . ." "That's a good point." "What you said makes the point very clear."		People directed their comments only to one or the other competitor. One particular person speaks only to contradict another particular person. One particular person speaks only after another particular person has spoken. One particular person interrupts only another particular person.			
		People implied, by tone of voice and body movement, that others' views were not worth consideration. They did such things as wave away					

Observing Small-Group Interaction

Behaviors related to Self-Fulfillment	Count	Behaviors related to Acceptance	Count	Behaviors related to Influence	Count	Behaviors related to Goal Achievement	Count
		what was just said, raise their eyes to heaven, cross their arms and purse their lips at what was just said, state an opposing or unrelated view with exaggerated emphasis. People made observations about how others were being treated in the group. People did not permit interruptions. People directed some of their contributions to those who had not spoken.					

who have been working together—in a class, in a team, in a continuing-education study group—and where the relationships have remained on a professional functional level. That is, the people generally have not developed strong personal-social ties.

Identify someone in the group whom you perceive as being quite different from you. If you are a man, you may pick a woman. If you are a Black person, you may pick a White person. Pick someone of another generation, or someone whose life-style seems very different from your own. Perhaps you have identified someone in the group whose childhood experiences were totally unlike those you had as a child. If you are struggling economically, perhaps you can find someone in the group who has never had to wonder how she was going to make ends meet.

The following situations illustrate different experiences of people's lives. Choose the one that fits your own experiences most closely. You may alter it to make it more accurate.

Now each of you take on the role of the other person and act out the situation to some kind of conclusion *as the other person*. You may do this in the privacy of your dyad, or in front of the rest of the group.

When you have finished a play, the role-players should discuss the following questions *with each other*:

1. How accurate were the role players in their presentations?
2. What specific errors were made?
3. What evidences of the other's knowledge and understanding about your life surprised you?
4. How did you feel about role playing the other person's life?
5. What did you learn that you didn't know before?
6. What more would you like to know about the other person's life?
7. What more would you like the other person to know about you?

After all the role plays and dyadic discussions are finished, the whole group should discuss the following questions:

1. What general observations do you have about this experience?
    •Do people generally seem to know a lot about those who are different?
    •Are there more differences between people or more similarities?
    •Do differences interfere with productive relationships?
    •How do you feel about this experience?
2. What commitment are you prepared to make to seek out experiences for increasing your understanding of other people?

MAN/WOMAN

Man's life experiences. I was taught early by the example of my father and by my teachers in school that the man is the breadwinner and the head of the household. As I grew older, the pressure from my friends and from media messages was to make as many sexual conquests as possible; to make as much money as possible; and to buy all the symbols of success, such as a big car, a big house, and a fur coat for my wife. Every time I fell short of these expectations, I felt like a failure.

Woman's life experiences. I was taught by my mother that a woman's goal in life was to be a good wife and a good mother. I married when I was eighteen and had three children within four years. When I was twenty-six, my husband and I separated, and I had to go to work. I found that there was very little I could do to make a living and support my children. I couldn't even establish credit to tide me over the rough spots. It took me a long time to learn a profession and get a decent job.

The situation to be role-played. The man and the woman meet at a party and begin to see each other regularly. After a while, they decide to get married. The subject of the roles of husband and wife has come up. The woman says: "I can't give up the job I worked so hard to qualify for. And I like the feeling of independence that working gives me."

The man answers: "Why do you need independence? You'll be married to me, and I'll take care of you and the children."

What happens now?

BLACK PERSON/WHITE PERSON

Black person's life experiences. Before I could really understand what was happening, I used to hear my mother and father talking about how hard it was for my father to keep a job. Though he was a skillful mechanic, it was years before he was permitted to join the union. When he finally got a job in a plant, he was let go at the first sign of business falling off. Because he was among the last hired (almost all the machine workers were White), he was among the first to be fired. As I got older, I experienced discrimination personally—my high school counselor told me there was no point in my taking an academic course, because I'd probably never be able to afford college. Anyway, no firm would hire a Black engineer.

White person's life experiences. When I was about twelve years old, a Black family moved on to my street. Everyone was very upset about it, and some of the kids threw rocks at their house and broke their windows. I knew this was a bad thing to do, but everyone on my block agreed those Black people had no right to move in where they were not wanted. My parents always said they'd never have moved in if someone hadn't paid them to do it just to start trouble. I've never really known any Black people personally.

The situation to be role-played. The agency supervisor introduces these two people. She tells the Black person, who has worked in the agency for two years, to take the White person under her wing and show her the ropes, to introduce her to everyone and help her to learn what has to be done. When the supervisor leaves them alone, they turn to each other.

What happens now?

OLD PERSON/YOUNG PERSON

Older person's experiences. Ever since I reached the age of fifty, I have felt that people look at me and talk to me differently. When young people distribute flyers in the street or stop passersby to sign a petition, they usually ignore me and stop only younger people. At work, I hear colleagues talk about how the agency needs "new blood," and they strongly imply that anyone over fifty is old-fashioned, rigid, reluctant to consider new ideas. I think I still have something important to contribute to the agency; I know my field, I'm energetic, I do a good job. When the younger people arrange parties or go out to lunch together, I am rarely included, and I feel hurt and outside of things.

Young person's experiences. I work in an agency where most of the other people are twenty or thirty years older than I am and make more than twice as much money as I do. Most of them are supervisors and administrators only because they've been around a long time, not because they're so great. Some of them don't deserve to make more money than I do. They're not doing the job; they waste a lot of time. They ought to retire and let young people with new ideas take over. The only older person I've ever known are my parents and a grandmother who died when I was four years old. I have nothing in common with older people—we're from two different worlds.

The situation to be role-played. The young person decides to take a night course at the local community college to upgrade some of her writing skills. The teacher of the course is the older woman who is working parttime at the college, teaching just that one course. After several sessions, teacher and student learn that they are both doing similar work during the day. One evening after class, the teacher suggests to the student that they go out together for a drink before they start for home.

What happens now?

POOR PERSON/MIDDLE CLASS PERSON

Poor person's experiences. I grew up on a farm worked by my family. The land belonged to a rich man who got a share of the crops we raised. Not only did he get most of our crop, but whatever we had to buy we bought in the only store in town, the one that rich man owned. I remember some bad years, when we went to bed hungry almost every night. One year it was because there was an early frost and it destroyed the crop. Another year, hailstones broke up all the young plants. We got into such debt at the store those times, that it took years to pay back what we owed. Though my mother and father and two brothers worked hard from early morning and into the night, we never seemed to be able to get ahead—have things a little easier or buy something that was not an absolute necessity. My mother finally died from just being worn out, I think.

Middle class person's experiences. We were never rich, but we always had everything we needed. My father owned a small business and he was able to provide a nice home and an education for my brother and me. He had six employees, and he always treated them well. Every Christmas, he gave each of them a nice bonus and a ten-pound turkey. And the wages he paid them were fair. Some of the people who worked for him years ago still come to see him when they're in the neighborhood. He's even the godfather of the child of one of his employees.

The situation to be role-played. The people in the town who are on welfare have been staging a protest against the decision of the town council to make every physically able person on welfare work for his income. This includes mothers of school-age children who are rearing their children alone. The work is street-sweeping and cleaning city property. The poor person described above is now a community worker attached to the city health and welfare department. He is out in the street demonstrating on the side of the welfare recipients. The middle-class person described above is a member of the town council. As he comes up to the city hall, he bumps into the community worker with a picket sign in his hand, and recognizes him.
What happens now?

MARRIED PERSON/UNMARRIED PERSON LIVING WITH A MATE

Married person's experiences. My husband and I love each other more every day. We have two fine children and we are doing everything we can to help them grow into loving and productive adults. Like most married couples, my husband and I have occasional disagreements and arguments. Once we were really mad at each other for a week. But we've learned to talk about our differences, and, because we really care about each other's welfare, we live through the differences and are stronger for them.

Unmarried person's experiences. John and I have lived together for seven years. We have a very good relationship. We help each other to grow and mature: We encourage each other to have new experiences, we meet new people all the time, and we do a lot of reading and talk to each other about what we read. Our two children are a joy to us, and they are part of our learning and growing. When we argue or fight, we have some real shouting matches, but we calm down eventually and compromise about our differences. We are all good together—a real, loving family.

The situation to be role-played. These two people meet in the elementary school on parents' visiting day. Their children all attend the same school. They know about each other, but they have never met formally. The married woman is the school secretary, and she knows the other woman is not married because the children's birth certificates indicate this. The secretary is in the classroom when she hears the other woman protesting to the teacher that her children are being taught that it is sinful for a man and a woman to live together without being married.

What happens now?

NOTES

[1] Kurt Lewin, "Field Theory and Experiment in Social Psychology: Concepts and Methods," *American Journal of Sociology*, 1939, Vol. 44, pp. 868–896.

[2] George Brager and Stephen Halloway, *Changing Human Service Organizations—Politics and Practice*, (New York: The Free Press, 1978), p. 33.

[3] Floyd Hunter, *Community Power Structure*, (Chapel Hill: University of North Carolina Press, 1953).

[4] Kenneth D. Benne and Max Birnbaum, "Principles of Changing," in Warren G. Bennis, Kenneth D. Benne, and Robert Chin, Eds., *The Planning of Change*, (New York: Holt, Rinehart and Winston, 1969), pp. 328–335.

[5] Laura Mae Douglass and Em Olivia Bevis, *Nursing Management and Leadership in Action*, 3rd. ed., (St. Louis: C.V. Mosby Co., 1979), p. 178.

[6] Adapted from Charlotte Epstein, *An Introduction to the Human Services*, (Englewood Cliffs, N.J.: Prentice-Hall, 1981), pp. 191–192.

[7] Rodney W. Napier and Matti K. Gershenfeld, *Groups: Theory and Experience*, (Boston: Houghton Mifflin, 1973), pp. 23–24.

[8] Douglass and Bevis, op. cit., p. 162.

[9] Warren F. Stevens, *Management and Leadership in Nursing*, (New York: McGraw-Hill, 1978), p. 91.

[10] Douglass and Bevis, op. cit., p. 178.

[11] Gwen D, Marram, Margaret W. Barrett, and Em Olivia Bevis, *Primary Nursing: A Model for Individualized Care*, 2nd ed., (St. Louis: C.V. Mosby, 1979), p. 49.

[12] Charlotte Epstein, *Affective Subjects in the Classroom: Exploring Race, Sex, and Drugs* (Scranton, Pa.: Intext, 1972), pp. 48–57.

chapter seven

The Nurse Leader in the Community

Unique contributions of nursing

Faye Wattleton, president of Planned Parenthood, herself a nurse, presents her observation on nurses as leaders:

> We (nurses) see people at the most vulnerable points in their lives, and I don't think anyone knows more about people without rights than nurses. We are uniquely in a position to see the need for change, and I think strong enough as a group to take an active role.
>
> But I think that as a profession, we tend to advocate professional issues to the exclusion of other important things. There is a bigger world out there. We need to address larger social issues—to take them on and work for change in more than just nursing.[1]

The nurse who wants to assume leadership in the community has opportunities unequalled in other areas of professional life. She may start with fewer handicaps than community workers from other disciplines, partly because communities have had positive past experiences with nurses and partly because the nurse comes to the community with clear and recognizable objectives easily shared by people in the community.

In general, community organization appears to have been suspended to some extent while people worry about energy and inflation. This may be the opportune time for the nurse to move in and use her unique role to effect important and lasting change. Even though the nurse may not be a resident of the community, her special skills are easily recognized as important to people's welfare. The nurse is not perceived like the social worker, who may be associated with the implied threat of discontinuing welfare payments, or like the agency outreach worker who may be viewed as manipulating people in order to defuse legitimate discontent and anger. She is not in the position of the teacher whose treatment has left memories of discomfort and failure, or the police officer whom poor people may see as an enemy soldier.

To many people in need it seems that the professional planner never implements his plans. The politician with his endless unkept promises has been written off by the poor. But the nurse has bandaged, healed, and alleviated pain. She has answered questions to reduce anxiety; she has offered advice to allay fears. If a patient has needed a clean environment, she has judged and lectured less and may have rolled up her sleeves to deliver what was needed. She has been the recipient of confidences from people of all ages and she has treated those confidences with the respect they deserved.

Whether or not she has been viewed stereotypically, the perception of the nurse has always been more positive than negative, and this perception can provide a strong base on which to function in the community.

Though it is the community health practitioner who has her base primarily in the community, the processes that move her must be the same for all nurses. A report on a curriculum for community nurse practitioners viewed a number of key concepts as essential:

1. *nursing process*—the methodology of nursing which identified it as a problem-solving process (assessment, problem identification, planning, implementation, evaluation).
2. *community development*—a process which parallels 1, above, but has as its base the community, and as its goal, the development of that community to solve its own problems.
3. *self-health*—applying the processes (1 and 2) to health—a goal of each process wherein individuals and communities are capable of making informed decisions and carrying out appropriate actions to improve their health.
4. *cooperator in change*—the CNP's role in the community. By applying the processes described and working toward self-health, the CNP becomes a cooperator rather than an agent of change.[2]

The hospital nurse who may spend most of her time on a unit must have links with her patients' community, or her nursing care will not be complete.

The nurse leader must inevitably find her way into the community to find support for institutional changes, to collect data contributing to greater understanding of patients, to educate community people in preventive health care, or merely to exchange information with other nurses who are based in the community and doing all these things.

Though the person who identifies herself as a community health nurse or a community nurse practitioner sees, as her major role, working to improve community health, rather than the health of individuals and families, any nurse can justify approaching her practice within the framework of community organization and community needs. The definitions of community health nursing are quite consistent with the role of the nurse leader who, though she practices independently or provides primary nursing care in a hospital setting, still perceives clients in relation to their community environment.

Before we examine in detail the potential role of the nurse in the community, I would like to point out that middle-class communities may be just as appropriate as targets for outreach and mobilization as poor communities. The nurse is uniquely qualified to take this new direction.

The unique qualification of the nurse lies in the nature of her skills and objectives. This needs no belaboring; who can argue that there are groups of people of any social class or other classification who cannot profit from the professional operations of the nurse? The greatest advantage she has is in this consensus: As soon as her profession is identified, a place is made for her in the community. A nurse would be as welcome in a high-income as in a low-income area.

If holistic concepts of treatment and a self-actualizing approach to human development are logically extended, nurse leaders will be concerned with global health needs. Many will work directly in agencies attempting to meet these needs and will find their way to communities in other countries to provide direct nursing care. A report of the World Health Organization in 1976 noted, for example, that *thirty-seven percent of the population of Latin America has no health services.* At the same time, they point to a growing belief in the right of everyone to health care. The report looks largely to the training of community health nurses to fill the need. The skills and functions they expect the nurse to supply suggest a view of a nurse leader who can change the direction of health care delivery. According to the report, community health nurses must be prepared to:

> Satisfy the health needs of populations with different socioeconomic and cultural characteristics.
> Teach in the health field and direct or provide care in cases of disease or rehabilitation.
> Experiment with new ways of extending services to rural and urban-fringe areas.
> Help people to discover their health needs.
> Promote changes in behavior with regard to individual and community health.

Meet the special health needs of people at all stages of the human growth and development cycle, from conception to death.
Help parents and children to meet the special needs of family living.
Supervise the care of normal growing children and of exceptionally gifted and handicapped children.
Help young adults to protect themselves against accidents and against chronic illness and its disabling effects.
Provide support and care for older adults experiencing health problems associated with aging.

Establish links between local health personnel and the health care system.
Help to organize local groups and volunteers.
Assume leadership and an executive role in the training of all types of auxiliary health workers.

Work in collaboration with other health professionals in the community.
Co-ordinate the care provided by a multiprofessional health team to individuals, families and the community.

Provide safe and effective care based on a broad and thorough knowledge of the health and public health sciences (epidemiological method, physical biological sciences, and behavioral sciences) and use this knowledge for effective communication with other community health practitioners.
Become proficient in applying public health methods for the purpose of identifying population groups with special health risks, and in evaluating community health nursing programs.
Exercise surveillance over the health status of population groups and of the population as a whole.
Develop the ability to mobilize community resources and participate in community development activities designed to solve health problems.
Make use of their potential in their own sphere and define the parameters for their own action.
Assume new functions relating to health care and relinquish old ones as the social needs of the moment dictate.
Evaluate the physical and psychosocial health of individuals and families.
Diagnose health needs and provide proper care for individuals, families, groups and communities of persons with similar needs: in the absence of disease; in the acute phases of illness; and in stabilized chronic conditions.

Project nursing needs and resources into community health planning.
Interpret the potential of nursing for community health programs.
Provide leadership in the health field and participate in educational programs for different community groups.
Secure the participation of users in the planning, delivery and evaluation of health services.

Participate effectively in intersectoral and intrasectoral planning at all levels, particularly the community level.
Collaborate in planning for and utilizing community nursing resources.

Participate with teaching staff in formal educational programs for new practitioners.

Design research studies relevant to the area of community health.

Apply their knowledge of the public health and nursing sciences in carrying out community health programs in accordance with community health needs and the learning requirements of the students.

Teach and apply the principles and concepts of public health and community health nursing, focusing on the community as a whole and on population groups with common health problems and needs.

Apply the psychology of learning in preparing curricula for community health nursing.

Apply knowledge required to produce teaching modules.

Design research studies on community health nursing.[3]

The linking function

The nurse leader who functions effectively in the community has a holistic approach to health service for the community, just as she does with the individual client. She is rarely the one who "points with pride" at the establishment of a first-rate open-heart surgery team in the fourth hospital in the area, especially when she knows that the incidence of tuberculosis is on the rise, or that old people cannot get to the health care facilities they need. She is a person who thinks systemically, so she is also the one to recognize that a rape unit in a local hospital is not sufficient to deal with the problem of increasing violent rape in the community. She recognizes that better street lighting and more effective deployment of police officers are also factors in the problem.

Similarly, she is sensitive to the feelings of people who refuse to accept help, who are apathetic and even antagonistic when it comes to accepting suggestions for better health practices. She knows that many people, especially poor people, are so discouraged and angry about their condition that harrying them on an individual basis is virtually futile. It is more reasonable to make efforts to alter some of the forces affecting them so they are freed to permit themselves to respond to offers of help. For example, both urban and rural poor people put health care fifth in priority after food, shelter, clothing, and education. Working to help them resolve problems related to their first four priorities will bring the nurse closer to her health care objectives.

These days, the nurse who works in any health care facility is concerned with what happens to the patient at home and in the community. The nurse leader can play an important linking function between the staff and administration of her institution and the people in the community. If other staff members are reluctant to walk about the community, get to know the people socially, and join in political action with them, a leader can do so.

She can then bring the knowledge, sensitivity, and skills she has developed back to her home base. She can share with her colleagues the concerns of the community; she can help them unlearn their stereotypes and develop new sensitivities to the feelings of the people and new appreciations of their strengths; she can encourage them to learn some of the skills she now has, such as skills of communication.

A nurse leader who is knowledgeable about the structure of community organization can bring together groups that will complement each other and cooperate for mutually desired objectives. For example, social and citizens' organizations in the community may have an interest in and concern about some aspect of health as part of their program. Where the health concerns of agencies overlap, the nurse can provide a basis for bringing them together to use their combined power to effect change. For example, the firefighters, the PTA, the scouts, Kiwanis, and Shriners could cooperate to clean up inflammable trash, since all have an interest in community safety from fire hazards. The school nurse could give impetus to the idea of cooperation in her health classes for parents and children.

In many communities, citizen action groups have health interests and would probably welcome the input of a nurse with her own interests in the community. For example, in one neighborhood the Black Panthers provide free breakfasts for school children who might otherwise go to school each day unfed or poorly fed. A nurse could help with nutrition information and diet planning. In another neighborhood a group of old people have organized themselves into a telephone communication system for keeping in touch with each other, to make sure that no one is lying at home alone, ill or hurt. A nurse who knows about the potential for such programs can provide leadership for starting them where they are needed.

Unions and industries have continuing health problems, many of which have never been solved. For example, as long ago as 1960, I noted that

> . . . people who are disturbed for any reason are likely to be less competent on the job. If they dislike, fail to understand or fear the people with whom they work; if they resent the boss; if they are discouraged by the depersonalization of mechanical and repetive work, they may injure themselves, do injury to others, or just not do the job that should be done. The industrial nurse is in a strategic position to take the lead in helping people solve their problems.[4]

Any holistic approach to health maintenance must include such factors, and it is not only the nurse in industry whose clients need help in solving problems generated by the work situation.

Nowhere are the skills of interdisciplinary functioning more useful than in providing leadership in the community. Though at one time, working to improve the health of a community was seen as the function of the public health team, it is clear today that there are a great many professions and roles that impinge on community health. The nurse leader must be aware of these roles and be able to work with the people who hold them.

Health and welfare councils are already established in many communities as agencies for linking most of the human service functions. They often publish a directory of community resources and are able to supply general information about agencies and services. Member agencies meet at the council and share information; this has resulted in some coordinated planning for human service delivery and action for change.

However, lack of organization, overlap and conflict of functions, ignorance of people's needs, and lack of input by client groups makes obtaining help—especially for people with multiple problems—a nightmare.

For example, Richardson and Scrutchfield found that older people in one community were more concerned with the cost of medical care and drugs than they were about the lack of facilities for treating specific ailments, although a physician who had assessed the community's needs had listed specific medical problems as of primary concern. What bothered other people was the problem faced by most Appalachian communities and other rural and poor areas—the lack of physicians. They were disturbed that help was not available in emergencies. They complained of long waits for appointments, and long waits in doctors' offices. When they did finally get to a physician, not enough time was spent with them to satisfy them that they were getting what they needed.[5] Perhaps nurses in the community are equipped to provide the integrating function that other human service professionals are not. The nurse's belief in holistic assessment with input from clients, and her assumption of responsibility to follow through on that assessment, may make the difference for individual clients, and provide the philosophical link between the community and coordinating agencies like health and welfare councils.

Probably the most valuable linking function the nurse can perform in the community is the one implied by the terms *outreach* and *referral*. Many human service workers are involved in efforts to identify people in need and see that they get to the appropriate care providers. However, in most communities consumers are still confused by the fragmentation of services and often become discouraged enough to give up their efforts to get help.

The nurse who has a holistic approach to care will not just give a client a name and address when it becomes necessary to refer him to another agency. She will discuss with him his needs and her own inability to help with those needs; she will make no referral until the client agrees; she will make initial contact with the referral agency if the client wishes her to do so, and perhaps even accompany him on his first visit. She will certainly follow up the situation to make sure that the client is not being shunted from agency to agency and that he is getting the help he needs. And she will hold out to him the offer of her continued availability as a lifeline in the maze of bureaucracies.

Outreach is the process of taking the initiative of identifying people in need, making contact with them, and then making plans with them to get the help they need. This means that the nurse, or other human service worker, does not sit in an office and wait for clients to ask her for help.

Some dangers are implicit in the outreach process, but these dangers are significantly minimized when the outreach professional is a nurse. Other workers have talked with neighbors of people who need help, and this has led to justifiable resentment on the part of the target family. Gang workers have taken on the dress and mannerisms of gangs they wanted to influence to accept help. Human service workers who live in the community have sometimes hidden their real function in order to gain the confidence of people who need help.

All of these behaviors are breaches of trust and almost inevitably reduce the effectiveness of the relationship between client and worker. The nurse in the community needs none of these subterfuges. She can function as a nurse from the onset of any relationship and be accepted for her knowledge, sensitivity, and skill. People may not immediately accept everything she has to offer, but good communication and initial successes in problem solving can provide a base on which to build expanded professional functions.

Thus, an independent nurse practitioner may be called out of her office to give emergency treatment in a street accident, offer to visit the patient to follow up her treatment, observe the need for parenting education in the home, and maintain the relationship until some pressing problems are solved. Similarly, a visiting nurse may observe that playground equipment in a public recreation facility presents a safety hazard. She may stop to talk to the parents of the children using the equipment, and continue to work with them to plan for approaches to the city recreation department in an attempt to rectify the situation.

Historically, the medical establishment has not demonstrated much awareness of what health care consumers consider most important in health care. In one study that graphically illustrates this point, a medical researcher made a priority list of health problems needing to be addressed in an Appalachian community. The list was at considerable variance with the health problems most important to the people in the community. The researcher listed the poor health of the children, including poor dental health, inadequate immunization, incidence of tuberculosis and chronic respiratory diseases, air pollution from local factories, and the high injury and death rates from automobile accidents.[6] Richardson and Scrutchfield, who went to the people in the community and asked for their priorities, discovered a wide gap between the two lists. They noted that the problems listed by Welsh were "primarily concerned with specific pathology in certain organ systems such as the teeth or lungs. No mention was made of the organizational problems regarding the delivery of medical care, 'which the community emphasized.' Even though the medical profession is becoming increasingly aware of public demands," they add, ". . . the dichotomy in priorities between organized medicine and the consumer is still pronounced."[7]

The nurse leader who is aware of this gap can assume an important linking function between the community and the medical profession. It requires, of course, that she have access to the organizations planning for health care delivery—local, regional, and state planning groups. Though most of these groups must, by law, have substantial lay representation, the nurse who knows the community knows that these lay persons are not always from groups whose voices are traditionally unheard—the poor and minorities. Therefore, the linking function of the nurse is defective if she does not also have access to grass roots citizen action groups that must fight to provide their input into the establishment systems.

Though one may not agree with all that Ivan Illich says about the medical establishment,[8] he makes some points that reinforce what many nurse leaders have been saying. For example, he contends in a recent interview that "Better housing, cleaner water, sewage treatment, better working conditions, better nutrition and therefore higher resistance seem to be the critical factors in improving the health of populations."[9] This is consistent with the sense of responsibility nurses feel to become involved in the community and with people who are trying to improve their socioeconomic conditions. He argues that "By turning patients into passive consumers, objects to be repaired, voyeurs of their own treatment, the medical enterprise saps the will of people to suffer their own reality. It destroys our autonomous ability to cope with our own bodies and heal ourselves. . . .The maintenance of health is a personal task that requires self-awareness and self-discipline." To the extent that nurses believe their major function is to help people increase their self-awareness and maintain control over themselves and their lives, they agree with Illich and his quest to "de-medicalize" society.

The teaching function

The nurse's ability to educate can provide a basis for important needed changes in the community. Education is rarely a rapid and radical process, so the accomplishments of nurses in this area may not, at first glance, appear to have precipitated great change. However, chipping away at small prejudices, filling small gaps in knowledge, providing a service to a few neglected people, contribute to a community's quality of life and prepare the way for acceptance of the nurse as a leader in larger changes.

Some education experiences that have been reported may make other nurses realize that they, too, have the ability to provide leadership in this area:

One nurse, Vivian Melham, of Illinois, put advertisements in local newspapers requesting that anorectics and their families get in touch with her. She instituted a program of meetings and lectures for them and also for health professionals, in an attempt to make some progress in ameliorating the condition.[10]

Gretchen Schodde, a family nurse practitioner in Seattle, Washington, developed a board game, *Winning at Wellness*, designed to interest players in making positive health choices. If it ever becomes as popular as *Monopoly*, we may see a measurable improvement in health in our country![11]

Nurses report that, under contract, they have taught ambulance drivers and psychiatric residents, given preretirement planning courses, and led retired persons' health workshops.[12]

A public health nurse who was the only nurse in a small, rural county health department conducted her own campaign to gain citizen support for financial subsidy of health care. "She carried the message throughout the county at public meetings and through individual contacts with the people whom she served in a 400-square-mile area, where efforts were being made to enact a special levy to support the health department. Her county's health levy passed by a handsome margin, and many of the voters admitted that their support would not have been forthcoming without the convincing actions of the nurse."[13]

In communities where there is great demand for babysitters, a nurse could teach courses in babysitting—a vital function for which there is even less preparation than there is for parenthood! Workshops for dealing with addiction to fad foods; programs for helping parents understand the importance of immunization; seminars for helping people deal with death and dying are all education services that the nurse leader is equipped to provide.

Home nursing care as an alternative to hospitalization must be seriously considered these days by all leaders in health care delivery. Even if all that were involved were the great expense of prolonged hospitalization, we would need some re-evaluation of the advisability of treatment in hospitals.

As noted recently by the congressional chairman of the United States House of Representatives Appropriations Committee for Labor and Health, Education and Welfare:

> Properly run home health care programs have demonstrated an ability to expand the capacity of a delivery system by providing needed care while conserving scarce, costly resources, both institutional and professional. . . . Evidence does point to significant savings when even a relatively small proportion of acute institutional care and long-term institutional care is replaced by responsive, mobile community services that are more closely adapted to the specific needs of individuals.[14]

There are considerations more specifically related to the province of nursing, and leaders in the field can articulate them for other professionals and for the general public. From the humanistic point of view, hospitals too often simply do not work. We can only estimate the number of injuries suffered and the number of iatrogenic diseases developed during hospitalization. It is not necessary here to belabor this; nurses have enough evidence of practices and policies that interfere with their attempts to provide adequate nursing care. But there are also indications that the very nature of bureaucratic institutions prevents the kind of recognition and care for an individual that he needs in order to recover and maintain his health. The stresses accompanying hospitalization may very well delay a patient's recovery and engender feelings of anxiety at the prospect of future hospitalization.

After initial hospitalization to treat a crisis condition, the nursing of the patient to bring him back to optimum health and to maintain him in that state might better be accomplished in his own setting, with the cooperation of the people who care about him. Recently, I heard a nurse asked what advice she had for people in choosing a hospital for themselves. She answered that, if it was absolutely necessary to be hospitalized, it was best to choose one to which one's family and friends had easy access, so they could monitor the patient's treatment. "Don't go to a hospital if there is any way to avoid it," she cautioned.

Instead of putting so large a proportion of resources into hospitals and then cautioning people to keep their loved ones close, it seems rational to plan a larger and more significant home nursing facility as an integral part of the system of health care. It could contribute immeasurably to raising the level of community health for the total population for a number of reasons:

1. Patients discharged from hospitals after crisis treatment would be followed up and helped to plan a program of recovery and health maintenance that could continue long after the period of hospitalization.
2. The home nursing process would also serve to educate the patient's family in their own health maintenance.
3. The presence of more nurses in the community could implement their outreach function, to identify people in need of help.
4. More nurses in touch with community needs could result in more effective education for health maintenance.

The Nature of Community

Living and working in the community

The professional goals identified by Brager and Specht for community organizers are not inconsistent with the goals of nurses working in a community: "(1) the increased competence of community participants; (2) the greater responsiveness of service organization to consumer needs, wants, and rights; and (3) small-scale or significant alterations in institutional policies and programs which impinge on consumer interests."[15]

The first goal relates explicitly to the education function of nursing. It implies that those who assume leadership in a community are committed to helping people grow in knowledge and skill so that, ultimately, they can lead their own communities. The second goal is consistent with nursing's humanistic beliefs, which posit the rights of individuals to define and get satisfaction for their own needs. Both goals contribute to autonomy and independence, freeing of people to enter upon the self-actualizing process. The third goal merely follows naturally from the first two: If there is need for increased competence of consumers and increased responsiveness to consumer rights, then change is also needed. Without it, the other two goals are not achieved.

The nurse working in the community will discover that limiting her concerns and activities to the narrow medical concept of care reduces the possibility of improving the health of the people in the community. When the central concern of people in a community is the extraordinarily high unemployment rate, especially among young men (a condition existing in most Black urban communities), the nurse would do well to find a place for herself in the actions surrounding this concern. Making herself available in the local public library for lectures on health maintenance will hardly provide her a setting for leadership that is responsive to the people's needs. This is not to say that lectures on health maintenance are not good and useful exercises. However, if young fathers are concerned about supporting their families and parents of teenagers are fearful that their children's idleness and feelings of frustration will lead to criminal behavior, a lecturer at the local library will be perceived—if she is noticed at all—as somewhat out of the mainstream of community life.

On the other hand, people will recognize and accept the leadership of a nurse who provides input for the statement by the local Committee for Action that the food stamp program fosters malnutrition in the recipients or the nurse who supplies epidemiological data to both the local health department and an active citizen's group on the incidence of rat bites in children. The nurse may offer to testify before the city council on the need for better enforcement of the building inspection codes; she may write a public letter to the chairman of the regional planning board pointing out the absence of facilities for recreation for teenagers in three contiguous suburban communities. On such matters the nurse can provide input from her area of expertise.

In 1943, when the Congress on Racial Equality was formed to organize nonviolent resistance to racial discrimination, nurses could have helped the protesters maintain their bodies at peak level efficiency. In 1978 when a middle-class community passed a local ordinance prohibiting families with children from buying homes in an area restricted to old people, a nurse might have pointed out the disadvantages to young and old of such segregation.

In a country where the segregation of school children continues to be a volatile issue, nurses, many of whom work in the schools, have been silent. What are the health maintenance implications for children of all races of attending segregated schools? What are school nurses, in the course of their daily work with children and teachers, observing about self-concept development, about fighting, about fear and anxiety as these relate to attending all-White or all-Black schools?

The Hispanic population in the United States is rapidly becoming our largest minority group. Nursing leadership is urgently needed in communities of migrant workers whose health is in constant jeopardy from their living conditions. Spanish-speaking communities often need links with local health departments, with hospital personnel, with landlords—leaders who can provide the data on community health needs. Spanish communities need better health care for women and children; nurses working in such communities could not only provide scientific information on needs, but could also help people develop the skills for communicating these needs to those who control the resources and for prying some of those resources loose from the controllers and allocators.

The Model Cities program made it clear that people indigenous to the community are in the best position to know what is needed. They may not always know how to get jobs, but they know that jobs are needed. They may not be able to organize effectively to convince the decision makers that a hospital is needed, but they are well aware of the problems associated with having to travel two hours for outpatient care or to visit hospitalized relatives and friends.

When people are experiencing the harmful effects of a problem, they speak with convincing force, and they resist attempts to put off solutions until a more propitious time. The community leader who is not only articulate and skillful in effecting change, but also a resident of the community, acquires a unique legitimacy. She can affirm, "Not only do I know this as a nurse and a scientist, but I know it as a resident of this community." Such a leader is difficult to co-opt.

In a small community, whether a city neighborhood or a rural area, the people may take the initiative in seeking out the nurse's services. One nurse recounts the beginnings of her independent practice in a community that knew she was in a graduate program and when she had completed her studies. ". . . upon completion of my program," she states, "they immediately began to say, 'Well, can you do this for me? Can you do that for us?'" And she began to work with patients.[16]

The professional who lives in the community where he works can more readily establish trusting communication with the people; he is more likely to know what they need and to respect their own perception of their needs; and he is accessible to them for many things that cannot strictly be defined as professional services. It is in his ability and willingness to stretch the parameters of his profession that he finds ways to feed the feelings of trust.

Thus the nurse can open the door to the knock of a new mother who is momentarily frightened because her baby will not stop crying. Or he can offer to teach first-aid techniques to the boy scout troop or CPR to an adult club. Since he is part of the community, these are neighborly services—a special level of services, of course, but services he is specially qualified to contribute to the life of the community. His neighbors offer him what they can—shared babysitting, a lift to the store, a surprise birthday party. In the neighborly give and take, the nurse as well as his neighbors see the need for his paid professional services, and agreements are made for their provision.

The advantage of living and practicing in a community was recognized by the traditional family doctor who lived among his patients and was able to provide them with comprehensive health care and also with the feeling of security that came from knowing the doctor was within call in case of emergency, and having a doctor who really knew you. Such an advantage has, in recent years, been recognized also in teaching. Teacher Corps members being trained for teaching, especially in poor neighborhoods, found that they functioned more knowledgeably and empathically when they shared the living experiences of the children they taught. Peace Corps volunteers, most of whom teach, engage in community planning, and provide other services, are assigned to live among the people they teach. Thus they understand the people better, establish bonds of trust, and generally work more effectively. The same applies to Vista volunteers, the domestic Peace Corps.

In law enforcement many people see the small-town police officer who works among his neighbors as more effective in keeping the peace than the city policemen who is sent to work among strangers. There is no doubt that fewer heads would be broken and fewer people shot if the confrontations were not always between strangers.

The nurse who lives in the community can help educate a whole new generation to the real meaning of nursing as a profession.

Assessing community needs

Initial observations in the community can provide a beginning for assessing needs. (See the last section of this chapter.) The nurse can ask some questions that fall within her professional purview even before she arrives to work in a particular community. For example, the primary means of livelihood in a community may pose some health hazards. In plastics work, the use of vinyl chloride causes genetic damage and cancer of the liver, respiratory tract, and brain. Dairy workers have a high incidence of brucellosis. Miners suffer from silicosis. In spite of health departments and workers' organizations like unions, there is still much to be done in the prevention of such work-related diseases—in education, so that workers may learn how to protect themselves; in community organization, so that laws may be passed to compel employers to install safety devices; in research, so that the diseases may be prevented and/or cured.

The problem of nuclear energy production has become a pressing one for whole communities. Nurses who work in those communities and have firsthand knowledge of the physical and psychological damage that is occurring have generally been silent. Just because the nuclear energy issue has taken a controversial form does not mean that the essential health problems are also moot. The nurse has strong scientific and empirical evidence for assuming leadership in dealing with these health problems.

If the people in the community are poor, it is likely that there are health problems associated with poverty. For example, dilapidated housing breeds rats; there may be a significant incidence of rat bites, especially in children. (If a community is plagued by rats, this can sometimes be observed in the initial observation walk. On more than one occasion I have had a rat cross my path in a city street, and seen dead rats near demolition sites.)

Poor communities, too, often have large numbers of unowned animals running the streets, rooting in garbage. Such animals may bite people and spread various diseases. Fear of them may be generalized to all animals and to the people who own them, and so interfere with optimum psycho-social development of children; it may interfere with learning (where animals are the subject) and with general well-being when fear is constant.

In our diet-conscious country, the poor are still beset with diet-associated ailments. The food stamp program apparently fosters starchy diets, and local stores in poor neighborhoods often do not even carry alternatives to foods such as over-processed flour and polished rice.

Poor rural families send their children out without shoes, often saving them for school and special occasions. Though we all know the pleasure and benefits of walking barefoot in the country, the incidence of hookworm makes this pleasure an expensive one.

The difficulty in poor areas of maintaining even the essentials of personal hygiene can produce an increase in many diseases, and the nurse can provide leadership by changing not only the poor, but also those who do not provide hot water, who do not enforce health codes, who do not make work available, and who keep the incomes of the disabled at inadequate levels.

General knowledge of a community can offer additional valuable information to the nurse. For example, people in a community situated in a low-lying, marshy area are prey to insect-borne diseases. People in a community without parks or other open spaces may be prey to behavior disorders, such as excessive irritibility. Communities with certain racial and ethnic groups seem to have a higher incidence of certain illnesses—like sickle-cell anemia among Black people and Tay-Sachs disease among Eastern European Jews. People caught up in the anonymity of cities may have a higher incidence of mental illness. (I remember recently walking through center-city Philadelphia and seeing the fourth or fifth person within a few minutes exhibiting bizarre behavior. A young man walking near me shook his head sadly and encouraged me to say: "There seem to be so many severely troubled people in this city—more than in other cities." "That's because," he answered sarcastically, "Philadelphia is such a loving, caring place." Apparently it was not to him!)

A community identified as highly mobile presents problems related to continuity of health care. Keeping track of children's immunization history becomes difficult. Emotional problems resulting from the need for repeated adjustment to new environments must be recognized and dealt with. (Many so-called "discipline" problems in schools are the result of such mobility; it will have to be the nurse who teaches teachers to abandon their emphasis on discipline in such cases and focus on teaching personal problem-solving skills.)

Examining census data and vital statistics can provide important evidence of needs. A high infant mortality rate may indicate unfulfilled needs for prenatal and child care, for parenting education, perhaps even for adequate housing and nutrition education. Higher incidence of certain diseases—stroke, for example—may indicate the need for preventive and rehabilitation programs.

One of the most neglected functions in the community relates to the problems of people in prisons. There is a breach in human service that the nurse leader may, if she chooses, fill neatly. If the nurse working in the community identifies families and friends of people in prison, she can begin to include in the planning and problem-solving systems the needs, feelings, and objectives of those who are away. Making contact with people in prison—in the company of relatives and friends or alone—can help include the prisoner in the communication system, and prepare families to live together again.

It is useful, too, to draw into the problem-solving process people in the community who are not immediately involved with prisoners. Most of the problems that beset people coming out of prison, and that may account for the high rate of recidivism, involve the fact that they are not accepted by the community. Employers are reluctant to hire them, people are reluctant to marry them, and even strangers such as physicians who treat them and social workers who admit them to service systems often perceive them with a certain suspicion.

Inside the prison, these community attitudes are clearly manifest. The quality of health care provided is of particular interest to nurses. People who suffer from untreated or inadequately treated physical and emotional ailments are certain to interact with each other in unproductive ways. People who feel inferior, unworthy, and useless cannot plan for effective living when they leave prison. (The new wave of sociological thinking that suggests that harsher punishment is the answer to rising crime rates, and concludes that "rehabilitation" programs have failed, are not making accurate needs assessments. A program will not "rehabilitate" if it does not address the needs of the people, especially if the program strategies actually violate those needs.) The nurse who becomes involved in upgrading the health care of prison populations may come closer to solving the crime problem than all the sociologists and social workers have.

Nurses who understand human behavior as at least partly a result of external forces over which the individual has little or no control can recognize that many people are caught up in the criminal justice system because of their own powerlessness and inability to find their way out of oppressive conditions. (For example, a young Black man who is repeatedly stopped by policemen "on suspicion," may, after the third or fourth stop, protest this treatment. This may escalate into angry words, a push, and finally with the youth being charged with resisting arrest and assault and battery on an officer. Most magistrates and judges fail to ask what crime had been committed to bring the officer to the scene in the first place. Since "suspicion" is not a criminal charge, we have a crime committed *after* the officer arrives on the scene—much like diseases caused by medical treatments. In jail, the young man is subjected to the conditions that may precipitate real criminal behavior both in prison and after he leaves.)

Community defined

The community a nurse works in may be in a city, several blocks where the people share interests and expectations. They trust each other, belong to the same organizations, and have similar points of view and life styles. Or, the community may be a collection of different neighborhoods that have been unified by events that have affected them all. That sense of belonging that characterizes a community is found in rural areas and small towns, as well as city neighborhoods.

Out of this sense of sharing and belonging comes a concerted action to achieve common goals. Such action is not without conflict, some of it unnecessary since communities do not appear to learn from the mistakes of other communities. In those places where there is little or no conflict, however, there is not likely to be change or progress. The more widespread the involvement in organizing and planning for action to solve the social problems, the more controversy there will be.

One thing the contemporary worker in the community must bear in mind is that more and more important decisions affecting local communities are made at higher administrative levels and in distant economic centers. Avenues of communication with these places must be opened up if local influence is to be felt.

The nurse who works in the community can utilize the knowledge of community structure and organization to plan her own professional interventions. Knowing the objectives of existing organizations can help her make a judgment about which ones are likely to be concerned about the needs she perceives. Knowing the history of organizational activities in a community can keep her from making mistakes that have been made before, and from going over ground that has already been covered. Knowledge of the power structure can keep her from planning her interventions blindly and dooming them to failure because she was not aware of where the real strength lay or where the real opposition was.

The future of the community

It is the poor who will force the professionals away from their overconcern with structure and coordination of services, which, though it results in some good, distracts us from the need for basic changes in our system of production and distribution of economic goods and in our provision of human services. They live with the real effects of our operation, and, to the extent that they make themselves heard, to that extent will evaluation of our economic and service functions be forced to submit to the hard test of reality.

The strength of the women's movement will also persist, and continued pressure from women's organizations will obtain for women a fair share of the opportunities in our society. Some of these pressures will continue to effect changes in the basic law, as pressures of Black groups resulted in the 1954 decision and other civil rights legislation.

The consumer movement will continue to grow in size and in power, through local and national organizations, and through successful attempts to put consumer advocates into political offices. More truth in advertising, more accurate packaging of consumer goods, more involvement in decisions concerning such things as use of nuclear power and experimentation on human subjects will continue to be demanded.

The mystiques of the various professions will be torn away, and patients, clients, constituents and students will increasingly demand full knowledge and the right to participate fully in the final decisions that affect their own lives.

A new development among professional planners sees an interdisciplinary approach to the solution of problems. People from education, race relations, urban planning, law, employment, and health are working together, pooling their interests and insights. This will probably result in fewer errors in planning, fewer omissions in providing for human needs.[17]

There is a new group of professionals who call themselves futurists whose purpose is to assess people's responses to change, analyze change trends, and plan for a future that we envision. The idea is that by understanding what is happening, assessing needs, and planning systemically, we can make our own future.

The future will be made in the communities of the country, and the nurse leader has an opportunity to contribute to the making of that future. For example, the dangers to health of food contaminants require more competent action than we have had to date. Some of these contaminants are added intentionally to enhance color or flavor, or increase shelf-life of food. Others come from industrial and agricultural processes and materials, and are eaten by food animals or directly by humans. A recent congressional report says that more information is needed about the effects of such substances, so that long-range plans can be made to deal with them.

Sometimes contaminants have long term effects that explode unexpectedly in crises. Perhaps we can avoid some of these crises situations—with resulting severe disability and death—if an observant nurse can begin to note early warning signs of trouble in community residents and feed this information to local or federal departments for further study.

Also, there is little or nothing in our laws to provide for immediate regulation of substances that are suddenly found to be toxic. The kind of systems planning that the nurse leader engages in should provide opportunity for more rational decision making rather than so many ad hoc responses to unanticipated crises.

Nursing Leadership for Neglected Groups

The aged

Though the states have funded demonstration projects to improve health care, too often health care agencies did not continue with the projects once funding ended, even though health was demonstrably improved during the experiment. For example:

> It was thought that care to patients in nursing homes could be improved through techniques used in rehabilitation, e.g., range of motion exercises, activities of daily living, and bowel and bladder training techniques. Several public health nurses were sent to enroll in a workshop of intense training in these techniques, as well as discussion of modern treatment for the most common disabling conditions: stroke, arthritis and fractured hip. Following their training program these nurses were assigned to nursing homes to educate nursing home personnel in the techniques mentioned, and to instill the philosophy of rehabilitation so that personnel would try these techniques on their own. . . . [A]fter a period of one year, the conclusion was drawn that utilization of rehabilitation techniques did dramatically improve the condition of these patients. The recommendation of the group working on the project was to have the nursing homes hire a consultant skilled in these techniques to oversee such a program, educate personnel as needed, and work with physicians and families to enlist participation. . . . Few nursing home administrators chose to enter such contracts, and those who did, did not do so for any length of time.[18]

The nurse leader can have a role in this kind of situation. If, for example, a nurse works in a local department of health, she is aware that her agency has a responsibility for health education in the community. A part of the education program could be focused on continuing education for nursing home personnel. Though this might not be the complete answer to the problem of not having a skilled consultant in each home, it could provide ongoing training and support for the ultimate purpose of improving public health. Physicians and families of nursing home residents could also be involved in programs; potential leaders among them and among nursing home employees could be identified and given special help to develop their leadership skills and to support them in their efforts at maintaining an acceptable level of rehabilitation activity in nursing homes.

Another demonstration project was done in a private hospital in an attempt to reduce the length of stay of patients with congestive heart failure. Four hypotheses were tested and all found to be true:

1. Patients were taking 2 or more medications daily.
2. Their poor health allowed them to 'mix up' the instructions for use of medications.
3. Home visits for instruction in the use of medications would result in better comprehension, better drug use.
4. Group sessions where mutual problems would be discussed would encourage closer adherence to their medical regimens. [19]

However, no agency would undertake to implement such a program. Here, again, a nurse leader might have become involved in a number of ways:

1. She could have provided the service as an independent nurse practitioner. Of course, the problem of third-party payment for nursing service would have to be settled.

2. She could have worked to convince state lawmakers of the value of continuing the program and perhaps money could have been allocated.

3. She might have interceded with the administration of the state health department and prevailed upon them to continue the project until local agencies could be persuaded to support it.

4. She could begin, in a limited way, to educate the patients in her own hospital or other care facility, and to develop materials for self-education. (The value of such materials—to be used by individuals or small groups in the community—has been recognized by the federal Administration on Aging. The Administration has funded a number of projects for the development and testing of similar materials, for example in the area of diet. The significant factor in developing this kind of educational material is that it is eminently consistent with the conceptual framework of nursing leadership suggested here: It provides an opportunity for further education for clients; it fosters autonomy and independence in that it encourages people to assume responsibility for their own health maintenance and supplies them with the enabling instruments; and to the extent that the materials are, in effect, plans for action, they constitute a systems approach to health maintenance.)

5. While she was doing 1, 2, 3, and 4 she would have been working with local citizens' groups to plan strategies for convincing decision makers to implement the program.

There is no doubt that care of the aged is needed in our communities, and that this need will continue to increase. Most people prefer care that will enable them to stay in their own homes. A nurse writing to the *American Journal of Nursing,* [20] makes a plea for nursing leadership to help establish a system of home health care, especially for the indigent old. (Though I would submit that it is not only the indigent who need and want this.)

It is possible that good nursing homes are necessary for those who absolutely cannot live alone and have no relatives to care for them. However, just because an institutional home is substituted for a private home, it should not become necessary to substitute the concept of disease treatment for the concept of health maintenance (which all people should be engaged in).

As Kinlein points out, physicians have historically set the standards of nursing home operation; and she suggests that if the standards of health maintenance were substituted it is likely that old people in nursing homes would be able to maintain their level of optimum functioning for a much longer period of time.[21] She herself went to work in a nursing home because she believed that it would be possible for her to practice nursing there, using self-care concepts for health maintenance instead of just following doctor's orders on disease states.

Generally, however, nursing leadership has not been evident in this area of health care delivery. Most professional nurses avoid working in nursing homes, and those who do often fall into the trap of stereotypic thinking about old people:

> . . . "after all," the reasoning went, "there is nothing to do in a nursing home except to keep the patient clean and give out pills." Such distorted thinking about the complexities involved in every situation in which human beings are caring for human beings produced the dismal result guaranteed by such an approach.[22]

The increase in the average age of the population, the articulateness and political sophistication of older people, and the heightened consciousness of younger people that they will either grow old or die may make problem solving in the area of aging a priority concern in this country. This is a good time for potential nurse leaders to start getting their feet wet in the rapidly moving waters. Nursing has some vital insights to contribute to the solution of problems concerning a group that needs to expend greater effort to maintain its health.

Opportunities for nurse leadership involve the aged patients of the physician or aged patients that he turns away. In my book I listed 45 questions that could be asked on the job to identify instances of discrimination against the aged.[23] A number of these questions are particularly relevant for nurses. They involve questioning beliefs that all old people have similar likes, dislikes, behaviors, and lifestyles merely by virtue of being old. They deal with the assumption that professionals and paraprofessionals may advise old people about how and where they should live, something they would not presume to do with younger people. They point up the fact that health care workers more willingly give younger people explanations about procedures they will undergo, and generally make those explanations more detailed.

The questions are designed to make staff members doubt the appropriateness of calling old people by their first names without asking them how they feel about it; pressuring them to submit to procedures "for their own good"; avoiding talking about their feelings about illness, about old age, about dying; and showing in a hundred ways that they believe the prevailing stereotype about old people. Even physicians who call themselves geriatric specialists fall into these errors, and the more sensitive, better educated nurse has the job of leading them to heightened consciousness and greater knowledge.

There are a number of things that the nurse can do to model appropriate behavior with old people. These behaviors are useful in physicians' offices, in waiting rooms of clinics and other health facilities, and even in hospital settings:[24]

1. Develop an ambience of relaxed use of time. Relaxed use of time is quite different from just keeping someone waiting for a long time. After waiting for an hour or two, it is disconcerting, to say the least, to have the doctor spend fifteen minutes with you, only half listening to your answers to his cursory questions while he examines you. If long waits are really unavoidable—and I am not at all sure that they are—the time spent waiting can be used to achieve viable therapeutic objectives. (See items 2, 3, 4, and 5.)

   The process, however, is quite different from the traditional one of seating the patient beside a desk and filling out a form as he responds to prepared questions. There is nothing relaxed about this process, focused as it is on "processing" patients in turn. In addition, the tension created in this kind of controlled situation often makes people respond in ways that are not quite accurate. Whether the reason is inability to recall accurately, or the felt pressure to complete the questionnaire, or the need to make a certain kind of impression on the questioner, the total information gathered is not as useful as the information given in a less formal, more relaxed atmosphere.

   The semisocial interchange when the nurse sits in the waiting room chatting with three or four patients may produce significant information of the kind that people are more likely to reveal to acquaintances and friends than they are to doctors and nurses. It also offers opportunity for patients to share some general expectations and anxieties and so alleviate the special tension that arises out of the belief that one is all alone in his misery.

   If the nurse's duties in the office involve her more technical professional skills, she can educate the receptionist to take over this function, arming her with the kinds of questions and comments that are calculated to encourage certain types of communication. The ringing phone and the bill typing can be reserved for those times when the doctor has no visiting hours.

2. Find out something about his expectations and anxieties. An opening gambit may establish the informality and make it clear that there are no taboo feelings or thoughts. The nurse may reveal something about her own anxiety in a similar situation and so encourage the patient's expression of feeling. One nurse tested this process by coming out from behind the partition that separated her office from the waiting room and offering lemonade to the two old people sitting there so patiently. After sitting down with them for a moment or two, she observed, "Do you know, when I've been waiting for a long time to see a doctor, I begin to wonder about all the other people on his mind, and all their ailments. I can't help feeling that I'd better not take up too much of his time with my little aches and pains. Then after I leave, I'm sorry that I didn't mention this or that, and it bothers me until my next visit."

   One of the patients responded, "He always seems to be so busy. It makes me nervous, trying to get out what I want to say."

   The other patient smiled sympathetically, "I used to stutter when I was younger. Now the only time I do is when I'm talking to the doctor. I try to talk fast."

   The nurse was able to provide information that might alleviate the apparent tension the patients felt by telling them, "The doctor plans for a full forty minutes for you on routine visits. That's more than enough time to talk to him about what's on your mind. And if anything special comes up, he's told me to just help the people who are waiting to be comfortable. So I know he hopes you'll just relax and talk to him as we're talking now."

3. Encourage him to put into words whatever questions he has. Sometimes, if the old person has had opportunity to verbalize some questions on his mind, he can get answers in the informal situation that are satisfactory and leave him free to communicate with the physician about more immediately relevant medical matters. One such patient, encouraged by the trained receptionist, asked, "What is leukocyst?" "Leukocyst. I don't know such a word. Maybe you mean leucocyte?" "What is it?" "A white blood cell," she answered. "Oh," said the pa-

tient, obviously enlightened and relieved. "When I went to the lab for tests, they kept talking about it, and I couldn't imagine what it was. I thought I had a rare disease."

Although I have no hard data on this, I would venture to say that receptionists behind glass, or even behind desks, are not often asked questions like this. And, on the rare occasions when they are, the patient is rebuffed by an admonition to save such questions for the doctor. If the patient feels constrained to respond only minimally to the doctor, then he is inevitably left with many unanswered questions that contribute unnecessarily to his discomfort.

4. Make some obvious efforts to see her as a whole person. The work she did before retiring can still be drawn on for interest and self-concept maintenance. It is good to continue to get recognition for activity that once defined your whole life. The request for an opinion about the current political campaign or a local labor dispute makes it clear that the old person is still considered to be tuned in to what is happening around her and is as concerned as any younger person might be. (There is evidence that a significant number of old people are even *more* concerned about political events than are many younger people!)

    A new movie or play, a best-selling book—how many younger people discuss these things with old people with whom they come into contact? It is no wonder that young people so often think that association with the old is dull; they assume that old people are not interested in the things that young people think about.

5. Interact productively with the friend, paid companion, or family member who accompanies the patient. The person who accompanies an old man or woman to the doctor's office has valuable information that may help the nurse and the doctor treat the patient more successfully. Unfortunately, however, there is often a tendency to talk to this person *about* the old person as if the latter were not present. The sensitive nurse can change the pattern of interaction by making it a three-way affair and, in the process, perhaps teach another adult to change a destructive form of behavior.

    Sometimes an altogether different attitude seems to manifest itself toward an adult son or daughter of an old person. Doctors and nurses could do much to alleviate the anxieties and frustrations of adults who must suddenly assume the care of aged parents who can no longer care for themselves. However, they often seem unaware of the need for such help and may even thoughtlessly exacerbate the difficulties with some of the things they say and do—or do *not* say and do.

    For example, there is a fear that is generated by the TV-perpetuated myth of the good old family doctor who knew you as a child and calls your mother by her given name (as she does his), and stops to have a cup of tea after a home visit to treat a mild cold.

The physician who treats your old mother these days is a very busy man. He can see her—after long waiting—when she is relatively well, or suffering from a persistent, chronic condition for which he needs to renew the medicine. The pervasive dread of the patient's family is that she will suddenly become acutely ill and need a physician immediately. There is no physician for this situation; there are only fire-department medics, hospital emergency rooms, or police wagons. Since one has no way of knowing if the symptoms are only alarming and not really serious, one may get involved with the whole emergency apparatus, including crowds in front of the house, and scare the old woman and the rest of the family half to death, when all that was needed was a simple remedy and some reassurance. No geriatrist ever seems to raise the matter with the family, and, somehow, one feels that talking about it would be an imposition on his time and his professional sophistication. He has more important things to do than respond to the fears of his patient's family—doesn't he?

An adult daughter cannot help remembering that once her father became ill when he lived alone, and nobody knew about it for hours. So now that he lives with her, she finds herself getting up several times during the night to see that he is all right, like a new mother with her child. Each nocturnal trip he makes to the bathroom, she listens to his footsteps, and turns back to sleep only when he is safe in bed again. When the night turns cold, she gets up to see if he has remembered where the extra blanket is, or, if the weather is warm, that he remembers how to open the sliding window; she doesn't want him catching cold. Aren't old people more susceptible to colds than younger people? (How is it that she forgets so completely that her father hasn't had a cold in twenty years, and she's had *three* since he's come to live with her?)

Most parents who respond to their infants this way learn to relax and be less fearful as time goes on. The pediatrician knows this and keeps telling the new parents that is will happen to them, too. Most fears prove to be groundless, and children are manifestly hardy survivors. But the geriatrist doesn't seem to recognize that it is difficult to develop this perspective about an old person. He so often does have aches and pains that make him as fearful as they make his family.

Has a nurse or physician ever asked a son or daughter how he feels about having a parent live with him? Just a recognition by professionals that there *are* feelings may help that person do better by the parent, and so influence the ultimate therapeutic objective.

6. Institute a process of informal education about old age and aging. The nurse can initiate a process of education to reduce stereotypic thinking and discriminatory behavior against old people. But the program in the physician's office will probably need to be an informal one, al-

though there is no reason why it cannot be as carefully planned and systematically executed as any formal in-service program.

The nurse can suggest to all the other personnel—including the physician—that they all watch for evidences or errors in thinking about old people and post a description of each error (without identifying the person who erred) on a bulletin board. If the target is one error a week, the nurse can encourage informal discussion of that error—at lunch, during coffee breaks, and during other moments of casual conversation—and bring to each discussion some information or observation calculated to increase knowledge about old age and aging and awareness of the needs of old people.

Selected readings can be brought into the office and left in strategic spots where personnel may pick them up. Lectures, TV shows, and other presentations of data about aging can be brought to everybody's attention, and discussions about them can be initiated on the following day. The results of the informal gathering of data from old people (see item 1) can be shared with technicians and receptionists, who do not ordinarily have access to patient histories, so that the pitfalls of stereotyping can be pinpointed in specific cases.

Women

Wherever nurses work with physicians, especially male physicians, the nurse who wishes to make some attempts at leadership has a ready-made place for herself if she wants to step into it. In the treatment of patients generally, significant changes appear to be necessary, changes that the physician himself has not been educated to consider. The physician's training is so technical, so focused on cure (and only recently on prevention) that the social-psychological aspects of his treatment modalities as well as his treatment situation do not become a part of his concerns.

But there are special areas of concern where the nurse can assume leadership by virtue of the unique nature of her own experience, especially if the nurse is a woman. One area involves the traditional sexual cognates of relationships. Where physicians are men and nurses are women, nurses can assume leadership in solving problems arising from the traditional relationships between men and woman. Women physicians may have been trained in a sexist milieu and may have learned the same prejudices and stereotypes that are so much a part of our culture. It is possible—and here I am on even more tenuous ground—that those men who become nurses have developed sensitivities concerning male-female relationships, unlike many other men.

At any rate, male physicians and female nurses are by and large in a situation where the nurse can identify some of the special problems that women have in coming to the physician for help, and can begin to identify objectives for changing the pattern of relationships in treatment. A number of questions can be asked to reveal the physician's attitudes toward women and the nurse's attitudes toward herself. Such questions may lead to additional objectives for change.

One question is: What kinds of things does a physician say to a woman patient when he is making a diagnosis of breast tumor or uterine tumor that might require mastectomy or hysterectomy? One physician I know joked about breasts being superfluous tissue, not to the patient herself, but to members of her family who expressed great concern at the possible diagnosis of cancer. Another physician recommended a hysterectomy for a woman and when she expressed dismay because she felt that removal of her reproductive organs was a reflection on herself as a woman and might interfere with her perception of herself as feminine, tossed off her very strong feelings by saying, "Well, you have two children; that's enough for anybody."

Another question the nurse leader might ask is: What does the doctor say and do concerning office appointments with women? Very often the attitude is that a woman can make an appointment to see a doctor at any time of the day that suits the doctor's convenience. The implication is that a woman has nothing else to do that can conceivably be more important than keeping a doctor's appointment. A man, as everyone knows, must go to work and has other responsibilities, so some care must be taken to make the appointments convenient.

Of course, the whole business of making appointments at the convenience of the physician relates not only to women but also to other patients. The pervasive attitude seems to be that people can be requested to make appointments at specific times at the physician's convenience; then there are no qualms about keeping them waiting one, two, and three hours after the time of their appointment. Usually there is not even a perfunctory apology for wasting their time.

The first stage of resistance to this practice is already apparent in so many of the humorous "how-to" books that prescribe ways of dealing with the everyday outrages perpetrated on us by people in power. One suggestion is to bill the physician for an amount of money based on the professional value of the patient's time. This is a first step in the change process; eventually some change will be made in the physician's practice of keeping people waiting for unreasonable lengths of time.

However, the nurse can provide a real leadership function by raising this question with the physician. She can also try to schedule patients in a more rational way so that they are not kept waiting except when a real emergency throws the schedule off.

Other assumptions are based on sexist attitudes. The insistence that a woman patient bring her husband when there is any consultation concerning abortion is an example. It may, in a general way, be salutary for partners in a relationship to confer with each other whenever an important decision must be made that can affect the relationship, but it is not the business of the physician to insist that the patient's husband participate in such a conference. The decision to confer is part of a process that involves the husband and the wife; the doctor has no right to interfere.

The nurse might ask the question: If a man were the patient would the doctor insist that his wife be a part of any consultive process? At any rate, with male-female relationships taking forms different from traditional marriages, the physician might profitably recognize that his formal education does not equip him to give nonmedical advice.

There is a certain amount of leadership skill in insisting that the physician, and other men in health facilities, not say things to the nurse that have a sexist connotation. Sexual harassment in business has become almost commonplace, as evidenced by the increasing number of complaints being made by working women. Similar sexual harassment can occur in health care settings against the nurse by the physician and even by male patients. To refuse to submit to such harassment, to insist that the nurse be treated professionally and with dignity is a leadership function.

Children

Leadership on behalf of children is a neglected area in the nursing profession, as in almost every other profession including elementary education. Some of the questions the nurse might ask concerning the treatment of children include: How justified is the physician in limiting his practice to adults? Aside from the fact that a physician or anybody else has the right to decide what kind of work he wants to do, is there some logical basis for separating an adult practice and practice with children? A specialty permits one to work in a narrow area where the rapid proliferation of knowledge can be processed by a single person. However, is there not also a responsibility to the population? Children do not, as a cohort, get the kind of medical care delivery that they need. Because so many childhood illnesses are self-limiting, there is a misconception that care delivery is generally adequate. However, the data reveal that many childhood illnesses are not treated; the implications for undetected, undiagnosed, and untreated illness go far beyond discomfort for short periods of time during childhood. It often means the onset of physical, psychological, and learning problems that persist throughout the person's life.

Children need to be part of a plan for total family health care delivery because the best way to detect many childhood illnesses is by talking to the child's family. The pediatrician who treats only the child and speaks perfunctorily to the mother or to another member of the family is missing the opportunity to detect such illnesses.

The nurse in the physician's office may ask whether there is provision in the office for children who are not themselves patients but who are waiting with parents or other family members. The assumption that children can always be left somewhere when adults have to visit the doctor's office is not realistic. The expectation that children who accompany adults to the doctor's office can sit and wait for an hour or two without disturbing anyone else is equally unrealistic. In addition, more and more in this country, children are seen in public and semi-public places and even sacrosanct circumstances heretofore marked "off limits" for them. They accompany fathers with working wives to their shops and offices; they sit in college classrooms next to mothers who have returned to school; they crawl about on auditorium floors while their parents listen to political candidates. Partly this happens because there is no place to leave them. Partly, however, parents are making a conscious decision to involve the children in all family experiences—not wait until some mythical moment in the future when they are supposedly "ready" to be taken about.

Another question the nurse might ask is: How are children treated in all health care facilities? What is the philosophical framework in which their questions are answered and their fears allayed? How much or how little information are they given about themselves? Does the behavior of doctors and other members of the staff imply that they believe children are somewhat less than human or, at best, imperfect human beings who don't know what they want, can't express their need to know, and, in fact, do not need to know much about themselves? I know of an instance where this kind of attitude culminated in an absurd situation, in which a seventeen-year-old girl was asked to wait outside while the doctor discussed her condition with her mother.

From what we know about how children deal with their own illnesses and even with knowledge of their own imminent death, we can conclude that the less information they have, the higher the intensity of anxiety and fear they experience. Because adults generally cannot dissemble their own fears and anxieties in the presence of children, the child's anxiety may increase beyond the bounds required by reality.

Patients as patients

There is much discussion of the whole area of patient advocacy in hospitals. New professionals called patient advocates are even being hired by hospitals to listen to patients' complaints and suggestions for improvement of hospital procedures and facilities and to relay these complaints to supervisors and administrators. Very little, however, has been said about patient advocacy in the doctor's office. The nurse, by virtue of her training and her introspection concerning nursing care delivery, is eminently prepared to act as a patient advocate. In the physician's office, she is also strategically placed to assume an advocacy position where it is desperately needed.

Unfortunately, the nurse often identifies so closely with the physician (who is, after all, her employer) that a situation arises where patients see the nurse more as adversary than advocate, or as an obstruction to channels of communication with the physician. (This is very much like the sort of thing that happens in business offices, where an "efficient" secretary "protects" her boss from the unnecessary encroachments from eager visitors.) For example, an office nurse is called by a patient who complains of feeling ill, and she tells the patient that the doctor is too busy to see her or talk to her and advises her to go to the emergency room of the nearest hospital. Certainly the nurse, in that moment of crisis, is perceived by the patient as an enemy.

Minorities

Nothing has been said so far about the treatment of members of other minority groups—racial, ethnic, and cultural minorities whose victimization by prejudice and discrimination has been written about in the literature of all professions. At the moment, the problems of these groups have been obscured in the public mind by the women's movement, concerns with the aged, and the fight against child abuse which is part of the child advocacy movement. It is not so fashionable as it was in the 1960's to express great concern about the problems of Black people, Hispanic people, Native Americans, and other ethnic and religious groups. However, those leadership skills that are put to use on behalf of women, the aged, and children can also be put to use on behalf of minority people.

One great advantage that minority groups can have in a health care system is a nurse who has knowledge of their history and empathizes with them in their struggle for equal treatment. The nurse who shares the language and culture of the community has an additional advantage in that she can work with clients in their own language and so profit from the subtleties of communication lost when one party to a dialogue must speak in a language not his own. Sharing the same culture can help the nurse make recommendations, such as for nutrition and health practices, within the framework of that culture. Thus the client can learn about health maintenance without having to unlearn behaviors with which he is comfortable.

Since education in health maintenance often requires the dissemination of written materials, the nurse who speaks the language of the community can see that pamphlets and directions are accurately translated and edited for cultural consistency.

Advocacy is a leadership function, and systematic efforts to protect the rights of those who need such protection flow naturally from the nurse's professional objectives. Though our sensitivity as a nation to the rights of many groups is increasing, we are left with a leadership vacuum. As examples, we agonize over the plight of old people and of children, but much of the associated activity seems to be unproductive, at least in the short run. We need people to help us get things stopped—old people living in boarding houses unfit for human beings; old people abused by their own relatives; old people dying of malnutrition; children being abused by teachers; teen-agers being tortured in the name of therapy. We need people to get things started—adequate physical protection for old people; systems of communication that children may use to protest mistreatment or just to ask for help; health care delivery systems that provide for those left out of current systems. We need people who can mobilize us to act in our own interests.

The special leadership skill involved in identifying objectives for change involves the clarification of relevant basic values that undergird the changes needed in the treatment of women, the aged, children, minorities, and patients. The first set of values involves traditional attitudes and beliefs concerning those groups of people that have traditionally been discriminated against in our society. The nurse, in the process of clarifying these values for herself and then drawing the physician into a process of clarifying his own values, is demonstrating leadership skill.

The second step is relating one's own values, now clearly articulated, to one's behavior and then helping others do the same. Very often, we profess to have a particular value, but are unaware of the inconsistency between the value we profess and the way we act.

The nurse can raise such questions as: "What are the errors of perception concerning various groups? What are the implications of these errors for adequate health care delivery to these groups?"

What are some of the behavioral objectives that can be identified before planning for change in the treatment setting? Some obvious ones include:

- People's waiting time will be cut from two hours to twenty minutes.
- Children will be addressed directly and honestly.
- Old people will be accepted as patients on an equal basis with people of other ages.
- Black people will be accepted as patients on an equal basis with people of other races.

Some of the modeled behavior and some of the questions raised by the nurse may be resented or resisted by physicians and other staff members. However, it should be borne in mind that nurses are in a particularly advantageous position these days. Because there is a shortage of nurses, they can pick and choose among situations in which to work. A competent professional who insists that she be permitted to behave like a professional, need have little fear of losing her job or of being unable to find another one.

Of course, some skills are needed to make the asking of questions and the modeling of new behaviors somewhat less threatening to the person who has never asked those questions of himself and who has acted in more traditional and more restrictive ways. Most skills, however, are secondary to the strong conviction that one has a right to speak up concerning the consistency of professional practice with professional philosophy. Why should a nurse spend two, three, or more years learning to practice her profession, and then feel compelled to compromise not only the quality of her practice, but also her integrity?

The poor and the middle class

Traditionally, those who committed themselves to community work concentrated on low-income neighborhoods where, presumably, the need for their help was greatest. They came to entice youngsters into playgrounds and schools, to identify people in need of counseling, to inform people about available facilities for health care and job training, to mobilize people for initiating needed change. They came also to study communities and people—to question, examine, draw conclusions, and then leave for unexplored and unmobilized areas. Though some needs in poor communities were addressed and alleviated, most persisted and others were added. The gap between the destitute and the comfortable continued to widen.

With the advent of the Model Cities program, poor people themselves were to take on community leadership roles and provide the impetus for defining needs and instituting change. Insufficient money from the government and lack of commitment to the idea by politicians and professionals eventually subverted the objective of community participation and control. It seemed that the cult of openness, of freedom to speak, of freedom to express emotion was being used as a device to sidetrack planning for change. In Australia I detected some of this among social workers who go into the outback to work with Aborigines. They provide forums in which the Aboriginal people can express their anger and frustration at having no work, no means of livelihood, no adequate living conditions, and no evidence that they are being given opportunities to prepare themselves to compete as equals with their countrymen of European stock. The social workers see this as a salutary kind of behavior—letting people blow off steam. There is no evidence that anything is done with the information gathered to effect any significant change.

In this country, a study of Community Action Programs found a similar process: The involvement itself obscured the fact that no social change was occurring.[25]

But the poor Americans who participated in the War on Poverty did learn that political activity and political power were the keys to community control. The nurse who wishes to offer some leadership to a low-income community must prepare herself with the knowledge of recent past history, or she will encounter cynicism and rejection of all but her most traditional services.

One thing she must know is that communities are rarely self-sufficient, poor communities less so than others. As has been noted about poor Black communities, "The economic and political self-sufficiency of the ghetto is severely limited. Ghetto people support themselves through relationships with outsiders and are dominated by them. Every morning brings white non-residents into ghetto territory and black people out of it, for a day's work. Considering the impact of the wider environment, the ghetto is only a part-community, as most overarching social institutions are not its own."[26]

People in a community generally feel that they are alike in important ways, that they share certain beliefs and norms of behavior aside from their socioeconomic circumstances. The outsider must be aware of these beliefs and norms, even if her ultimate objective is to change some of them. If she does not know what the people believe, what they approve of and disapprove of, she will fail without ever knowing why.

Take, for example, the nurse in a rural community in Appalachia who attempted to get the people to reject the ministrations of a local healer by ridiculing her and debunking her prescriptions. She was herself rejected by the community. What she thought was rational argument and scientific thinking was perceived by people as narrow-minded arrogance and derogation of them and their traditions.

Most human service workers concentrate their activity in urban areas. Nurses, too, have largely neglected regions such as Appalachia, the nonmetropolitan areas of the north central states, Florida, and California. "Florida and California have large concentrations of old people, and the younger professionals may be reluctant to spend so much of their lives with the elderly. Appalachia and the nonmetropolitan areas lack many of the cultural and convenience amenities found in cities. So there are large areas of the United States that may offer exciting opprotunities for community workers who can resist the lure of urban life."[27]

Other community workers have traditionally gone into low-income neighborhoods for reasons that may seem specious in retrospect. It is obvious that poor people have more pressing material needs than people with money. But I have never believed that providing money and food requires vast professional bureaucracies that spew out red tape to justify their continuous expansion. It is not an original observation that if there were fewer people hired in the welfare system, there would be fewer people going hungry and our welfare costs would probably be much lower. (The costs in loss of privacy, resentment, frustration, and feelings of failure traced to the nature of providing welfare need more space than we have here for adequate assessment!)

When we leave the basic material needs and examine the other human needs that could be addressed by community workers, I think we will find the socioeconomic boundaries breached. Just as poor people need to organize in order to control and affect their environment, so do middle income people. In our complicated world, where high levels of technical knowledge and political sophistication are necessary if we are to understand what is happening to us, middle-income people are not much better equipped than poor people. Middle-class people are prey to anxiety and alienation because they feel powerless, just as are poor people. Perhaps the results of these feelings are more apparent among the poor in the higher incidence of violent crimes, of suicide, of hypertension, and of mental illness. But most poor people do not commit such crimes, and many middle-class people do. Many middle-class people commit suicide and suffer from other dysfunctions traced to extreme stress. Middle-class people may commit crimes for which they are less likely to be apprehended, for example, stealing goods on the job, embezzlement, or food adulteration. (The very way we perceive poor people makes them more vulnerable to contact with the law enforcement system, and more likely to end up in jail for longer periods of time than middle-class people jailed for the same offenses.)

The point is that there is a large overlap in needs between the poor and the middle class, and professionals who restrict their community work to poor communities are overlooking large areas of need. (We are not even discussing the rich and their needs; often the assumption is that, with enough money to buy the necessary help, needs are automatically fulfilled. A short period of working with the children of the rich can correct such a misperception!)

There are other factors that should be considered in the argument for making middle-class neighborhoods targets of community work. In looking at the distribution of socioeconomic levels, it becomes clear that there are poor people in suburbs as well as cities, in small towns as well as in outlying rural areas. Often the poor are "hidden," insofar as the surrounding middle-class people generally ignore them and government agencies do not seem able to improve their condition. Experience seems to have proven that working exclusively among the poor has not achieved whatever objectives professionals have had.

Perhaps the answer lies in extending our target areas. Working in both poor and middle-class neighborhoods to help people develop the skills they need to improve their lives may facilitate cooperation among people across socioeconomic boundaries. People of all groups may more readily realize the universality of human needs and be less likely to perceive other groups as enemies if community workers themselves cut across those boundaries. The more people heretofore psychologically separated from each other begin to view each other realistically, the more they will begin to think about pooling their resources to effect change. Such a power pool, reinforced by knowledge and skill, can result ultimately in meaningful change.

Socioeconomic barriers are not the only ones to be breached by changing the approach to community work. Racial segregation, whether physical or psychological, can also be mitigated. An example of practically wasted effort in community organization has been going on in urban areas for some time. Largely poor Black populations, left behind as more affluent Whites move to the suburbs, have become more and more powerless to prevent the rapid deterioration of the cities. It would appear that any effective organization would have to be launched by the cooperative effort of suburban Whites and urban Blacks.

The fantastic mobility of our society in itself suggests that community workers should function everywhere. In our movement from one place to another, we need some assurance that our new locations provide the amenities to which we are all entitled. We need room to move with confidence in the schools, in the integrity of political organizations, and in the availability of health care. Focusing community organization efforts only on poor neighborhoods can never result in the improvements needed in all neighborhoods nor provide us with the assurance that when we move we do not worsen our condition.

Once in a community, the nurse interested in providing leadership can begin to gather information to help her assess community needs and give clues to where her own efforts may best be used. As has been suggested, any systematic approach to planning and change depends upon accurate information to initiate the process, to define objectives, and to build the system. The nurse should gather only the information needed for her own first steps. Subsequently, the people who will be affected by the changes should be involved in the information gathering. Like any other situation in which information is to be learned, facts have little meaning if they are discovered by others and presented in indigestible chunks. It is much more likely that those who feel the need for information, search for it, and discover it will finally use that information to solve their problems.

As a first step, though, the nurse needs to know something about how the community functions. Much of the information for this can come through her normal professional channels. For examples, if she is associated with a hospital, she can identify the nature of health needs in the community, assess the availability of private physicians and other primary care deliverers, get some idea of the adequacy of recreation facilities for children, and learn about the income level and occupations of the people.

She can make contact with other community facilities in which health practitioners are employed: family planning agencies, mental health centers, schools, public health agencies, recreation centers, even industrial plants. Through these other practitioners she can learn much, not only about the health of the community, but also about people's beliefs and feelings about current issues, their attitudes about education, and about the kinds of labor and professional organizations they have.

From the people she herself treats she can learn how they feel about the various agencies, institutions, and organizations in the community. She can learn what is worrying them about their children and what they feel good about. She can get some clues to children's attitudes toward their parents. From older patients she can learn something about how old people are viewed and how they are cared for when they can no longer care for themselves. She may be able to discover who is trusted in the community, which individuals are perceived as leaders.

All of this information gathering goes on while the nurse is providing bedside care, supervising her team, administering her unit, making house calls, or running a medical clinic.

Out of all this she begins, tentatively, to identify some needs that are not being adequately addressed. I say tentatively because in the final analysis, the identification of needs and the setting of priorities must be made by the people in need. However, the nurse must set some preliminary objectives for herself on the basis of what she thinks needs to be done in the community. Her leadership, however, is not for the purpose of accomplishing what *she* thinks the people need. Leadership is for the purpose of helping people accomplish what *they* think they need. What effective leadership does is influence people to make their decisions on the basis of sound information, using methods that have the greatest chance for success.

After developing for herself some knowledge of the community, the nurse defines one or two objectives based on that knowledge. These objectives must be defined in behavioral terms, so that she can easily determine whether or not they are achieved.

The nurse in the community may act as a leader outside established organizations, or she may choose to become a part of one or more existing organizations and establish herself as a leader through them. Her objectives will depend on which way she chooses to exercise her leadership function.

Community Institutions for Nursing

Health centers

"Along with our encouragement of HMOs, we are looking upon community health centers as a desirable way to deliver health care services in many communities. CHCs provide coordinated, comprehensive, integrated care to communities in great need of that service, and I believe they do a very good job. They are also significant in their services to reach out to the community, trying to involve community people in the delivery of health care services and to educate the community served by that center. Again, CHCs serve far too many people and are available to far too few."[28]

An interesting example of such a health center functions in the Appalachian Mountains, emphasizing "outreach into the community, programs of preventive practice in health maintenance and health education, student programs, and involvement of the entire family in the care of the client . . ."[29] In spite of the historical reluctance of health professionals to work in isolated rural communities, this center in one of the most isolated and poverty-stricken counties in the state, attracts and holds a staff of twenty-five people.

Their concept of team functioning is especially interesting, depending as it does less on traditional role definitions than on functions as they are currently performed. In Stumbo's own words: "The term 'management team' is used . . . to identify that group of individuals involved with the health care management of a patient. The team is organized around functions to be performed rather than specific titles an individual must possess, such as dentist, nurse, physician, to become team members. The philosophy . . . is that the center's staff delivers the highest quality of care to all clients. Any member of the center's staff who performs any procedure must be the best member of the staff, or equal to the best member of the staff, in performing that particular procedure."[30]

The center originally had a problem in educating clients to accept nursing care. "The people in our area had not been used to a nurse's doing anything but taking temperatures and blood pressures."[31] Unfortunately, the staff seems to have perpetuated the concept that the nurse and other health care professionals are merely helping arms of the physician. They actually call them "physician extenders," and rely primarily on the constant monitoring of total patient care by the physician. At the beginning the physician even made a point of telling all new patients that he trusted the nurse, that she was well trained. The net effect seems to be that nurses practice a great deal of medicine, managing stable patients with chronic diseases according to developed standing orders and educating patients and their families on the knowledge of disease and its treatment. (Though the writer maintains that "The nurse has not become a 'super R.N.' or a 'low-class M.D.' but simply a provider of care concerned with the total family needs—a traditional concept in nursing."[32])

However, the nurses are engaged in a program of patient education that focuses on prevention and health maintenance. They run classes for weight reduction and a program of education in prenatal and well-child care. Their work with individuals suffering from the prevalent chronic lung disease, and with their families, has helped people live more comfortably with the consequences of the pulmonary impairment and reduced the need for repeated hospitalizations. They even began an education program to reduce inappropriate use of emergency room service by teaching clients how to deal with common problems at home.

Outreach is engaged in by all members of the staff. One interesting example of outreach that follows a patient from the center back into the community (instead of going out into the community to find her) shows how useful it is for a nurse to resist limiting her functioning to the four walls of any institution. "One mother and her infant repeatedly visited the emergency room with the complaint of diarrhea and vomiting on the part of the child. No one on the clinic staff could determine what was causing this child's illness, so one of our nurses made a home visit to this family. She found that the family had no electricity or refrigeration and kept the child's milk in the creek to keep it cool!"[33]

What a classic illustration of the uselessness of medical treatment in isolation from knowledge of and involvement in the patient's community!

There have been examples of community health centers established by nurses who recognized the desperate need for primary care in poor urban areas (for example, a clinic established by the College of Nursing of the University of Delaware in Wilmington), a number of privately-owned centers run by nurses in outlying areas, and many centers in all areas where nurses are part of the regular staff. In many of these centers, nurses made home visits when necessary to evaluate the care being given within the context of the client's living situation. Very rarely does there seem to have been any reluctance on the part of clients to accept primary care from a nurse. What is significant is that the care provided by nurses who have broken away from the traditional model has been a new kind of care, utilizing community resources and emphasizing the concepts of education and client autonomy. A large part of the work these nurses do is essentially with well people. Also, much of what they do involves interdisciplinary communication and cooperation, first in reassuring members of other professions who feel threatened or otherwise disturbed by the new nursing role, and then in drawing together—through referral of clients, consultation, and information feedback—the various professionals whose combined efforts constitute integrated human service delivery.

Mental health centers

In 1963, Congress authorized the construction of community mental health centers. States are supplied with matching funds to provide inpatient and outpatient care; day, night, and weekend care; diagnostic and rehabilitation services; foster home placement; home visits; halfway houses; and training and research. Planning continues for comprehensive mental health programs.

Unfortunately, the mental health movement, by developing separately from other aspects of health care delivery, has muddied the concept of holistic care and has further fragmented the health maintenance function.

Considering the estimate that half the people treated by physicians and surgeons may also have emotional problems, and that almost everyone could profit from mental health counseling at some time, it seems that mental health care should be a part of total health care. Nurses could take the lead in providing such total care. They are admirably situated to identify people in need of mental health care, provide some kinds of care, make appropriate referrals, and collect epidemiological data.

Much mental health counseling is an integral part of good nursing care. Helping people to learn the skills of problem solving increases coping ability and prevents the escalation of frustration, fear, and anxiety. The nurse who teaches parenting to young mothers may contribute to the amelioration of child abuse in a community; the nurse who helps the stroke victim become proficient in the activities of daily living may demonstrate to the community a viable and preferable alternative to the total deterioration and need for total care of the aged ill. Such treatment serves the mental health of the community by reassuring people that succumbing emotionally to illness and stress is not inevitable, and that help is available when needed without extensive psychiatric consultation or hospitalization in a psychiatric facility. In addition, counseling and skill development in solving of everyday problems can prevent many physical ailments that have their genesis in emotional factors.

There are times, of course, when special psychiatric treatment is needed. The nurse who recognizes this need can make a referral in such a way as to allay the anxiety that may exacerbate the person's problem. The family of the patient, too, can bank on the unique trust they have in the nurse to help them accept the referral. The nurse, too, is committed to following up on the referral; thus psychiatric hospitalization is not extended beyond the time necessary.

There is evidence that more than thirty percent of those in outpatient psychiatric treatment programs drop out without the approval of the staff. Unless a health center or clinic has an effective outreach organization, these people are lost to treatment and may continue to get worse. The nurse who functions as an integral part of her community knows both the people who live in it and the service agencies established to deliver care. One way or another, she will learn about the person who has interrupted his treatment. She may make efforts to establish more solid communication with him, or observe him from a distance. She may know people who are important to him and work with them to influence him to resume treatment. She may also, in the process, receive information about the functioning of the mental health facility that needs to be fed back to the system in order to improve service. The professional with strong ties in the community and with good communication with health care consumers has vital information to feed back to institutions that may be functioning with minimal community input.

The nurse leader who not only recognizes the value of systematic nursing research, but also wants to contribute to the body of new knowledge, has an appropriate research function in the area of mental health. She can collect data on the incidence of untreated emotional problems and follow up discharged psychiatric patients as well as those who drop out of treatment to assess and compare their adjustment in the community. She can also document the general level of mental health in the community from the wealth of empirical data that comes to her, and feed it back to the school system and the judicial and law enforcement systems, as well as the medical and psychiatric systems, thus providing material on which to base needed changes.

In many areas, a problem arises which may ultimately be solved by the establishment of adequate community mental health facilities. However, there are still communities where a person undergoing a mental crisis has nowhere to go. A family may become alarmed at an individual's bizarre behavior, and may also perceive the behavior as potentially dangerous to the person or to themselves. Not knowing where to turn, they call the police, who may take the individual to a hospital emergency room. He may be given medication, but the police who brought him are told there is no place for him in a general hospital. The police, on attempting to bring him back to his family, find that they do not want to take him back. They insist that he needs treatment and that they can do nothing for him. They may lock their door and refuse to open it.

Here is the kind of community situation where a competent caring nurse can provide essential leadership in a number of ways:

1. She can become known in the community as someone who works in a person's home to help him through crisis situations. If she has had psychiatric training, she can provide one level of help. Even if she has not had such specialty training, there is still much she can do to allay the fears of the family and help them to accept the presence of the ill person.

2. If the incidence of such cases is significantly high in the community, she can feed this information systematically to mental health councils, planning boards, and to the public health department so that it can be incorporated in whatever plans for health care are being made.

3. She can bring her information to citizens' organizations concerned with community health, so that they may bring pressure to bear on the health delivery system to provide facilities for such situations.

4. She can work with the staff in the general hospital to consider ways of providing even minimal inpatient help for people in crisis.

5. To all these organizations, she can suggest ways in which they might help people in crisis be cared for: offering further education in psychiatric treatment to a cadre of public health nurses who will give home care; establishing a team of nurses to work systematically in the community to prevent mental health problems and crises; giving nurses the means for training paraprofessionals in the community to detect mental health problems that can be dealt with before the onset of crisis; setting up walk-in clinics and telephone hotlines for people in trouble.

Providing counseling on demand in a community is probably the single most useful service in helping people function on a day-to-day basis. High school students, for example, are worried about the challenges they face to learned moralities and the new interactive skills they need to maintain or develop positive self-concepts. A knowledgeable and sensitive adult can provide them with the confidence to make viable choices and the feeling that they have someone to turn to. There are younger children who cannot make sense of their world and do not even know what questions to ask, young adults with concerns about parenting, and older people struggling to continue productive lives in a culture that makes this very difficult.

This kind of counseling need not wait upon a fully-equipped consultation office. Merely the opportunity to stop and chat with a nurse who is known in the community can defuse anger, reduce anxiety, provide information about a community resource. The cumulative effect on the mental health of the population can be significant.

One nurse recounts her experiences in a rural community in Alaska, to which she came specifically to provide mental health services. Because she was interested in working with children, she negotiated with the school administration to secure a room and with this as her base in the community, she conducted play/talk sessions with individual children and group sessions with gifted older children, made home visits and counseled parents. She also trained Head Start and other school personnel, developed training aides, arranged for psychological testing, and held case conferences on individual children with the appropriate teachers, public health nurse, school nurse, and state social worker. She even organized a karate/counseling group for children, to help them deal with deaths in their families. Throughout her experience, she lived and worked in the community, accepting the teaching of the community people about their ways and their values, and trying to address the needs they felt."[34]

Becoming Involved in the Community

Initial observation in the community (1)

The nurse who is new in a community may feel more comfortable if she has some systematic process for getting to know the community and finding a place for herself that will afford her opportunity to function as a leader. Whether she has just come to work in a health agency established in the community, or is a student on assignment to become involved in the community, there are ways to minimize the anxiety and confusion that one feels on coming into a new place.

There is no substitute for just taking some time to walk around the community looking into the shops; noting the existence of organization offices and service institutions, the presence of physicians, nurses, lawyers, and police officers; the size and age of the school buildings; and the condition of the residential areas. There are clues in this kind of observation that can offer the observer important information about life in the community, and information, too about the observer herself, if she cares to examine her own behaviors and feelings.

CLUES TO HEALTH SERVICES

Shingles of professionals with offices in the community

If there are no physicians, nurses, and dentists in private practice, one must look for other evidence of health care provisions. Must people travel long distances to get the care they need? Are there nearby hospital or health center facilities where they are welcome? (When people without accessibility to private practitioners are forced to use hospital emergency rooms for routine health care, their treatment often indicates to them that the hospital is losing money on the facility and resents the community's inappropriate use of it.)

Hospitals

Is there a large general hospital offering the whole range of hospital service? Is it a public hospital where the poor can get care? Is the hospital a small one, obviously inadequate for serving all the people in the area?

Commercial health centers

What do the advertising signs on the buildings say they provide? Is everything offered, from foot care to prescriptions? Is there a list of the professional staff that can easily be seen? Do the apparent qualifications indicated on the list seem to be consistent with the services advertised? Are the windows of the center open to the view of passerby? (How comfortable might the patients be feeling about having their presence part of the advertisement? An answer to this would require closer investigation.) How crowded does the center appear to be? (How long do you think people have to wait before they are treated?)

Community health centers

Where is the center located? Does it appear to be in an easily accessible part of town? (If there are no old people living in the vicinity of the center, it might be worthwhile to look into what difficulties the aged in the community are having in getting to the center.) Is it easily identifiable from the outside? Does there appear to be constant traffic of people going in and out, or does it appear rather quiet and deserted? (If the center's hours are limited only to certain times of the day, it is possible that there are segments of the population who cannot use it because they work, because they have small children they cannot leave alone, or because they want to keep their visit to the center secret from their families. Further investigation may reveal the existence of such excluded people.)

Pharmacies, Opticians, and Optometrists

Is there more than one pharmacy in the area? More than one fitter of eyeglasses? Are they one-owner businesses or cut-rate chains? (If there is only one, it might be productive to look into the comparable cost of pharmaceuticals and eyeglasses; where there is competition, prices may not be as high as with only a single, one-owner business in the area.) Do the display windows of the pharmacy carry information about the advantages of asking that prescriptions be filled with generic brand drugs? (There are still people who are not aware of the enormous difference in the price of a prescription filled with a brand name and a generic drug. Physicians and pharmacists do not always give this information to their patients and customers.) Must people travel a long way to get their eyeglass prescriptions filled? (We know that, if it is difficult to get to an optometrist, people often wear ill-fitting and out-of-date eyeglasses.

CLUES TO ECONOMIC SERVICES

Houses

Do the houses seem isolated from each other, with blinds drawn and doors closed? Are there very few people on the street and little or no communication between neighbors? (Many people have moved to suburban communities in the belief that they would be living among friendly neighbors and participating in lively social interaction among people much like themselves. Often, this has turned out to be more myth than reality, with neighbors keeping pretty much to themselves and interaction more limited than in many urban areas. The boredom of women who stay home all day, the absence of recreation facilities, the political apathy have all been widely observed in suburban communities.) Are there many abandoned, boarded-up houses? (These constitute some of the greatest health hazards in urban communities, with vermin spreading from abandoned to occupied houses, with danger to children who play in and near abandoned houses, with crimes committed in them. Not infrequently, the owners of these properties, including local and federal governments, are holding on to them until the neighborhood deteriorates so badly that it can all be condemned for renewal. Even requests to local governments that they clean up these fire, health and safety hazards often bring a laconic observation that the neighborhood is slated for renewal and that is doesn't pay to invest any money in it. In the meantime, people live there for years in misery and danger.)

Stores

What kind of food stores exist in the community? What kinds of clothing and hardware stores? (Generally, supermarkets and department stores are able to sell their merchandise at lower prices than small one-owner shops. However, a small grocery store may sell on credit to regular customers who are temporarily out of money. It should also be borne in mind that store owners as well as managers of large stores have been known to raise prices in poor neighborhoods on the days they know that welfare checks are issued. Though some of them maintain that they do this to make up for the amount of money they lose from shoplifting, the available evidence indicates that the incidence of shoplifting is not greater in poor neighborhoods than it is elsewhere. At any rate, poor people often are trapped in their neighborhoods because they do not have cars and public transportation is either inadequate, nonexistent, or not practical for carrying bags of groceries. If people do not have the choice of going elsewhere, they may be taken advantage of. At least one supermarket administrator, asked why meats that were considered not fit for sale in an affluent neighborhood were sent to the branch in a poor neighborhood—to be sold for the original price—insisted that there was nothing wrong with the meat. It was just that, he said, the people in the affluent neighborhood wouldn't buy it after if had been on the shelf for a couple of days.) Do stores have heavy iron screens on their windows? Have the windows been replaced by plywood? (These are clues either to the incidence of crime in the community or to the *fear* of crime, which very often goes far beyond any realistic assessment of the incidence of criminal behavior. However, such fears are real and can affect how willing people are to meet with each other, to plan for change. If people will not leave their homes after dark, if storekeepers lock up and leave the community before dark, it is well to be aware of this before arranging community meetings.)

Public transportation

Do people need automobiles to get around? If there is public transportation, does it seem to be well maintained? overcrowded? If people are not easily mobile, it is more important for them to have all kinds of services and amenities within convenient walking distances. If they have neither convenient transportation nor amenities, they are truly disadvantaged, even though they may not be very poor. In reference to public transportation, people who live in the older cities have an added burden these days: the public transportation systems are rapidly deteriorating. The result is that buses, trolley cars and subways continually break down, burst into flames or simply never leave the barns for their appointed routes. A number of psychosocial consequences have developed from this: people are afraid to use public transportation for fear of getting stuck between subway stations and getting hurt in a stampede of panicky passengers, or being stalled in a bus far from home, or being late for work again and again. They are also very angry, with the anger that comes from the frustration of waiting unconscionably long periods of time in rainy, snowy, cold or blazing hot weather for buses. When a bus does stop—and many do not because they are too crowded to take on additional passengers—people are so disturbed that they forget to hold tightly to their pocketbooks and other belongings. They push their way into the crowded buses and trains, and have their pockets picked—a very common occurrence. Complaints to the transportation companies, whether they are publicly or privately owned, could not fall on less interested ears. The police can do little more than reiterate their warnings to people to hold tightly to their valuables.

Banks

Are there any banks in the community? (These days, conveniently located banks are a necessity to people of all socioeconomic classes. Old people have their pension and social security checks mailed directly to the bank so they will not be robbed of them. Welfare checks need to be cashed and deposits need to be made regularly in retirement funds. For everyone, given the increase in holdups and burglaries, it is wise not to carry much cash, so it is necessary to go often to the bank to withdraw money for day-to-day living expenses.) Are there people outside, waiting in line for ten minutes to half an hour before they are permitted inside to conduct their business? (At first, banks in poor neighborhoods put up guide ropes within which people had to stand while they waited their turn for service. Now banks in other areas have begun to do this, keeping large numbers of waiting people under control rather than hiring a sufficient number of tellers. Just recently, in some poor neighborhoods, I have begun to see people waiting outside. Perhaps banks in neighborhoods where there is some competition will not be so quick to copy *this* practice.)

Industries and office buildings

Industries or even small businesses may cause noise, air, or water pollution, or create safety hazards for children and adult pedestrians if the industries are close to residential and shopping areas. In small towns, the establishment of industry has caused a variety of problems that may be associated with health; wages and working conditions are often minimal because there are few labor organizations. Farmers may be driven out by the rise in land values and be left with no saleable skills. The cost of living may rise so precipitously that the many old people who live in small towns on fixed incomes are unable to get along. Many of the industries employ mostly women, which not only results in large numbers of unemployed men, but causes the kinds of family disruption that results from inability to manage rapid changes in role expectations. Mining industries have destroyed arable farm land by strip mining and, after depleting the coal deposits, have refused to reclaim the land and have abandoned the towns to economic depression.

High-rise office buildings create psychological hazards for people who must walk through canyons forever dominated by piles of concrete. There is little doubt that the sense of powerlessness is exacerbated for those who spend their whole lives in this environment. In addition, the practical hazards of miles of streets that are dark and abandoned at five o'clock cannot be minimized, especially in cities where personal crimes increase after dark.

CLUES TO LEGAL SERVICES AND LAW ENFORCEMENT

Public legal services

If you know that the community is largely made up of low-income people, you might look for a branch of Community Legal Services, the law service established by the federal War on Poverty legislation that has survived in many communities. (People pay little or nothing in fees. But, even more important, there are often paraprofessionals indigenous to the community who act as links between the people and the professionals and between clients and litigants. For example, in dealing with landlord–tenant complaints, it is clear that the lawyers and landlords are often on the same socioeconomic level, which may cause lack of trust between lawyers and the poor clients.

Lawyers in private practice

Is it clear where lawyers in private practice have their offices? Are there "legal clinics" that have easily identifiable signs on the building? (When people need legal help, it seems to require a certain amount of sophistication to find that help. Lawyers' offices may be virtually hidden in office buildings, and, unless one enters the building and searches the directory, one does not know they are there. Somewhat more knowledgeable people know enough to call the local bar association to get help in finding a lawyer, but others often feel helpless, not knowing where to go for help. Recently, lawyers have begun to advertise, so in some communities, it may be easier to find legal help. It is still important to have advocates of all professions in the community to refer people to lawyers when legal help is needed.)

Police officers

Do you see police officers in the community? Do they seem at ease? friendly? hostile? tense? Can you detect any feelings toward them on the part of the people? Are the officers approached and spoken to, or ignored? Do the officers seem to know the people they pass? Do they appear to be of the same racial and ethnic groups as most of the people in the community? (Historically, the police in minority communities have been perceived as the enemy, and often with good reason.) A look into a police operations room can provide some sound data on police attitudes. Is the person at the desk courteous to people coming in with complaints? Are suspects who are brought in treated as if they were innocent or as if they have already been found guilty?

CLUES TO EDUCATION SERVICE

Schools

Do school buildings appear to be in good condition? (From a rational perspective, it would seem that in a community that cares about its children, that is truly as "child-centered" as our society claims we are, the school buildings would be among the most beautiful and the best cared-for. Yet, in most communities, this is certainly not the case. Actually, schools are often the first institutions to have their support substantially reduced at the first sign of economic recession. It might also be considered that certain kinds of damage to school buildings may be read as indications of children's feelings about what is happening to them in school: broken windows and obscenities painted on the walls may be labeled vandalism in law enforcement terms, but can be read more accurately by those who are more knowledgeable about human behavior.) Do the children seen entering and leaving the school buildings all appear to be of the same racial and ethnic group or is there a mix of groups? (Children of different groups who are kept separate from each other often show the effects of such separation by ignorance of other groups, fear and hostility against other groups, and unrealistic self-concepts. If a viable health care objective is self-actualization, then racial and ethnic separation of children interferes with this objective.) Are there private and parochial schools as well as public schools? When the children from different schools meet at dismissal time, how do they relate to each other? (In some communities, the intermural sports between public and parochial schools are pointed to with pride as evidence that the two populations of children get along well together. More accurate indications of how they get along may be found in the confrontations at dismissal time, in the interactions after school in the neighborhoods and recreation centers, and after the games when one side has lost.)

Higher education

Are there many people in the streets who are obviously students? Although a pleasant town near a university may appear to be an ideal setting to prospective students and their parents, there may be serious conflict between students and townspeople. Is the university in a large urban area? (In recent

history, conflict with universities in urban areas has been between communities, generally of poor people, and university administrations who were identified with forcing people out of the neighborhood to provide land for university expansion. Students—those who were involved at all—sided with the
community. Currently, the prevailing conflict in urban universities has re-
volved around the rising crime rates in urban areas.)

Continuing education

Are there commercial, public, or nonprofit voluntary schools for training and retraining in various occupations? Are there schools for adults, for
the teaching of basic skills, language (for immigrant groups), and liberal arts
for those who wish to learn more about the world?

CLUES THAT TRIGGER SELF-INSIGHT

In inner cities

1. Are you surprised when a passerby smiles at you? (Have you always believed that city people were unfriendly? Did you know that city neighborhoods are often as close-knit as any rural village, and people friend-
   lier than they are in many suburbs?)

2. Do you clutch your pocketbook to you when a teenager passes? (Do you
   believe that the high crime rate in cities means that most people are
   criminals? Are you particularly suspicious of teenage males? Did you
   know that in the highest crime area of a city, less than two percent of
   the people are criminals? Most of the people in poor urban areas are the
   victims of crime, not the perpetrators. Also, how many teenagers do
   you know personally, and how much of your distrust is based on what
   you have heard from others?)

3. When a man of another race ogles you or makes a suggestive remark,
   do you feel more frightened, more angry, or more flattered than when a
   man of your own race behaves in a similar way? (What are you afraid a
   man of another race may do that men of your own race do not? You
   might be interested to know that rape, for example, is largely an intra-
   racial crime. Why are you more flattered or more frightened at attention from a man of another race? Do you think the other race is superior to yours? Inferior?)

   (Though, intellectually, you may be convinced that you are free
   of racial prejudice, those of us reared in our kind of society are inevitably affected by the pattern of prejudice and discrimination. We can
   never relax our vigilance over what we say and what we do, lest our
   early learnings betray us. I found an interesting example of this in a

book by a competent and well-known nurse leader. In answering questions at a conference, she is proud to say that she has minority people as clients.[35] But, in noting what to look for in the physical examination, she states, without qualification, that "The skin of the face should be clear and pink . . ."[36])

4. Do you feel apprehensive because you think the people in the community are looking at you with hostility? (As two teachers put it after walking around the community of their school: "Since it is an all-White neighborhood and very prejudiced against Blacks, I didn't feel very comfortable at any time. I was very apprehensive about what the people in the neighborhood did and would do." and "When I first started out I was frightened . . . I thought I would feel extremely 'White' walking in the neighborhood . . ."[37] The first teacher said she would continue to go into the neighborhood because she believed "it would get easier each time." The second teacher said the "feeling seemed to ease up," and that she was "extremely satisfied" with the experience.)

5. Do you feel angry, guilty, or repelled by the evidences of poverty? (People who have never been so poor or who have risen in the socioeconomic scale may feel anger and contempt for those who live in poverty, believing that they could change their lives if they really wanted to. They are largely unaware of, or choose to ignore, the factors that stand in the way of learning, of self-actualization, and of just plain getting a job. Others may feel guilty at their own good fortune. Guilt is a dangerous emotion; it may turn to anger against the people who precipitate the guilt feelings. Those who feel guilty may end up justifying the poverty as well as their own lack of involvement in attempts to eradicate it.)

In city fringes and higher-income areas

1. When you see the size of the houses, the wide streets, the cleanliness, do you feel envious? (If you have never been able to afford to live in such a neighborhood, your envy may color your needs assessment of the people: "They have no problems that require my help." Or your behavior with people may reveal evidences of antagonism that you believe you are hiding from them.)

2. Do you feel very much at home? (Are you so comfortable because the style of life and the behavior of the people in the area are so much like your own? This is understandable. However, if you are also equating "your own" with what is generally most desirable, most appropriate, and most healthful, you should look a little more closely at the basis of your comfort.)

3. Do you note people and occurrences that "don't seem to fit" in the set-
    ting and find yourself providing explanations for them without addi-
    tional data?

    (From the following quotation, can you assess your own reason-
    ing in this regard? "I saw a Black boy pushing a lawn mower and hold-
    ing a broom. I was stunned to see him in the neighborhood. I thought
    he came from somewhere else to do the lawns for extra money. As I was
    wondering where he came from, two Black girls walked by. One looked
    about ten and the other was about seven years old. I smiled at them and
    they smiled back. But I felt guilty as I realized that they and the boy
    probably lived in the neighborhood. Although the girls were well
    dressed and smiled sweetly, I felt that they were saying to me through
    their dress and smile, 'See, we can live in a nice neighborhood, too!'
    I'm sure they weren't thinking that but because I felt guilty about my
    prejudiced observation of the boy, this is the way I interpreted their
    smiles."[38])

In suburbs

1. Are you surprised at the apparent crowding and lack of country am-
    bience, and even the presence of poor people? (Many suburbs look very
    much like their adjacent cities. Your expectation that suburbs all have
    space and trees and grass is based on old data. Also, there are probably
    more than half a million suburban poor people in the New York City
    area alone. The best available information is always vital as a basis for
    professional assessment and planning. Serious errors in planning are
    often caused by inaccurate data.)
2. Do you feel guilty that you have chosen to work in such an affluent
    area? (Human service agencies concentrate their efforts in poor areas,
    under the assumption that their services are not so desperately needed
    in the suburbs. Professionals generally gravitate toward more affluent
    areas partly because they feel more comfortable working in areas where
    people are more like themselves, partly because of the physical ameni-
    ties in higher-income neighborhoods, and partly because of the oppor-
    tunities to earn more money. On the other hand, if they are at all aware
    of the trouble and suffering in the world, they may feel guilty about of-
    fering their services to people who are not desperately in need. Nurses
    can resolve this conflict by considering their objectives within the con-
    text of our total national and world systems. It is true that, whatever
    problems the affluent suffer, the poor also suffer, but always with the
    added problems generated by poverty. So we can safely generalize that
    the poor need more help than the rich. However, the more affluent who
    have not been helped to become self-actualizing can seriously hamper
    local, national, and world efforts to improve the quality of life.

In rural areas

Are you aware of a feeling of intellectual superiority? (Though there is no doubt that rural communities generally lag behind urban communities in their adoption of new ideas and practices, rural people are not less intelligent than urban people. The reasons for the lag may be found more in isolation from the mainstream of change and a lack of money than in any differential in potential for thinking. It might also be considered that there are people in all parts of the United States who share a belief in the value of some traditional ways.)

Initial observation in the community (2)

The next step in learning about the community is to select one or two things you have observed from the outside and arrange to spend a little time inside, gathering additional information from another perspective. Armed with information from your walks about the community and with additional general information, make up a form to provide guidelines for your more intense observation of one or two places in the community.

If you decide to observe how the education system works, write to the superintendent of schools and ask for permission to visit a school for an hour or two over a period of several days. While you are waiting for permission, go to the school, introduce yourself to the principal, and tell her that you work in the community and are trying to learn more about the institutions and the people. Tell her you have written for permission to visit, and would like to get her permission, too. (You may immediately be invited to visit any time.)

Your observation guide may look something like this:

OBSERVATION GUIDE FOR SCHOOLS[39]

The children

1. Do they smile and speak to each other?
2. Do they hit each other?
3. Do they complain about each other?
4. Do they smile and speak to strangers? (e.g., to you?)
5. Do they make a great deal of noise that does not seem to relate to learning activity?
6. Is there much running about in the halls?
7. Are the children standing outside classrooms or sitting outside the principal's office, and looking rather unhappy?

8. Are there obviously handicapped children in separate classrooms?

9. Is the lunchroom a pleasant, social situation?

10. Do children of different ethnic groups sit together in the lunchroom and play together in the schoolyard?

11. Do boys and girls sit together in the lunchroom and play together in the school yard?

12. Do handicapped and "normal" children sit together in the lunchroom and play together in the schoolyard?

13. Do adults and children speak easily and informally to each other? (The following information is more available after you get to know each other.)

14. How do the children feel about attending the school?

15. What is the absentee rate?

16. How do the children feel about the nurse?

The teachers, the principal, and other adults

1. Do they smile and speak to strangers?

2. Are they polite to the children when they speak to them?

3. Is there shouting in the classrooms?

4. Do the adults seem friendly to each other?

5. Are there people of different races and ethnic groups?

6. Are there men and women in most positions?

7. Do the teachers seem tired, worried, annoyed? (The following information is more available after you get to know each other.)

8. How do the teachers feel about working in the school?

9. What is the record of achievement of the children?

10. What is the absentee rate?

11. What is the prevailing strategy of teaching: democratic? autocratic?

12. What is the role of the nurse?

13. Do the parents of the children participate in the running of the school?

14. Are any of the adults—parents, teachers, principal, classroom aides, etc., involved in local government or citizens' groups? What recent changes or decisions have they been connected with?

The plant

1. Are the floors and walls clean?

2. Is the building in need of repairs?

3. Does the building have a pleasant odor?

4. Are the rooms too hot? too cold?
5. Are the walls esthetically decorated?
6. Is the parking lot for staff merely a section of the children's playground?

Initial observation in the community (3)

Local newspapers and television and radio programs are excellent sources of information about the community. Here, too, it is useful to have a framework for observation, keeping in mind that there are clues here for understanding your own agency, for identifying influential people in the community, and for getting a sense of community attitudes and values.

Guide for learning from the mass media

1. Which local names crop up repeatedly?
2. Which organizations in the community have their activities reported?
3. What are the current local controversies being reported in the media?
4. What public service information is supplied by the media?
5. Is there evidence of racial or other prejudice in the community? (e.g. criminals identified by group if they are not White and Anglo-Saxon; most people in public office and administrative positions being White or male; commercial advertisements showing White spokespersons, pictures of Whites, and men and women and old people in stereotyped roles; minority-group newspapers detailing instances of discrimination.)

First steps in community involvement

Gathering information about conditions in the community is a process that may initially take several weeks. However, it is a never-ending one because, as one becomes involved in the community, getting to know people and taking part in activities, one must refine original observations and revise hastily-drawn conclusions. For example, an initial observation of deteriorating housing and dirty streets may make the casual observer conclude that the people who live here are lazy and dirty and care little for maintaining a clean and wholesome environment for themselves. But further investigation may disclose the following facts and lead to quite a different conclusion:

1. The houses in the area are at least sixty years old.
2. They had originally been built as single-family homes.

3. In the last six or seven years, the houses have been bought by builders who divided them into apartments and rented each apartment to a family.

4. The original basic plumbing and lighting installations were not changed; some new bath and toilet fixtures were added. Material used for partitions was of minimal standard, providing very little noise insulation, and was already in need of repair.

5. Though people paid very high rents compared to those in other areas of the city, owners provided very little maintenance. They generally did not even provide adequate heat and hot water, and there were times when the cold water came out of the taps in a small trickle.

6. Repeated complaints by individual tenants to the city's Department of Licenses and Inspections brought occasional inspectors around, but produced no indication that anything would be changed.

7. The city garbage and trash collection had not increased its pickups because the neighborhood was ostensibly still made up of single-family dwellings. It is estimated that ten times as many people are living in the same area as were twelve years earlier.

In another instance, a pleasant town in a rural area with neat-looking houses, attractive gardens, and clean streets might indicate that people here were economically comfortable and concerned about maintaining a clear and healthful environment for themselves and their neighbors. Here, again, further experience in the community might disclose the following information:

1. A disproportionate number of old people live in the community. They have inadequate incomes and are often alone and malnourished.

2. In the small end-of-town streets and in the same areas not far out of town people are living in abject poverty.

3. Seepage from the garbage dump has found its way into the water supply, which is making people sick. They know that the water often tastes bad and makes them feel nauseated, but they have taken no steps to correct the situation.

It is important then, for the nurse to learn more about the community than she can from just walking through it specifically to observe, or on her way to and from work, or in the course of her life with her small group of friends and family. Learning about one's own situation is probably the best way to uncover the basic data on community decision-making. It has the advantage, too, of needing no elaborate argument to justify asking questions, since there is general agreement on the theory that it is useful for professionals to know their own institutions. Using her own hospital, health center, health department, or even her own independent practice as the focal point, she can start to understand how the community functions.

One important thing for the nurse leader to know is how the community makes its decisions. Does a group of elected officials tell the people what is to be done? Is there a group of wealthy and influential businessmen who are known to make the decisions? Is there a vocal citizens' group that has the greatest influence on decisions? Are most decisions made outside the community at the county, regional, or state level? How much involvement of the citizenry is there in the decision-making? Only with answers to such questions can planning start for assessing needs and instituting changes. Even in gathering data to be used for needs assessment, the nurse may find that there are people in power who refuse to release information, pressure others to withhold cooperation, and even lie in order to prevent change.

Trying to track down the most influential individuals in the establishment of one's own agency can provide data for making general observations about the community's decision-making.

In later stages of planning, it is necessary to determine if the decision makers are in agreement or disagreement with one's goals. In order to develop adequate strategies for change, it is necessary to know if the strategies must deal with basic antagonism or friendliness of the people in power; to know this, the power structure must be identified. This is not an easy thing to do. Writers in the field have used various techniques which may account, in part, for their different conclusions as to who makes the decisions in communities.

A nurse will generally not have the same resources as a team of sociologists in her attempts to identify the decision makers, though her need for the information is probably more immediately relevant. (Sociologists study a community to develop general theory. The nurse leader needs the data in order to take specific action.) Therefore, the nurse will find useful some uncomplicated processes for identifying them:

1. Ask people from all walks of life and all professions whom they perceive as influential in community affairs. Keep a running tally of the times each person or group is mentioned.
2. Talk to people about specific recent changes in the community (that you have read or heard about) and ask them who they think was influential in effecting change in that particular instance. Keep a running tally of the times each person or group is mentioned.
3. Ask people whom they would go to for help or advice of various kinds: e.g., to find a lawyer, to get a child into a school, to get redress from a landlord, to fix a ticket, to get a permit of any kind.
4. Talk to the people who work in the polling booths and political party headquarters. Ask them these questions, and note whether their names

appear on your lists. Check the tally of the names you identified in the media.

5. Ask the people who have been in your own agency for some time how the agency got started. Read whatever internal publications are available about the history of the agency and the ongoing news of the agency. Did the idea for the agency come from people in the community or outside it? Are any of these people currently involved in the activities of the agency? Keep track of the names mentioned as leading, exerting influence, speaking out either for or against.

6. Ask people in your agency about changes that have been instituted or proposed and rejected recently. Ask them to detail the process of instituting or rejecting the change, and keep a record of the names and organizations they mention. Was there concerted (organized) community involvement in the process? Did an individual (like the chief administrator) or a small elite group (like the Board of Trustees) prevail over a large community group? Over sporadic individual community protest? Where did the local news media stand on the issue? Did any professional organizations take part in the change process? Did all professionals line up on one side of the issue and all community people on the other side? Were there professionals who sided with the community? Is the issue settled?

7. Put all the names collected into a single list, with the most-often-mentioned name at the top.

8. Try to talk to the first five people on your list. Tell them you're working (and perhaps living) in the community, and you would like to know more about it. You can tell the people that you have heard their names very often in the course of your work and you think they can best help you find a way to make the best contributions to the community. Don't be afraid; they'll probably be flattered when they find out you're not asking them to use their influence in your behalf.

NOTES

[1] *American Journal of Nursing*, Nov. 1979, p. 2026.

[2] Elizabeth T. Anderson et al., *The Development and Implementation of a Curriculum Model for Community Nurse Practitioners;* DHEW Pub. No. HRA 77-44, Hyattsville, Md.: Division of Nursing, August 1977, p. 6.

[3] *Teaching of Community Health Nursing,* PAHO/WHO, Pub. No. 332, 1976, pp. 6-10.

[4] Charlotte Epstein, "Intergroup Relations in Occupational Health Nursing." *The Canadian Nurse,* 1960, Vol. 56, No. 11, pp. 1010-1020.

[5] J. David Richardson and F. Douglas Scrutchfield, "Priorities in Health Care: The Consumer's Viewpoint in an Appalachian Community," *American Journal of Public Health,* 1973, Vol. 63, pp. 79-82.

[6] Kenneth S. Welsh, "Initiating Community Health Development in an Appalachian Community," *American Journal of Public Health,* 1968, Vol. 58, No. 7, pp. 1162-1172.

[7] Richardson and Scrutchfield, op. cit.

[8] Ivan Illich, *Medical Nemisis* (New York: Pantheon, 1976).

[9] Ivan Illich, "Medicine is a Major Threat to Health," *Psychology Today*, May 1976, pp. 66-77.

[10] *American Journal of Nursing*, Feb. 1979, p. 227.

[11] *American Journal of Nursing*, Oct. 1979, p. 1761.

[12] Ada K. Jacox and Catherine M. Norris, Eds., *Organizing for Independent Nursing Practice* (New York: Appleton-Century-Crofts, 1977), pp. 95-96.

[13] Evelyn Rose Benson and Joan Quinn McDevitt, *Community Health and Nursing Practice*, 2nd ed., (Engleside Cliffs, N.J.: Prentice Hall, 1980), p. 263.

[14] Daniel J. Flood (U.S. Rep., Chairman, House Appropriations Committee, Labor and HEW), "Some Priorities in Appropriations for Health Care Delivery," *People Power, Politics for Health Care* (New York: N.L.N., 1976), pp. 13-14.

[15] George Brager and Harry Specht, *Community Organizing* (New York: Columbia University Press, 1973), p. 42.

[16] Mary Gray, in Jacox and Norris, op. cit., p. 47

[17] Charlotte Epstein, *An Introduction to the Human Services* (Engleside Cliffs, N.J.: Prentice Hall, 1981), pp. 162–163.

[18] Ilse Leeser, Claire Techalski, and Rosie Carotenuto, *Community Health Nursing* (Flushing, N.J.: Medical Examination Publishing), p. 16.

[19] Ibid.

[20] *American Journal of Nursing*, Feb., 1979, p. 245.

[21] M. Lucille Kinlein, *Independent Nursing Practice with Clients* (Philadelphia: J.B. Lippincott Co., 1977), p. 122.

[22] Ibid., p. 20

[23] Charlotte Epstein. *Learning to Care for the Aged* (Reston, Va.: Reston Publishing, 1977), pp. 141-142.

[24] Ibid., pp. 130-134.

[25] Kenneth B. Clark and Jeannett Hopkins, *A Relevant War Against Poverty: A Study of Community Action Programs and Observable Social Change* (New York: Harper & Row, 1970), p. 256.

[26] "Soulside, Washington, D.C., in the 1960's: Black Ghetto Culture and Community," in Colin Bell and Howard Newhy eds., *The Sociology of Community* (London: Frank Cass and Co., Ltd, 1974), p. 150.

[27] Charlotte Epstein, *An Introduction to the Human Services*, op. cit., p. 159.

[28] Susan Stoiber, "Remedies and Initiatives in Health Care," *The Emergence of Nursing as a Political Force*. (New York: National League for Nursing, 1979), p. 44.

[29] Jan Stumbo. "For the People of the Mountains: A Model Rural Health Center." in Anne R. Warner (Ed.), *Innovations in Community Health Nursing*. (St. Louis: C.V Mosby, 1978), p. 212.

[30] Ibid., p. 216

[31] Ibid., p. 217.

[32] Ibid., p. 222.

[33] Ibid., p. 220.

[34] Marianne Stillner, "Providing Mental Health Services in Rural Alaska," in Warner, op. cit., pp. 202-204.

[35] Kinlein. op. cit., p. 48.

[36] Ibid., p. 78.

[37] Charlotte Epstein, *Affective Subjects in the Classroom: Exploring Race, Sex and Drugs* (Scranton, Pa.: Intext, 1972), pp. 124-125.

[38] Ibid.

[39] For more information about schools, see Charlotte Epstein, *Classroom Management and Teaching*, (Reston, Va.: Reston Publishing, 1979).

chapter eight

Political Leadership

One thing we rarely deal with systematically is the process of getting into politics. Minority groups in our society, trying to counter exploitation with a variety of strategies, have discovered that the best way to effect change is to become involved in the political structure, both locally and nationally. But professionals, generally, are reluctant to become engaged in politics. They seem to feel that there is something incompatible between politics and professional functioning. This is different from other countries, such as France, where professionals have often been viewed as having special skills that could contribute much to the organization of the country.

Political activity is merely the practical application of the products of theoretical scholarship in universities—the use of knowledge of human behavior and of systems functioning to effect change. However, when a university needs an analysis of its business system, an outside organization is hired to do it; within the university there are professional educators proficient in systems analysis and in business management who are not called on to do what they could do much better and for little or no financial outlay.

Throughout the nursing literature, nurses are continually scolded and exhorted for their political inactivity, as if there were something about nurses that made them different in this respect from other professionals and from other people generally. However, aside from the fact that there is a great need for the active participation of nurses in this period of rapid

change in the profession, I don't think nurses should feel particularly dere-
lict; even as a nation we let a small proportion of our numbers run our governments and institutions.

Of course, this does not mean that we are always, or even usually,
pleased with the quality of our organizations or content with the way they
are run. Why, then, do we not commit a portion of our time to communicating dissatisfaction, to organizing opposition, to offering alternatives to the
movers and shakers?

Attitudes toward political activity

The most significant cause is probably that we are generally unaware of our
own ability to create and use power. Wherever there are people, there is potential power, and there is nothing mysterious about mobilizing this power.
It takes only a knowledge of the people and a willingness to take the time to
apply that knowledge for a particular purpose.

Nor is there something reprehensible about mobilizing power to
achieve desired ends, as long as the knowledge of people is not used to ma-
nipulate them, and as long as the power is not used to achieve immoral
goals. Democratic, humanistic power can move us into a future of our own
making, not one made for us by those who love power for its own sake.

Another reason why so many of us stay out of politics—either the politics of our own employing institutions or the politics of government—is that
we feel so hopeless about the possibility of making any changes. The more
complex our institutions become and the further removed we are from the
decision makers, the more we are convinced that our own feeble efforts cannot make a difference in the scheme of things. Part of this feeling stems from
our lack of knowledge of the processes of making change. But a large part
stems from feeling so overwhelmed at the enormity of the needed change that
we are too discouraged to ask the first question: How does one start?

The secret of dealing with this is to avoid contemplating the awe-
inspiring difficulty involved in "fixing" the whole world, and to concentrate
first on a subsystem close to home, where the faces of the people are recognizable and identifying processes is a manageable task.

A leader is one who has learned how power is generated, has recognized
that change is possible, and then proceeds to raise the level of consciousness
of the other people involved in the subsystem.

Lack of unity in the profession has also been a source of much breast-
beating and self-condemnation. But why? Has there ever been a large group
of people who agreed with each other on everything and worked as one to
achieve what they wanted? Especially when great change is occurring and
even greater changes are needed and contemplated, there is bound to be emotional disagreement and even internecine warfare. A part of the change process involves the working through of differences of opinion, sometimes com-

promising, sometimes holding out for one decision. But differences within the group do not preclude mobilizing to oppose the arbitrary decision-making power of those who would control us. It is a matter of rationally distinguishing between issues on which we disagree among ourselves, and the process of decision-making that must be changed to admit our active participation.

There is no doubt that leadership behavior directed toward introducing change in a situation may cause those who engage in such behavior some anxiety, guilt, and fear. Everything most of us learned as children about obeying authority, not causing disruption, being "polite" and "respectful" (whatever those terms meant to the people in charge of us) causes us to feel discomfort at resisting those in charge and demanding changes in the situation. We feel that we are once again "problem" children in school or "naughty" children at home. We have been taught that those in charge have a right to run our lives, and we are supposed to respect that right no matter how loudly our reason calls to us to question what is happening.

For those of us who are middle-class Americans, this attitude has become a cultural given: Nice people do not call attention to themselves by disrupting the status quo. Though many middle class people have rejected this precept, many still look with distaste on those who are perceived as "aggressive," "opinionated," "activist," or "militant."

Add to this all the sexist constraints put on women, and we have a powerful deterrent to political activity. Certainly, it is not "ladylike" to be aggressive and militant. It is part of the woman's role to be passive and obedient. Women do not have the ability for rational thinking. Women use feminine wiles and tears to win their points. (Even though seventy-five percent of people in the health field are women, they hold few positions of power; sexist attitudes—their own as well as those of men—have kept them at low levels in the power structure.)

So leaders, especially women leaders who wish to change current practices, are almost inevitably a prey to anxiety and guilt; they must recognize their need for help, support, and reassurance as they become involved in leadership activity.

The fear that leaders feel is often a function of what they know has happened to people who buck the system. However, as we have noted, confronting opponents with the various forms of power provides good protection against the dangers of advocating change. Often, too, in assessing the power of those in control, we overestimate their ability to do us damage; we may overestimate also their desire to hurt us. (Generally, they would prefer to co-opt our skills and energies and so neutralize them, while saving themselves.) As one radical activist has put it, "Power is not only what you have, but what the enemy thinks you have."[1]

Superimposed on these human-cultural factors discouraging leadership is the nature of traditional nursing education emphasizing obedience—

to physicians, to supervisors. Such training never suggested that political sophistication was a goal of professional education.

Unfortunately, mere awareness of the factors underlying attitudes toward political activity does not cause the attitudes to disappear. However, knowledge may give us the ability to examine our attitudes and feelings somewhat objectively, and to recognize that we share them with other individuals, other groups, and other professions. This may help us stop berating ourselves, as if we were the only ones who had these feelings and so were somehow inferior to other professions and groups.

We might then proceed to take steps to live effectively in spite of those feelings: by offering and accepting support from colleagues and others; by realizing that it is possible to survive even with feelings of anxiety, guilt, and fear (and that the longer we survive and the more successful we are in our leadership endeavors, the more are these feelings diminished); and by glorying in the fact that our behavior will save the next generation from the need to struggle with such feelings and attitudes.

The nature of political activity

What does political activity consist of? What does the nurse have to do if she is to become involved in political activity? For one thing, she must get rid of the notion that political activity is, somehow, unprofessional. Political activity is merely exercising skill in analyzing a system as it functions; identifying the objectives of the system; discriminating between the real, measurable outcomes of the system and the ideal objectives; and then determining where she can fit in most effectively to influence the changes needed in the system. Whether she becomes involved in changing the objectives of the system or moving the real outcomes closer to the ideal outcomes, she will need to know something about areas of power and influence; she will need to know where to speak, when to speak, and how to speak so that what she says will be heard and acted on.

There can be no effective political behavior on any wide scale unless the individual develops a way of working politically within his own immediate surroundings. Developing the skills and understanding how the system of which he is a part operates enables him to become a representative of his subsystem to the next higher subsystem, and then to the next higher, and so on. Eventually, through his employing institution and his professional organizations he can become effective enough on a national political level to change criteria for professional operation, for funding student scholarships, for the functioning of hospitals, or for licensing new kinds of practitioners.

If one learns Roberts' Rules of Order at a departmental faculty meeting, one can use that knowledge at the convention of a national professional organization. If one learns to assess accurately the power structure in a hospital, one can use the knowledge of how that power operates, whether in a national professional organization or in the Congress of the United States.

Knowing where, in an organization, the power resides and acquiring some of that power is the essence of both political activity and of leadership behavior. Like the meaning of political activity, the meaning of power is often misunderstood, and the idea of power is equated with using people and manipulating them for nefarious ends. But the sources of power are varied and the way power is used must determine the morality of the user. For example, there is no doubt that much power derives from the ability to force people to do what they do not wish to do and to punish them if they resist demands. If this kind of power is exercised over children by parents we see it as legitimate because, supposedly, parents know what is good for children and so should have the right to wield power over them. In this case, supposedly the good ends justify the means.

Similarly, coercion may involve making children feel shame or guilt at their behavior. Many of us are familiar with the "If you really loved me, you wouldn't act this way," ploy, calculated to rouse guilt at violating such a basic moral dictum as "You must always love your mother."

However, if we are consistently democratic in our decision making and behavior, and if we believe in the desirability of leaving people free to become self-actualizing, then the means and ends will be consistent; force and coercion are not justifiable merely because the ends are "good." Of course, as in all philosophy and human events, we must be wary of foolish consistency. The toddler who walks into moving traffic must be snatched away, regardless of his screams. Precautions must be taken to protect him while he is learning to use the available data to make the reasonable decision on his own that walking into moving traffic is not advisable; punishment is not the best way to achieve this end. The right to hem adults about with external protection on the premise that they do not yet know what is good for them is *not* a right held by any other adult. A leader is not a father, and followers are not toddlers.

Similarly, power that has its source in the ability to reward desired behavior can be as coercive and as morally questionable as the ability to punish. Here, too, what we do with children needs careful evaluation. The whole idea of rewarding children for appropriate behavior (the essence of the behavior modification approach in education) has come under some attack as manipulative. Perhaps, though, it may be justified on the basis that there is general social agreement as to the desirability of certain behaviors, and that children need to learn them if our society is to survive. On adult behaviors there is far less agreement. In addition, there is the legal precept that adults must be free to decide for themselves how they shall behave, within certain very broad limits.

These broad limits involve the basic legal philosophy on which our society rests. The legal mechanisms we have devised set the limits of our behavior based on that philosophy, and, as times and situations change, the parameters of those limits change. Thus, the law can state that a Black man has no right to use public places with White men, and that attempts to exercise such rights are subject to punishment. It has the power to back up this proscription. But the people retain the power to question the validity of this law and to change it, so even the power of the law is not absolute. It must be remembered, however, that coercive power is the law's, and does not belong to individuals. Our philosophy is clear: the law is supreme, and when there are differences between people, the law is the final arbiter. The more democratic we make the law, the more democratic will our decision-making processes be, and the more consistent our decisions will be with the human need for self-actualization.

In a job situation, where an administrator has the power to promote, or in a governmental situation, where an officeholder has the power to allocate scarce resources, the use of such power to reward those who do as they are told to do is undemocratic. The obvious goal is to change the situations so that such power does not lie in the hands of individuals. The point is that the democratic leader does not depend on this kind of power to achieve his ends.

A particular source of power that is abundantly generated in the nursing profession is sometimes known as referent power. It is power that may be said to be owned by default, because it resides in individuals by virtue of the attitudes of others. Thus, physicians have power because patients may see them as infallible in all things. They also have power because nurses defer to them and accept as their right the final decision-making function even in nonmedical matters. The nurse may have power in her relationship with patients who feel that her profession implies that she knows all there is to know, not only about patient care but about family relations and care of the aged and dying, and who follow her dicta without question. To unquestioningly follow a professional's recommendations is to assign her power by default.

The kind of power most consistent with democracy, self-actualization and rational thinking is the power that comes from knowledge and expert skill. The person with relevant knowledge and skill can provide data and strategy necessary for solving problems. He also relies upon skill in teaching to help others develop needed knowledge and skill. Such a leader's relationship with his constituency, then, is a reciprocal one, as he learns from them what they need and want and as they learn from him what he knows. Together, they move toward mutually desired goals.

Some individuals with knowledge and expertise are not successful in becoming leaders. This is why it is so important for the knowledgeable person also to be a good teacher and skillful in communication. Without teaching and communication skills, he may be forced to sit by and watch the coercive uses of power and power by default cause an unqualified person to be enthusiastically followed up the garden path.

The political leader and her constituency

At all levels of political functioning, the effective leader will not be the one who is merely voted into representative office or one who has been hired as a supervisor or administrator. She is the one who keeps in touch with her constituency and continuously uses the feedback she gets to define her constituency's position and incorporate the experience of the people she is representing into identifying and achieving objectives.

When difficulties arise, when bars are put in the way of change, the leader who has been in constant touch with her constituency can draw on the power of the people she represents to support her in a number of very practical ways. They may meet on a local level, pile into buses and descend on the state capital, or help to buy advertising time to justify a position to the public.

If she is aware of the range of differences within her constituency, she can develop a systematic, organized approach to the solution of problems. This requires not compromise so much as an understanding of the broader principles upon which the people are willing to function. A clear definition of those broader principles can encompass, in a varied constituency, a great many differences in approaches, in ideas, and in solutions to current problems. The leader must be totally committed to those principles in order to operate effectively as a leader. Otherwise, she will vacillate from principle to conflicting principle, from one value-implicit approach to another, in order to satisfy the individual idiosyncrasies that are a part of any constituency. However, if she is committed to the essential principles, she will know when pressure to act in a certain way or to adopt a particular objective is inconsistent with those principles. And she can, in all integrity, refuse to go along. As long as she can connect her decision to consistency with a basic principle, she is on solid ground.

When enough of the constituency reject these basis principles, of course, she is no longer effective as a leader and should not be the leader of such a constituency.

This does not mean that, if an individual finds herself in a group whose principles and values she does not share, that she should abandon attempts to lead the group or that she should leave it altogether. A large part of the leadership function is to communicate successfully to the group what the leader knows so that ultimately the group will reexamine its principles and values and make a decision to change. If the leader is successful, the group will identify its objectives in terms of this new knowledge and will incorporate the leader's knowledge and skill into its problem-solving processes.

In the history of communication between leader and followers, the leader may learn things from the group that require him to modify his own principles and values. Both leader and followers must continue to examine the bases for their thinking and acting, must continue to learn more about their own and each other's motivations, must clarify their values and add to their knowledge from advances in the different disciplines. All of this must go on in an atmosphere of candor, openness, and mutual support in the painful process of self-examination.

It is not unusual for people in positions of leadership to decide that this or that piece of knowledge should be kept from the constituency in the interest of progress, safety, or some other expediency. Not only is the very concept of secrecy by leaders antithetical to the concept of self-actualization, but there are some very real dangers associated with its practice:

1. Secrets are usually badly kept. Though it has become part of our sexist culture to attribute the inability to keep a secret only to women, the obvious fact is that in institutions controlled by men, such as the United States government, "secrets" are forever coming to light.

    It would not be quite so detrimental if it were merely that information invariably leaked out. In the process of coming to light, information is almost invariably distorted, and what people come to "know" are different versions of the secret. So the accurate information vital for people's planning and decision making is lacking, with the inevitable effects on the quality of the decisions being made.

2. The keeping of secrets reduces the level of trust in a constituency, not only in the general public but also in the inner circle of the privileged. Just knowing that secrets are being kept from others makes the privileged individuals maneuver to retain their privileged status, forever fearful that they may lose that status at the whim of those who are more powerful. This kind of maneuvering and distrust is what many people think of when they hear the word politics; it is this sort of situation that makes many people avoid political involvement as something distasteful and beneath them.

3. The keeping of secrets encourages and reinforces adversary relationships between people on different sides of an issue. The aim then becomes to keep knowledge from the other side rather than to inform everyone involved so that decision making may be based on the best available knowledge. The more we persist in adversary relationships, the less likely are we to view issues as matters for problem solving, rather than for attack and defense, for winning or losing. A curious example of this becomes apparent in our legal system: Presumably, a trial is for the purpose of bringing all knowledge (evidence) to light, so that the truth of a matter can be determined. In reality, however, a trial becomes a contest between two lawyers, who do whatever they can to win and to cause the other side to lose; not infrequently, this involves keeping pertinent information from the other side. As a society, we probably lose more often than we win in our legal confrontations.

It sometimes seems as if our ultimate reliance on war to resolve problems influences our whole approach to problem-solving and change, so that we begin, at the outset, to view change as a process of beating the enemy. We approach the change process as we do a war, determined to win and to cause the enemy to lose. Since we will all feel the effects of any change, we had better get everyone involved in learning and problem-solving, or—win or lose—we will be doomed to spend our lives in a system menaced by enemies.

Opportunities for Political Leadership

Political activity and political leadership may take place at every level of organization, from the small, as-yet-unorganized group of people at one end of a floor, to the top level of political organization, the United Nations. It may be necessary to organize a group of like-minded people in order to effect change, or it may be necessary to become active in a well-organized group, utilizing existing mechanisms to introduce new ideas and change behaviors. Wherever you find yourself, there is opportunity for political leadership. It remains only to assess the situation realistically and then to remember some general procedures for effective political action.

Employing institutions

Political action in hospitals or other social agencies deals primarily with influencing changes in policies, and then using those policies as reference points for effecting changes in practices so that they are consistent with the stated policies. Whatever the problem is in what seems like a limited area of the institution, involving few people, the chances are that it has some institution-wide causes. Therefore, it is an essential function of the leader to help people make the connection between their immediate interest or concern and the wider condition.

However, it is first necessary to get the people who have a focus of complaint or interest to meet with each other to discuss their problems. People may be reluctant to commit themselves to a meeting; the time to get them to do so must be strategically chosen. Generally, if an incident has occurred that is related to informally articulated complaints, it is a propitious time to suggest that all those concerned meet to discuss the incident. People can begin to see that voicing their complaints in a group not only provides more catharsis and satisfaction than individual, isolated griping, but it can lead to planning for changing the situation.

Though personal charisma is probably not sufficient to cause people to follow an individual for very long, a friendly, well liked leader has a better chance of convincing people that coming to a meeting will be worthwhile for them.

If the situation has been accurately assessed, one or two who have power and influence in the upper echelons of the organization and who share the concerns of the group will have been identified. The leader may contact these individuals and get their cooperation in providing a suitable meeting place. A person in power may act as the communication link between the group and the administration. He may even be asked to attend subsequent meetings and participate in the planning for change. It is a mistake to assume that any work group concerned with improving the quality of its service has no support from any of the power people in the organization. The group must not, however, rely on that person to take the initiative for making the change. Chances are that he is somewhat cushioned, by virtue of his position, from feeling the discomfort caused by the need for change; those who are hurting are most likely to persist in their efforts until their goal is achieved. Also, though he may have power in the organization, there are others who also have power and he will need the support of the group in his attempts to influence those others.

What the leader and the group must be wary of is any attempt to make them compromise with essentials. Those who are powerful, comfortable, and out of the line of fire (in that they are not performing the basic services for which the institution is designed) almost inevitably find it easier to postpone change, even while they claim commitment to the need for it. The classic example of this differential perception of groups ostensibly committed to the same objective is the matter of racial equality. At one point in our recent history, Black people said, "We have had enough. We want our rights *now*! We want to vote now. We want equal access to public accommodations now. We want equal education now." It is amazing how many so-called liberals who claimed to believe in equality, were able to demur at the demands, to temporize about how unrealistic it was to expect change overnight, to advise patience. Only someone at some remove from the anguish of the situation could, in effect, counsel a Black person to wait for the right to vote: "So, maybe you won't get the chance to vote. But your children probably will. Be patient."

When an influential individual agrees to help the group—by providing a meeting place, for example, or permitting time off from work for a meeting—and then changes his mind and does not follow through on his offer, there is a danger that the morale of the group may plummet, and that the original enthusiasm for meeting will disappear. It is safer to plan for alternative meeting places and times so that the group does not fall to pieces at the news that the expected support is not forthcoming. The rescinding of help provides additional information about the situation.

It is important, when a leader and those following his lead complain about a policy or a practice, that they have in mind a constructive alternative before they begin to establish communication with supervisors and administrators. This requires that those with the complaint meet and work together for the time it takes to arrive at a usable alternative. If this is not done, there is danger that the choice of alternative will be left to the administrator, who may choose it without checking it against the information and opinions of the people affected. The resulting situation may be no better, and may even be worse, than the one that caused the original complaint.

Much of the literature on organizational management, as well as the codes of professional practice, emphasize the importance of "going through channels" when one wishes to communicate dissatisfaction with the working situation. However, there are pragmatic factors in the experience of social and institutional change that suggest that it is often far more expedient to bypass the lower organizational echelons and go right to the top to make your communication.

Limiting complaints, protests, and suggestions for change only to immediate superiors undoubtedly helps to maintain the established order of the organization, the status quo. The communication may never get any further than the immediate superior; if she has neither the wish nor the power to make a change, the effort has been wasted.

Information may also undergo change as it is filtered through the individual cautions and needs of the supervisor. It is likely that the intensity of delivery may be reduced; the feeling of urgency of the protestors may be lost. Unless the supervisor has been part of the group's deliberations, has contributed to the process of arriving at the group's decision, and has offered to represent the group before the administration, it is wiser for the group to do more than just turn over the responsibility to her. Additional steps should be taken to publicize the group's position and reduce the danger of miscommunication.

For example, the group might write a position statement, undersigned by everyone who subscribes to it. A copy of it might be given to the supervisor acting as the link with the administration, so as to reduce the possibility of distortion. Copies of the statement could be shown to colleagues by group members in the course of informal conversations.

The statement need not be hostile or intrinsically threatening in tone; it need only express a need and a desire to address that need. It may be couched in the language of a newsletter, to keep others in the organization aware of the activities of the group. It may even result in the recruitment of more members, though it should be borne in mind that it may also result in attempts to stop the group's activities.

Ignoring "channels" and taking a group's suggestions for change right to the top may outrage the proponents of "law and order," and lower-level proponents of the status quo. Lower-level personnel may not have a grasp of the whole structure of the institution, and so may make their decisions on the basis of insufficient information. Also, experience has taught us that these "reluctant gatekeepers" often interpret the policies of institutions to coincide with their own beliefs and values, and they attribute these same values to the top administrators. Though they are not always in error in their attribution, they sometimes are. Communication with the top level, then, may result in change that lower level people are reluctant to permit.

A rather mundane example of the value of bypassing the lower levels is in consumer affairs. Complaints to an automobile dealer about a defect that should be remedied can be ignored in the face of anger, tears, and threats. But a short note to the president of the company that manufactured the car (and that distributes the dealerships) can prompt a call from the dealer offering to replace the defective part free of charge.

In a hospital, the nursing service supervisor may resist all attempts by the other nurses to discuss with her the validity of their making assessments and judgments for the Professional Services Review Organization while they are not permitted to participate in the PSRO at the policy level. In her opinion, policy making is for physicians and administrators, and she has never questioned the fact that she has never been asked to sit in board meetings and provide the information that she has and that the board needs to make hospital policy. Such a supervisor, it seems to me, must be bypassed if any change is to be achieved. The concerned group that sends a representative to the PSRO chairperson and asks for time at the meeting to present its case may very well get a hearing and some encouragement to pursue the efforts for change.

Professional organizations

Participating actively in professional organizations contributes to the process of social and professional change by increasing the political power of the profession, and so may be defined as leadership behavior. However, such participation can also provide impetus for developing mechanisms to encourage leadership behavior in individual members of the profession.

For example, built into conferences and conventions at local, state, and national levels should be work sessions designed to provide nurse leaders with the support they need to strengthen their resolve, refine their leadership skills, and fulfill other needs that nurse leaders are discovering as they struggle to effect change. Jacox and Norris suggest that "It might be that consultation clinics for nurse practitioners would be a useful component for meetings of organized nursing at state and local levels."[2] Their idea is that practitioners can, in such clinics, present some of their cases for peer review, something they have great difficulty obtaining in their home situations. I might add that such peer review clinics could reduce the feeling of being alone and unsupported in leadership positions, and provide the leader needed reassurance that she is operating effectively.

But such practical instruments for encouraging leadership need not be limited to peer review clinics for independent practitioners. Consultation clinics for presenting other kinds of leadership attempts might prove of value. Nurses could get feedback on their effectiveness and further help in planning for change. For example, a nursing supervisor might present her plan for changing her unit over from team nursing to primary nursing, and get input from clinic participants on pitfalls and additional information she needs to be successful. Another nurse might ask for suggestions to get started on a plan for changing the pattern of interaction between nurses, physicians, and other staff people in a hospital from one of hierarchical relationships to more democratic, autonomous relationships.

Such instruments would have to be quite different from the usual kinds of sessions prevailing at professional organization meetings. That is, they could not be held in rooms where, for an hour or two, registrants would sit and listen to speeches and have an opportunity to ask a question or two or make a corroboratory comment.

Nor would the usual "small-group discussions" that so often follow speeches serve the purpose. These would have to be highly-structured sessions with a limited number of people, all of whom have prepared in advance for the planned presentations, so that those requesting the consultations can come away with some solid input that they can immediately put to practical use.

This is not to suggest that the usual speeches and small-group discussions at professional conclaves have no use. On the contrary, information on the state of the profession, opportunity for catharsis for pent-up frustrations, and encouragement for continuing the fight are three important gains for participants. However, peer review leadership clinics can help more directly in developing the leadership potential in the profession.

Volunteering to work on the planning committee for a professional meeting is a leadership initiative. A committee member, for example, may introduce the idea of having a leadership clinic and so provide the support for and education in leadership that is so needed. This one idea may change the nature of all future professional meetings for that organization.

One cannot readily provide political leadership in the profession unless one is an active member of a professional organization. (There are exceptions to this, of course. If a nurse is on the staff of a government health agency or is an elected representative to the local, state, or national lawmaking body, there are opportunities for providing leadership in the area of health service delivery. However, even in such circumstances, the effective law-maker or government official who is not in touch with what is happening in the professional organization is probably not in a position to know what the concerns and needs of the profession are.)

For those nurses who work in local health care facilities and want to exercise some leadership in the profession, being an active member of a professional organization is mandatory. Witness, for example, the work accomplished at a recent meeting of the House of Delegates of the Alabama State Nurses Association.

It passed resolutions on the entry level for professional nursing, mandatory continuing education, the status of the association as a labor organization, and the development of sound personnel practices in employing agencies.

The BSN was endorsed as the entry level to professional nursing practice for the future. A detailed study is now being conducted to assess the availability and accessibility of educational programs for nurses interested in obtaining the BS degree and of ways to implement the change.

A resolution was also approved to direct the association's legislative committee to seek legislation by 1984 that would require not more than 15 contact hours of continuing education for RN relicensure in Maryland.

Focusing on the nursing shortage, the delegates passed a set of Recommended Employment Standards for Registered Nurses in employing agencies. By doing this, they reaffirmed a belief that recruitment and retention of qualified nurses is dependent to a large extent upon the development and administration of sound personnel practices in employing agencies.

The recommended employment standards note that nurses have a responsibility to promote and maintain educational advancement and work together with organizations to secure the best possible nursing care for all people.

Recommended standards include the following:

• Salaries and benefits comparable to those of employees in other fields in the community.

• Time off and leaves of absence to attend education programs, conferences, and seminars.

• Regular channels of communication between nurses and management for salary administration, review of personnel policies, program planning, and implementation and evaluation of such policies and programs.

• Nurse input in written job descriptions.

• Job titles that reflect the responsibilities of and qualifications for each job.

During the convention, a resolution submitted months before requesting that the association be decertified as a labor organization was withdrawn. The issue had caused heated debate throughout Alabama prior to the convention.[3]

Consider the effects on the profession in Alabama of the decisions made during this meeting, and the effects on the profession nationally. If you disagree with the idea that the professional organization should also be considbered a labor organization, then your opinion was not heard as long as you had no part in the discussions and deliberations that led to the final decision. If you believe that the decision has a direct effect on your professional functioning, as do those who argued on both sides of the issue, and you had no part in it, then in a very real way you permitted others to run your life. You may have been able to present an illustration from your own experience or make a point in such a way as to change the balance in the debate. In discussing the issue with other nurses in your unit, you may have heard a cogent reason given that you might have communicated if you had been a delegate to the state body. You may have started the train of thinking at the meeting that resulted in a completely different decision. Without fireworks or some mystic charisma you could have changed the course of history. All that was required was that you be there. In most professional organizations, it takes little more effort than an announcement of willingness to win an election as a delegate.

Participating in local and state professional organizations inevitably enables one to influence the decisions made at the national meetings. For example, when the ANA Commission on Nursing Education is charged with presenting reports at a national convention, it calls on state and local groups to send representatives to discuss the preliminary reports. At these discussions, suggestions are made for modifications in the reports; these suggestions are brought by the representatives from their constituencies. Those who have voiced opinions at local meetings as well as the representatives to the national discussions all provide input for the final report. At the national convention where the final report is presented, there is still opportunity for influencing delegates to make changes in it. Keeping your opinion to yourself or griping to your best friend seems ludicrous when political activity can be almost as easy, and much more satisfying.

Unless one is involved in a professional organization, it is virtually impossible to keep track of the hundreds of bills that can affect health care, and to provide nursing input to lawmakers responsible for refining those bills and voting them into law. The American Nursing Association maintains an office in Washington with full-time lobbyists to influence legislation. If one does not work to influence the decision of ANA, then national planning and decision making go on without one's ideas and concerns being included; an organization that purports to represent the profession actually may be representing only those whose voices are heard.

The National League for Nursing is a tax-exempt organization, and so cannot lobby. However, it does provide information to legislators. Such information, again, does not include the perceptions and ideas of those who are not involved in the ongoing deliberations of NLN.

Much is written about continuing education for nurses, but little is said about the implications for continuing education in involvement in the affairs of professional organizations. There is information about changing current practices to be obtained from people in a variety of positions working in different geographical areas. There is heightened awareness to be achieved from sharing the experiences of individuals who are striking off in new directions. There are skills to be refined by watching others' behavior in groups and practicing one's own. There is strength to be gained from giving and receiving support from colleagues—strength without which there is no effective professional functioning. In what course in a university, in what seminar for continuing education can one get so much opportunity for learning and for growth?

Involvement in professional organizations is important even for reasons that may, on the surface, appear trivial and mundane. For example, the American Nurses' Foundation announces the creation of a nurse researcher award. If nurses are unaware of this new development, the nurses in one's own institution or region who are doing research may go unheralded and unsupported except for the few nurses in their immediate area who know and appreciate what they are doing. In addition, most nurses will never know how many of their colleagues are actively struggling to push back the frontiers of knowledge in the profession. Just having nurses unaware of the award is a loss to the profession. Attending the meeting where the award was announced, or reading the professional journal where the announcement was published, or being a member of the committee where the decision was made to issue the award all constitute different levels of political activity that contribute to the development and stature of the profession.

In the education of nurses, strong orientation in organizational affairs can set the pattern for future involvement in the governance of the profession. Students involved in the National Student Nurses' Association have an opportunity to develop political sophistication even while they are taking a hand in controlling their own lives. If their teachers are involved in political activity they can build into the education program mechanisms for testing ideas, practicing skills, and sharing perspectives that will help prepare their students for involvement after graduation.

Educational institutions

In 1976, the Center for Nursing was established at the University of Southern Mississippi as an "intellectual arena" for nursing students, professional nurse practitioners, and nurse researchers. In 1979, it was proposed to establish a National Center for Excellence in Nursing at the Rush-Presbyterian-St. Luke's Medical Center in Chicago ". . . to facilitate the selection of future leaders in nursing . . . and to provide recognized leaders in the nursing profession an opportunity to study, do research, and teach . . ."[4]

Not only do such centers serve the profession by providing opportunities to develop and practice leadership skills, but they also serve a particularly useful purpose in the institutions where they are established. Faculty and students in university schools of nursing often are not part of the professional communication network. Though deans receive information from professional organizations about legislation and other professional concerns, they do not always send that information along to faculty and students.

A hospital administrator may receive new research data and information on changes in technology and thinking, but may not share the information with staff nurses. Thus, data that are important for effective leadership behavior never get to those who might be moved to act as leaders.

Similarly, deans and administrators do not often communicate new data about nursing to other university administrators, who are thus unaware of new developments in the profession and may make administrative decisions on the basis of outmoded knowledge and concepts.

A nursing center, highly visible in the university setting to all components of the university, including its affiliated hospitals, can do much to keep the vital information flowing to all concerned persons. There are many potential leaders who, if they knew all that was going on, would find a place for themselves where they could make their ideas known.

Citizen policy and planning boards

If nurses are to emphasize health maintenance as a primary goal of the profession—as opposed to curing disease which is the medical goal—then they must be closely involved with other citizens in their various planning and policy making activities. Moloney observes that nurse leaders are reluctant "to use their power to inform the public . . . about the concerns of nursing in its efforts to bring about quality health care."[5] She suggests that it is because nurse leaders are not familiar with the political, economic and social issues involved. I would suggest that it is because, like most practitioners in other professions, they (a) do not realize that it is the public that ultimately decides how a profession will practice and (b) believe it is, somehow, *infra dig* to debate professional matters with "lay people."

Even before the advent of the War on Poverty, it should have been clear to more of us that the recipients of our services inevitably defined the parameters of our practice and determined the success or failure of our efforts. There is not one service profession that has not finally had to come to grips with the evidence of its own massive failures to achieve its goals. The teaching profession knows that, for most children, the education system has failed. (Some teachers believe that where people succeed in becoming educated they do so *in spite of* teachers and schools.) All the "burned-out" social workers know very well that their contribution to the improvement of the quality of life has not materially changed that quality. And no one knows better than nurses that day-to-day health care delivery has not improved the nation's health.

If we were to identify a single overarching cause of this universal failure—or, at least, absence of notable success—I think it would be that the consumers, the recipients of all this service, have not permitted that service to become optimally-functioning aspects of their lives. They have rejected prescriptions formulated without sufficient information about them, but they have not insisted that human services deliverers seek additional information. They have ignored advice without demanding that advisors help them develop the skills they need in order to use the advice. At the same time they have fostered the belief in professionals that they are all-knowing and so awe-inspiring that they are to be listened to with unquestioning respect.

The War on Poverty gave extraordinary impetus to the involvement of citizens in policy making and planning for change. Though our national political heritage includes a belief in democratic participation, in actual practice (especially as our population increases, our government grows in size, and our technology becomes more and more complex) the political involvement of the general population has continued to decrease, and citizen power has been eroded. The Economic Opportunities Act articulated a belief that the problems associated with poverty could more effectively be attacked and poverty more expeditiously be eliminated if poor people were themselves involved in identifying the relevant issues and planning for the solutions to the problems.

The same period of history has seen the spread of the belief that people have the right to make the decisions that affect their lives. It is a belief that reduces reliance on the omniscient expert, and relegates him to the role of providing the information that he has for use in the problem-solving process, a process in which those affected by the solutions are active participants.

Even children, who are among the least powerful members of the population, are currently believed by many to have rights that should not be violated, even in the name of parental love. Children are also being encouraged to participate actively in the decision-making, problem-solving systems in their lives.

Some of the most articulate proponents of this philosophy have been members of the health care professions. Given the name The New Professionals by some writers,[6] they believe that the consumer has the right to be fully informed and, on the basis of that information, to make the decisions that affect his life.

Though we are a long way from full citizen participation in all aspects of decision making, the consumer movement is too powerful to be stopped, and the glib professional observation (heard in some form in *all* professions) that the consumer doesn't know what is good for him is evidence of an outmoded commitment to paternalism and exploitation.

It is, of course, part of a realistic assessment of people to recognize that we are not always in possession of the available pertinent information and that our use of the information we do have is often circumscribed by prejudices, anxieties, and disabilities in thinking. The new professional, then, must commit herself to filling in the gaps in information and helping people become more skillful in using that information. This cannot be done without interaction with citizens in decision-making situations.

The law that provides for setting up local Health Systems Agencies made up of health care providers is where most local planning for health care delivery goes on. Though nurses are involved in these agencies, it is not known just how many there are because, in counting members, the Department of Health, Education and Welfare lumped nurses with other health and allied health professionals.

It is at the meetings of the Health Systems Agencies that local concerns are voiced and decisions made about what is needed in the health care area. If hospital and other agency administrators are neglecting to appoint a fair number of nurses—and not just nurse administrators—to the agencies, it is time that staff nurses requested appointment. The rationale for such a request is not difficult to define: Nurses are in the best position to know how effectively current delivery systems are working. They are daily faced with the frustrations of unmet needs, of people who need help and are not getting it, of efforts that are wastefully duplicated, and of expensive machinery that goes unused.

The consumers in the HSA's are natural partners with nurses, for, while consumers can recount their individual anxieties, frustrations, and needs, nurses can round out that information with corroborative data accumulated in their close contact with many consumers. They can lend scientific credibility to the data from their professional knowledge of health care provision. If there are not enough working nurses on the HSA's, then health care planning systems are seriously defective.

Boards made up of "lay people" are running hospitals, universities, and community health care institutions. They make up part of the membership of local, regional, and national bodies planning improved service delivery, urban renewal, and rural industrial development. They sit on policy councils for improving human services delivery of all kinds.

It is amazing that nurses are almost never members of such planning and policy boards, even when the board happens to be making policy for a particular hospital in which nurses make up the largest part of the staff. If our democratic heritage and our developing philosophy of self-actualization lends credence to the practice of controlling one's own life, how is it that nurses are still permitting the decisions in their lives to be made by boards of trustees and community councils that include no nurses?

Nurses have a real leadership role to play in convincing other professionals of the value and importance of involving citizens in the planning and policy making for health care delivery. Too often, the attitude among managers of health care facilities (not always *themselves* health care professionals!) is exemplified by a recent article by Steckler and Herzog.[7] In it, the authors call citizen boards a fad and give advice on how to neutralize them.

In the light of what we believe about self-actualization and autonomy, and in the light of what we know about the limited effectiveness of human service delivery, this viewpoint is truly myopic. However, it is consistent with the maintenance of institutional hierarchies, and the conviction that "we" always know better than "they" what is good for them.

On planning and policy boards, nurses may have opportunities to interact with other health professionals and to help them become aware of the changing role of nursing in health care. They, in turn, may bring the message to their own professional organizations, to other departments of the university, and to other professionals on hospital staffs.

For example, a physician sitting on a local citizens' planning board meets another board member, a nurse, and hears from her about the success in the community of a nurse practitioner who is providing primary health care. Some of the other citizens on the board speak with enthusiasm about the great need being fulfilled by the nurse practitioner, and express the hope that·they can attract additional practitioners to fill the community gaps in health maintenance, health education, and health counseling. The physician, until now unaware of the community's enthusiastic acceptance of the nurse practitioner, brings this information to the next meeting of his local medical association. Though there are sporadic attempts by individuals to stop the nurse from practicing what they call "medicine," the attempts come to nothing. Other physicians, approached by nurses to accept referrals from them, are not taken by surprise, and are able to express interest in the work of the nurses. They may begin to reevaluate their expectations of the nurse's role in health care.

The World Health Organization, examining the need for more and better primary health care in Latin America, urges that sanctioning of the nurse's new role be speeded up by fostering "awareness of this need in the professional associations."[8] Given the general lack of opportunity that nurses have to speak to other professional organizations, it would seem that sharing membership on citizens boards with other professionals can supply the communication link with those organizations, and provide them with the new knowledge about nursing.

If it is true, as Jacox and Norris maintain that there are those who ". . . are afraid that nurses will use their power to move the discipline ahead in terms of prestige and national influence rather than moving ahead in terms of health care delivery . . ."[9] then it would seem that participating in the decision-making of citizen boards can put that fear to rest where it exists. If there is anyone on the board who is afraid ". . . that nursing may be more interested in its own benefit than in public need," the contributions of the nurse to the board's deliberations can make it clear that nurses are concerned with improving the quality of life. An actively involved and articulate nurse can convince the board that nurses are prepared to help identify the health needs of the community in terms of factors that go beyond the identification and cure of disease and include environmental concerns, lifestyle influences on health, and the quality of education. There is a growing body of evidence that, as people become aware of the true scope and nature of nursing, they are enthusiastically accepting what the profession has to offer.[10]

Professional organizations generally keep themselves informed about new planning and policy groups being formed, and active participation in the organization will provide information for individual members who wish to volunteer to serve on the boards or who wish to recommend colleagues for such service. Also, being involved in community organizations and activities puts one into the communication system for learning that boards are about to be formed. There is no reason why an active, informed nurse cannot write a letter to a government official and let him know that she is qualified and prepared to serve. Those in power who select individuals to serve on committees and boards really do not enter upon a scientific process for evaluating all potential selectees and deciding upon the best. Rather, they choose those who are in the same communication system with them. So if they hear from a person directly, or hear about a person from someone in their system, that person is considered for appointment. Putting one's name into the system may be all that is needed.

Action in local government

Not so long ago, a local politician running for the state legislature asked me to write a paper on education that outlined the education needs of the community and pointed out areas needing change. He used the paper as the education plank in his campaign. Why did he ask me to write the paper? Only because I had served with his campaign manager on a neighborhood school committee, and he had heard some of my ideas. If there had also been a nurse on that committee, she might have been asked to provide ideas for improving health care in the community.

The point is that political involvement is a natural concomitant of community involvement. The nurse who recognizes the importance of working with the community in which she practices her profession can easily develop communication links with those who make the decisions and pass the laws. The process is neither mysterious nor esoteric, it merely takes a commitment of a certain amount of time and energy. If you are a professional, you already have the knowledge and skill. You realize that you cannot utilize the knowledge and skill to the best effect if you do not maintain ties to the community in which you practice.

Local politicians are always interested in having people help them when they are running for office. Volunteering such help even if, initially, it is for mundane chores that do not require your professional skills can bring you closer to the ear of the candidate.

Getting to know the ward leader in the community is very easy to do; the ward leader's strength comes from his contacts in the community. It is through the ward leader that you can become aware of the local political process—the meetings of party members, the committees for gathering information on local attitudes and needs, even the arguments about who should run for a particular office. Again, there is nothing mysterious about the process, though you may discover that the most powerful people are not always the ones who hold political office. The name that may come up most frequently may be that of the president of the bank or the chairman of the board of a local corporation. A letter to this person about the need to include health care planning on the agenda of a planning council may not only get your suggestion on the agenda, but also get you appointed to the council.

City and state health departments are political entities. A good way to make initial contact with a department is to make a request for some information that they are empowered to gather. It may be information that is needed by a citizens' group of which you are a member, for example. You can get to know the person who provides the information and, in the process, inform her of the work your citizens' group is doing. When the department needs a pipeline into the community for disseminating or collecting information then your group may be contacted *because someone in the health department has heard of it.*

When a committee of professionals is to be formed by the department for some purpose, such as writing new guidelines for health care delivery, your name will also be known and perhaps you will be chosen to serve on the committee.

Obviously, not all communication lines put out to local politicians and political appointees stay open. However, the more such lines you put out, the more chances you have that someone at the other end will return the call. When people maintain that it's whom you know that matters, they fall somewhat short of a realistic assessment of political and social involvement. More often than not it is who knows your name, who has met you at a meeting and talked with you, who has received a number of letters and calls from you, who has heard your name mentioned several times in the context of health care delivery.

Action in national government

There is no nurse on the National Health Planning Council. There is not one nurse with a political appointment in Washington. Perhaps this situation will change in the near future. Certainly the opportunities being provided by the National League for Nursing for nursing students to spend time in government offices learning how they work are producing nurses who are knowledgeable about national political and administrative processes and are sharing their knowledge with other members of the profession.

However, at the present time, there is great pressure because of economic conditions that make money hard to get, and pressing health care needs that persist to find creative solutions to improving the quality of health care delivery. Jeffrey Merrill, Director of the Health Care Financing Administration of the Department of Health, Education and Welfare in 1979, said that his agency was ". . . committed to a new focus on primary care." He goes on to say ". . . it means the participation by other people in the decision-making process." And he asks that nurses, for example, give input to the Congress and to the agency from their different perspectives. He decries the fact that physicians continue to dominate the decision-making process, and that "nurses have always been viewed somewhat as outsiders . . ."[11]

It would seem that the 205 regional Health Systems Agencies, set up by national law, would be an ideal medium for providing input to national administrators and lawmakers. The concerns of local care providers and consumers, systematically fed to the Department of Human Services, can provide a wealth of data for planning and legislation at the national level.

As Leda Judd points out:

> The emphasis by this Administration and others is on cost containment. When health care issues are debated in Washington, there is no talk about accessibility or need or equality or underserved populations. Washington talks about money and how to keep the spending down. Very few voices are heard on the other side of the debate, and that is a very serious lack. We may become so cost conscious that we will devise a very efficient system that will not provide the level of care that is needed or serve the people who need it most. I think nurses have a vital role to play; they add to this debate the voice of the person who is out there delivering the care, who understands the needs of the people, who understands what it means to be in trouble or in pain and who have a need for compassionate care. If the voice of nurses doesn't bring these concerns to the debate, then I submit to you where will it come from?[12]

One area of political leadership and intervention in national decision making occurs in administrative agencies by people who use their professional expertise as staff members in government agencies. According to Barbara S. Christy, "Nurses working in federal agencies have opportunities . . . to influence the ways that program goals are perceived and the purposes defined. Suggesting and working on model legislation, expressing concerns and sharing information during planning meetings, drafting regulations and influencing the vigor with which program objectives are pursued are . . . ways by which nurses employed within the executive branch can have impact on the goals and programs of an agency."[13]

Christy makes an interesting point that those who have not worked in government agencies may be unaware of. She reminds us that there are always members of the public who request information and raise questions about programs that a nurse is best able to answer. "Every nurse who has ever answered a patient's questions following a physician's explanation to the patient can identify with the need for an interpreter role in health care, and the same need applies to the federal government."[14] If, as we have noted earlier, the interpretation/education function constitutes leadership behavior in other settings, then it does, too, in this one.

Political Problems in Nursing

The problems that nurses are concerned with involve not only the continued development of the profession, but are intimately related to the improvement of the quality of life for all people. There are problems that require pressure and planning for social change, some local and minor and some on national and international levels. Other problems require only convincing an individual supervisor or administrator of the advisability of instituting a new practice or eliminating an old one. But wherever problems need solving in institutional and social settings, political action is required of those who care enough and are willing to assume leadership.

The following matters crop up again and again in the literature of the nursing profession. Most nurses can also give personal evidence that members of the profession are concerned with them. I present them here primarily to make clear the connections between professional concerns and broader social concerns. The more clearly these connections are perceived by all people, the more easily will alliances be made—between professionals and other citizens, among people from different professions, between management personnel and those they manage—to deal collaboratively with those concerns and achieve objectives that are beneficial to all.

Maintaining professional independence

The problem in today's world is not one that involves choosing between independence and subservience. If this were the choice, it would be an easy one, especially if our frame of reference in individual development is the striving for self-actualization. The real problem is maintaining a productive balance between independence and interdependence, as individuals and as professionals.

While it makes no sense for physicians to regulate the practice of nurses, neither does it make sense for nurses and physicians to work apart from each other. Continuing communication between the two professions is needed to check on each other's changing perceptions of illness and wellness, to collaboratively shift the areas of responsibility from one to the other as needs are redefined and technological and human resources change, to offer skills and knowledge to one another, and to struggle together to solve human problems.

However, this kind of communication and collaboration is not possible between groups of unequal status and of differential power, except in relatively rare, isolated instances between individuals.

To suggest that the problem can be resolved by having nurses insist on complete political and economic independence in isolation from doctors is to try to pick up past history and have the profession of nursing very rapidly recapitulate the development of the medical profession. Since the history of medicine was not a planned one, and its current practice and organization hardly the most efficacious one for optimum public health, what sense does it make to repeat the same errors?

Nursing has the benefit of all we have learned in recent years about human functioning, all we have come to believe about self-determination and autonomy, all that we find good about honesty and interdependence. Surely, in the quest for professional independence, we can find better models than the traditional ones.

At the same time, a nurse who practices in an area where there are no other health practitioners has a right to be reimbursed for her services by the same government sources that would reimburse a physician or a teacher. Often, what is required is political activity, especially in rural areas with unique problems. A nurse may be licensed to practice under state law and under the same state's law not be covered for reimbursable services. Such conflict requires that legislators be informed, and that nurses make opportunities for themselves to serve in policy-making positions.

A nurse who is part of a health care organization has a right to assert herself as an independent professional; to raise questions about policy and procedure from the vantage point of her professional knowledge and expertise; and to resist the expectations of others that she is absolved of responsibility because she follows orders.

The rights of women are also inextricably bound up with the rights of nurses, as long as women make up such a large part of the nursing profession. As a society we are still trying to overcome the debilities of generations of sexism, and those nurses who are women have a right to keep denying that the stereotype of the female of the species is an accurate picture of them. They need not defer intellectually to men, no matter what their professions are.

Third party payment

The whole matter of independent practice and fees for service is far from settled. Some lawmakers criticize the emphasis practitioners are putting on their demands for equitable third party payments, as if independent nursing practice were somehow less deserving of a fair fee than independent medical practice. Before we arrive at total government health insurance, decisions must be made in the matter of payment for nursing care delivery. It is likely that, if the law does not provide for complete third party payment for nursing care, not only will nurse practitioners continue to have great difficulty in maintaining their independence, but something even more basic will be perpetuated. That is the continuing emphasis in health care delivery on the treatment of disease, and the neglect of health maintenance and education for health maintenance. The chances are, too, that nursing's attempts to focus on changing the nature and quality of health care delivery to neglected groups will stay at a minimal level, as nurses are compelled to adjust their practice to the parameters of established medical institutions.

It has been suggested that clients need to have opportunities to learn what nursing has to offer before they will seek out nursing service and be willing to pay for it. Also, only when they have experienced nursing care (outside of the traditional institutional care) will they, as an electorate and as consumers, demand payment under public and private insurance provisions. The profession is urged, then, to consider means for financing nurses who want their own practices until there is general acceptance of such practice.[15]

This kind of financing, encouraging as it does new models of health care delivery, can set a precedent for encouraging those who, with a little money to keep them going, are willing to take the lead in new approaches to health maintenance. Nurses, working as independent practitioners, may be interested in starting school programs in health education, community based screening programs, community needs assessment projects, and other health maintenance activities. If they can get support for practicing their profession in these ways until the public begins to truly appreciate the unique contribution that the nurse can make, the quality of our lives should change materially in a very short time.

Allocation of professional resources

The geographical areas that are without adequate health care delivery continue to be of concern to many professionals as well as to the communities going without. Some fair way of getting primary providers of all professions to those areas must be devised. Latin America is looking more and more to nurses, but there is a danger in having nurses as primary providers in areas where there are almost no other health care professionals. It is possible that, with the need for emergency treatment and curing illness, the broader activities of health care maintenance may go by the board. If the need is to save people in imminent danger of death, there may never be enough nurses, or enough time—to achieve the long-term objectives that involve education, planning, and social change.

Allocation of resources is not only a problem geographically, but also socially. That is, plans must be made to achieve health goals for neglected groups, like the poor. Within the group designated as poor, the aged, women, and children have special problems that have never been adequately addressed by the medical establishment. That is partly why, despite the advances in immunology, medical technology, pharmacology, and surgical techniques, the general, day-to-day health of the American population has not greatly improved. Nurses, as a profession, are more visibly concerned than any other health care profession about getting to these underserved groups and working with them to improve their health. There is much to be done politically before enough money is allocated for maintaining the health of the poor.

Not infrequently, though we have health laws on the books, the standards laid out are not being maintained. The argument often advanced is that not enough money is provided to pay professional personnel to oversee the law. However, it must be considered that there are professionals, among them nurses, who are not assuming the kind of leadership responsibility the profession calls for. They are seeing these things happening and, for one reason or another, are keeping silent. Others, of course, are speaking up in community groups, professional meetings, and in the literature. Thus, we have stories about mentally ill patients discharged from hospitals who are not receiving the care they need, old people in so-called nursing homes who receive neither nursing nor home care. We have a law that provides for mainstreaming handicapped children in schools for the purpose of providing them with better education, but they are being put into situations where things are worse for them rather than better.

Quality of health care

Nurses are concerned with the general quality of life and of health care as it contributes to that quality. They are raising questions that other professions have not raised, questions that strike a responsive chord in consumers and that could pave the way for further cooperation between nursing and the public.

We have mentioned the terrible condition of "nursing homes" for the aged and infirm. Nurses have expressed great concern about them, though it is also true that most nurses refuse to accept employment in them, or will work in them only for very brief periods. Thus, instead of staying and exerting leadership for change, nurses leave them to continue the abuses.

Questions are being raised about the very large differences in the cost of hospital care in different areas of the country, that cannot be explained by the smaller differentials in general cost of living. Nurses are in the best position to know what the day-to-day practices are that would cause such cost differences.

Nurses are asking questions about why, for example, someone in New York state is much more likely to have surgery (a one in two chance) than someone in Michigan (a one in five chance). In their contacts with patients, they are in a position to learn about pressures to submit to surgery, use of second and third opinions, and the quality of presurgical information given to patients.

The asking of such questions in places where they are likely to result in further action exemplifies leadership behavior.

The whole matter of comprehensive health care as opposed to the fragmented, specialist approach that does not do justice to the holistic nature of the human being is of deep concern to the nursing profession. At present, our institutions, laws, and the money allocated for health delivery do not provide for a holistic approach to health. The more nurses participate in policy- and law-making, the closer our provisions will come to comprehensive health care.

We know that the medical establishment has not dealt adequately with dying. It is no accident that hospices, where people can go to make their final time a peaceful, reasonably comfortable and even productive part of their lives, are largely run by nurses. More needs to be written by nurses about the experiences they are having, so that research questions can be defined and further research undertaken. Quality care when we know that we have not long to live is a part of comprehensive health care, and nurses have demonstrated leadership in this area.

I would suggest that professions have an official responsibility to disseminate all the available data on both sides of a controversial issue. Just because an issue is controversial, with strong emotional support for conflicting points of view, people are left to fight it out on an emotional basis. The professions that have the scientific and clinical data to contribute to the debate generally keep out of it, except for individual leaders who continue to try to educate the public, and small groups that organize to provide a service on one side or the other. Perhaps it is not always necessary to take a side on an issue, especially if the profession feels that all the evidence is not yet in. But to publish material on the treatment of radiation poisoning without also publishing all the evidence available on incidence and circumstances of poisoning and some inescapable inferences from the evidence is abrogation of professional responsibility. Such behavior is not likely to promote trust between nursing and the public—especially as nursing presents itself as a public advocate for the common good.

Similar cases might be made for publishing the best available data on abortion, euthanasia, and other controversies, instead of leaving it to individuals to publish individual points of view.

Dissemination of new nursing data

All these areas of concern in the profession must be systematically disseminated if public policy is to be based on accurate data and a realistic assessment of what the nursing profession is equipped to provide. At the same time, whatever research is done in nursing should also be made public, to lend weight to the stances taken on different issues by professional organizations and individual nurses.

For example, research might be conducted to determine systematically what constitutes nursing practice, to define what differentiates the work of the independent nurse practitioner from other health care delivery, to pinpoint the relationship between different kinds of professional experiences and the quality and scope of nurses' practices, and to evaluate the quality and effects of nursing practice. This last is more calculated to demonstrate a commitment to the public good than any other single activity in this age of heightened consumer consciousness and skepticism.

Taking Action

Throughout this book, we have emphasized the identification and learning of specific skills that constitute leadership behavior. This seems to be an appropriate point at which to take stock of the skills you now have, so that you may plan some action with a good chance of carrying it through to a successful conclusion. Those skills that you do not yet have can be learned as time goes on; you need not put off your leadership activities until you have learned them all.

Self-assessment on some leadership behaviors

Read the following hypothetical situations, identify the leadership behaviors used by the people involved, and state the purpose for which they were used. Put a check mark next to each behavior that you believe you could demonstrate in a similar situation.

The key at the end of the exercise identifies each leadership behavior and its purpose. These leadership behaviors are discrete behaviors subsumed under the three major aspects of leadership: systematic thinking, teaching, and interdisciplinary functioning. Though they have not previously all been explicitly named, they have been described and illustrated throughout the text. In this section, they are lifted from the illustrations and listed. The list (i.e., the key) may then be used as a permanent reference of most essential leadership behaviors.

If you are not sure about your ability to use the behavior, try it out by role-playing the situation with your colleagues. Then discuss how you felt using the behavior, letting the others give you feedback on how effectively you demonstrated the behavior.

	Leadership behavior	*Purpose*	*Check your skill*

1. The most popular pastime among the nurses on the medical-surgical unit was complaining about Ms. Green, the head nurse. "If she doesn't stop looking over my shoulder every time I check an IV, I'm going to let her have it," Jean Hammond told Betty Maston, for the hundredth time.

   "I've been thinking," Betty answered. "We all gripe about Green. We're good nurses. We know our business. Why don't we get together and try to figure out how to get her off our backs?"

2. Joan Masters repeatedly demonstrates sloppy sterile techniques. The other nurses talk about it, but no one has said anything to her or to the supervisor. Apparently the supervisor is either not aware of what she is doing or just has not corrected her.

   Sara Judd watches from the doorway of the room as Joan puts a prepared hypodermic syringe on the bedside table while she talks to the patient. Later, Sara sees her having lunch in the staff dining room and brings her tray to Joan's table and sits with her. Sara starts to eat, and for a minute or two they speak desultorily about how quiet the floor is today, how tomorrow it will probably be a madhouse. Then Sara says, "You know, I think you're a good nurse. You know your stuff, and I don't want to put you down. But I can't help noticing that you don't always follow through on sterile technique."

	Leadership behavior	*Purpose*	*Check your skill*

3. For weeks there has been a rumor in the hospital that there is to be a change from team nursing to primary nursing. The talk has all been among the floor nurses; no administrator has mentioned the matter. The nurses have various opinions about how nursing care is best provided, but most of their talk has been colored by resentment that none of them are involved in making the decision. When, several times, Sally Rosen has suggested they go to the front office and ask what is happening, she has had no response, except for a shrug or two or a smile. She finally decides to take the step herself, and at a team meeting she announces her intention to several of her peers and their supervisor. "I really want to know what's going on. Is there any reason why I can't just ask Miss Markin?"

Her peers tell her they think it is a good idea. The supervisor says nothing.

Sally asks her directly, "Would you have any objections to my finding out?"

The supervisor answers rather cooly, "I'm sure if they want us to know, they'll tell us. But, of course, I have no power to prevent you from going to the front office."

Sally makes an appointment with the secretary of the director of nursing service, and is finally sitting in the director's office, facing her across the desk.

Ann Markin, B.S., R.N.,

	Leadership behavior	Purpose	Check your skill

M.S., Ph.D., smiles tentatively and says, "Miss—uh—Rosen. What can I do for you?"

"Miss Markin, we have been hearing rumors for weeks about changing over to primary nursing. I would just like to know what is really happening."

"Well, nothing has been decided yet."

"I'm happy to hear that and I know others will be, too."

"Oh, you are opposed to primary nursing?"

"No, that isn't it. It's just that I'd like to have a chance to discuss the pros and cons before the decision is made."

4. The nursing team meetings are managed and run by the nursing supervisor. She distributes assignments, makes announcements, asks if there are any questions or problems, answers the questions, renders a solution to the problem, and sends everyone on her way.

It is after the meeting that the staff express feelings and identify problems they never bring up at meetings.

Finally, at one meeting, the supervisor asks, "Are there any questions or problems?" Dorothy Londen, a staff nurse, answers, "Well, it's not exactly a problem, but I have a request to make."

"Yes?"

"I was wondering if we could use part of the team meeting to share some of the new ideas and new knowledge in nursing. A lot is happening in the profession

	Leadership behavior	*Purpose*	*Check your skill*

that we could put to use here. Most of us don't get to professional conferences; maybe those who do can tell us what they learned."

5. Dr. Smith has a policy of telling his patients almost nothing about their condition or treatment, and telling members of their families only a very little more. He has made it clear that attending nurses are to give no information unless specifically requested by him to do so. He has refused to respond to any suggestion from nurses that he permit them to inform the patients and answer their questions.

Ms. Spitzer is a forty-year-old woman hospitalized for treatment of peptic ulcer. She keeps asking the nurse who cares for her, Ms. Anelone, questions like: How can I tell when I'm improving? What happens if the medication doesn't work?

Ms. Anelone has used evasive tactics, making responses like: "Try not to worry. I'm sure the doctor will tell you what you need to know." But she has become increasingly angry with herself and has finally decided to do something more productive. The next time Ms. Spitzer asks her a question, she says, "Ms. Spitzer, Dr. Smith has told me that I am to give you no information that he does not instruct me to give you. I think you have a right to know the details of your condition and your treatment. Also, I know that the better informed you are the better able you will be to maintain your

	Leadership behavior	Purpose	Check your skill

good health. If you like, I will stay with you the next time he comes in and together we will insist that you be informed."

6. John Rush is twenty-four years old, and has been admitted to the hospital for treatment of bronchial asthma. He has been told that it is inadvisable for him to continue to live in a cold climate, and winter sports are strongly contraindicated. However, skiing, skating and bobsledding are very popular activities in his social group, and he is very angry each time it is suggested that his rejection of the advice is bound to make him very ill.

Up until this hospitalization, the asthma has been kept under control. This is the first hospitalization, resulting from a prolonged, acute attack that occurred after a skating race on a local pond.

Carol Mander is the nurse assigned to care for Mr. Rush. She feels that the care plan must emphasize teaching the patient to accept his condition and minimize the possibility of future attacks.

Before she finalizes the items on her care plan, she asks the patient, "How do you feel about having bronchial asthma?" Then she says nothing and just listens to the answer.

7. A seminar in continuing education is being held in a hospital for twelve staff nurses who have volunteered to meet for ten sessions to explore new developments in nursing. They have a small allot-

	Leadership behavior	Purpose	Check your skill

ment of money from the education fund of the hospital to pay for three or four speakers. The planning of the seminar and the decisions about how to spend the money are being left to them.

For this first session, they have spent an hour mentioning first one topic for study, then another, without getting beyond this pattern of discussion. Finally, one of the group members says, "Let's just decide to get more information about primary nursing. I know someone at Memorial who is into that, and we can ask her to come and speak to us."

Another answers impatiently, "Oh, for goodness' sake! That's the third time you've made the same suggestion! We're not getting anywhere with this!"

Rosemary Marks, one of the nurses in the group says, "Those are two good ideas: Studying primary nursing is a timely suggestion; we'll be faced with a change-over soon, I imagine, and we ought to be prepared for it. Also, we can't spend too much time deciding what we want to do, or we won't have enough time to do it.

"I have an idea: Let's get down all the topics we're interested in. Then we can sort them out and set priorities for ourselves. I'll write on the board as fast as I can; you just spill out all the ideas."

8. The health team meetings are held once a month. The team is an interdisciplinary one. There are four

	Leadership behavior	Purpose	Check your skill

R.N.'s (one of them is a unit supervisor, one a clinician specialist, and two are nurses providing primary care), one staff physician and one resident, a pharmacist, a dietitian, an LVN, a social worker, an inhalation therapist, and a physical therapist. The team has met three times and has dealt with a variety of problems. The chair is rotated, and the chairperson for each meeting assumes responsibility for making up the agenda. Generally that person and the nursing supervisor between them select the problems for discussion and ask individual members to prepare presentations of cases and problems.

Each time somebody completes a presentation, raises a question, or makes an observation, the chairperson responds to it in such a way as to effect closure: the presenter is thanked, the question is answered, or the comment is acknowledged.

Caroline Jerome, one of the nurse members on the team, has been increasingly frustrated by the lack of responsiveness of the members to each other's contributions. She is worried that deep concerns will not be brought up and interest in attending team meetings will begin to decline.

At this meeting, after the social worker has presented data on the incidence of old people who are leaving the hospital to go back to apartments and furnished rooms where they live alone, the

	Leadership behavior	*Purpose*	*Check your skill*

chairperson says, "Thank you, Miss Levine. That was very informative. Something really needs to be done about the situation."

"The next item on the agenda is . . . ."

Caroline Jerome interrupts. "Before we got to the next item, do you mind if I ask Miss Levine a question?"

The chairperson shrugs his shoulders, apparently indicating that it is all right with him. Miss Jerome then turns pointedly to the social worker to ask her a question: "Is the inference to be drawn from your report that there is a problem here that we may be able to solve?"

9. Callie Howard is attending a state meeting of her professional organization. About three hundred nurses are sitting in a convention hall listening to the speaker enumerating the defects in nurses that prevent them from taking an active part in the politics of the profession.

After forty minutes, there is general applause and the speaker asks if there are any questions. Callie has never asked a question or said anything in this kind of group. She has always felt intimidated by the large number of strangers looking at her; she has believed that this kind of situation did not provide a commentator with opportunity to make a clear statement or even to clarify a request for information.

However, she felt that, if she

	Leadership behavior	Purpose	Check your skill

did not speak this time and if no one else expressed what she was feeling, everyone in the room would leave with the idea that the speaker spoke for them all.

She rose to her feet and was recognized. She spoke directly to the speaker:

"I speak only for myself. I am here because I care about what is happening in the profession. On my job I am assertive and caring and involved in the institution and the community. I do what I know how to do and I am learning more all the time. I appreciate the sense of urgency that you have communicated; there is a lot to be done. But I don't think I will be moved to do more by being told over and over again how apathetic, fearful, and brainwashed I am."

People began to applaud, but she held up a hand to stop them. "I know about you, Dr. Ament," she went on. "You are a very competent professional and have had much experience in leading the profession to make significant changes. I would like you to teach me some of the knowledge and skill you have."

KEY TO LEADERSHIP BEHAVIORS AND PURPOSES

Leadership behavior	Purpose
1. *Leading peers* describing the problem situation	•to help a peer move from expression of feeling to recognition of the unproductive behavior

suggesting a rational alternative

articulating a common goal

- •to start the problem-solving process
- •to hold out the possibility of achieving a desired objective

2. *Leading peers*

giving negative criticism when necessary

focusing on the inappropriate behavior and not on the person

stating the limited nature of the criticism (just one inappropriate behavior)

- •to improve patient care

- •to maintain friendly, open communication

- •to preserve morale
- •to reduce the possibility of egothreat caused by criticism

3. *Leading power holders*

not asking for permission to take action

taking action openly

initiating professional communication with a person in a power position

- •to forestall almost inevitable refusal

- •to get whatever support people are ready to give
- •to begin to establish autonomous, democratic interaction

4. *Leading power holders*

intervening to change a set pattern of operation

taking action consistent with expressed needs of people

asking for continuing education

- •to initiate a process leading to optimum involvement
- •to suggest a way for immediate fulfillment of some needs
- •to improve patient care

5. *Leading patients*

giving a patient (the leader's constituency, in this case) an honest professional opinion

supplying data to justify the need

offering advocacy and supportive action

- •to maintain professional integrity
- •to teach the patient that professionals disagree with each other
- •to promote trust
- •to promote patient autonomy and help her assume responsibility for her own health
- •to provide strength in stating the case for change

6. *Leading patients*

expressing interest in the feelings of the patient (the leader's constituency, in this case)

listening

- •to gather data for understanding the patient's point of view
- •to develop trust
- •to initiate a process of involving the patient in formulating his own care plan

7. *Leading small groups*

neutralizing the effects of an attack	•to minimize the possibility of withdrawal by a group member or the establishment of an unproductive pattern of attack and counterattack
ego building	•to establish a pattern of acceptance of members' contributions
	•to make people feel good about themselves and each other and so encourage regular attendance and productive activity
moving the group forward	•to reduce the frustration of not knowing what to do
introducing a strategy for getting the job done	•to achieve the original general objective

8. *Leading small groups*

intervening to change a shared role perception speaking directly to another member and using body language to inform the chairperson that he is not expected to respond	•to illustrate a different pattern of communication in the group. (Apparently the members believe that the job of the chairperson is to announce each presentation and respond to each member's remark before moving on to the next item on the agenda. The leader's behavior changes the pattern of communication by opening communication with a fellow member.)

9. *Leading large groups*

speaking out in public	•to shift the focus of a group from feeling guilt to considering productive action
ego building	•to divert people from the usual practice in large groups of taking a side and denigrating the opposing side

Assessing the setting

Knowing what leadership skills you have and practicing those you are not yet comfortable with are part of learning to be a leader. Another part of the process is learning to recognize the factors that may affect your chances of being successful in your leadership efforts.

Almost any professional concern may be addressed through political activity on any one of a number of levels and spheres: institutional, community, local government, state government, national government, or professional organization (local, state, national). Since the first rule of political activity is to work with what you have, you must assess the factors that indicate the advisability of working on one or another level, in one area or another.

Following are lists of factors in different areas of professional activity that have significance for change efforts. Before deciding where you want to use your knowledge, skill and energy, check to see what factors and systems are already operating in the situation and can be utilized as entry points for potential leaders.

INSTITUTIONAL FACTORS AFFECTING SUCCESS IN LEADERSHIP

Peer factors

1. *A universal shortage of qualified personnel*

If nurses have an advantage in the labor market, they will probably have more freedom on the job to violate institutional norms and effect changes. If they can, at the same time, justify their change efforts by achieving improved patient care, higher personnel morale, etc., administrative resistance can be kept within reasonable bounds.

2. *A problem or problems making many people uncomfortable*

The analogy to biological homeostasis is, I think, valid. If there is enough discomfort, the body politic will move to achieve some equilibrium. Influencing the direction of the move is a leadership function.

3. *A number of peers who are willing to work on solving the problem*

It is not necessary to have one hundred percent of the work force ready and willing to engage in problem solving. A small, active group can carry the day.

4. *A pattern of trusting, friendly peer interaction*

People are more willing to be led by those they think well of and more likely to respond to suggestions for getting together if they like each other. Lack of trust can cause people to suspect the motivation behind initial leadership attempts and make success very difficult to achieve.

5. *A variety of leadership skills owned by peers*

If a number of people have the skills, leadership efforts can be shared from the outset. Multiple leaders are able not only to make contact with a larger number of followers, but they can support each other, learn from each other, and improve each other's effectiveness.

6. *A certain amount of autonomy and involvement in decision making*

Obviously, if a democratic system for problem solving already exists, there are many opportunities for assuming leadership in the ongoing processes.

POWER FACTORS

7. *One or more people in positions of power who are willing to communicate*

Power people who have authority to make changes or who can influence those who make the decisions are important assets in attempting institutional change from the bottom. However, leaders and their constituents must be careful not to lose sight of their objectives. It is tempting to respond to persuasive arguments of a friendly power figure that nurses keep a low profile while he works behind the scenes to achieve the desired change. People who do not feel very uncomfortable with the status quo, even though they are intellectually committed to change, are able to wait for that change for long periods of time. They are also able to compromise easily on what those on the line consider essentials.

PATIENT FACTORS

8. *An articulate clientele*

People who are so intimidated by institutions and by professionals that they suffer in silence whatever is done to them deprive problem solvers and change agents of important information and supports. The change process must ultimately involve clients and patients or it will have dangerous defects. However, if a number can be identified who are ready at the outset to work on problem solving, the leadership job is greatly facilitated.

9. *Continuing, productive interaction between people in the institution and community people outside*

Any health care institution purporting to serve a community must have input from that community. If the mechanism already exists for that input, leaders can tap it for information and support.

10. *Receptive people outside the institution who are in positions to influence people in the institution and are willing to exert that influence*

A similar caveat obtains here as in factor No. 7. It should be borne in mind that power people must always be worked *with;* responsibility for working for the change should not be left to them while the professional staff retires and waits.

FACTORS IN PROFESSIONAL ORGANIZATIONS AFFECTING SUCCESS IN LEADERSHIP

The factors here focus on a basic condition of professional organizations: They are too often closed corporations, run by a small group like some kind of private club. Channels of communication are severely circumscribed and, in some cases, nonexistent, so that the general membership often feels powerless to make its feelings and observations known to the inner circle.

Though members of the profession are exhorted to join and to come to meetings, there is generally insufficient opportunity to participate actively in those meetings. People come away with the feeling that they are not the organization, but that the organization is something operating on them.

Members can more easily exert leadership to the degree that the following factors exist in organizations. Potential leaders might keep in mind that making changes to achieve these factors can help involve more people in the business of the profession, and so increase its power and effectiveness.

1. Local, state, regional and national chapters, with opportunities for representation at every level.
2. Open agendas at every level with opportunities for members to contribute items.
3. Potential office holders for local levels drawn from the local membership in open elections, with state, regional and national chapters run by representatives from each level.
4. Newsletters published and distributed locally with regional and national news inserts.
5. Local financial support for holding office at every level.
6. Viable committee structure at every level, with periodic publication of committee openings which all members are encouraged to apply for.
7. Substantial common recognition of problems that need solving.
8. Substantial agreement on basic philosophical precepts.

COMMUNITY FACTORS AFFECTING SUCCESS IN LEADERSHIP

Though the factors listed here emphasize existing community organization as facilitating opportunity for leadership, this does not mean that disorganized, fragmented communities cannot rally behind effective leaders. The occurrence of a critical incident or the pressure of a painful situation can quickly mobilize the most apathetic community to action.

The nurse leader, however, will find that working through existing organizations can generally help her make her influence felt more quickly.

Even without organizations, systematic search will uncover leaders that the community people recognize, even if outsiders are not aware of them. The following factors affect success:

1. Substantial common recognition of problems that need solving.
2. Active grass roots organizations.
3. Communication among organizations and overlap of membership.
4. Members of power structure interested in solving problems.
5. Existence of planning groups with active grass roots members.
6. Grass roots leaders.

Identifying a problem for political action

1. Identify an unresolved professional problem that has disturbed you for some time.
2. Speak to one person at each level and in each sphere of your work situation. Get some sense of how people in each area feel about this problem.
3. Pick the three levels in which people seem most sensitive to and concerned about the problem.
4. Check each level against the factors lists to determine the practicality of working on that level.
5. You may decide to work in more than one area. This is all right if you are prepared to spend the necessary time. As others become involved, the responsibilities will, of course, be divided among you.

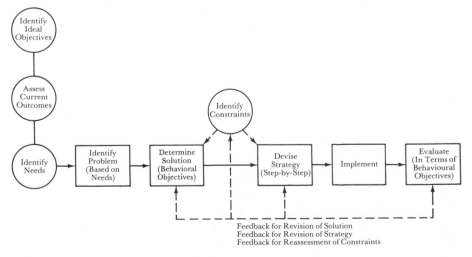

Figure 8-1.

Preparing a plan for action

Figures 8-1 and 8-2 show blank outlines of simple system models to help you plan for solving the problem you have identified. Fill in the boxes and circles with descriptions of the needs you have identified, a definition of the

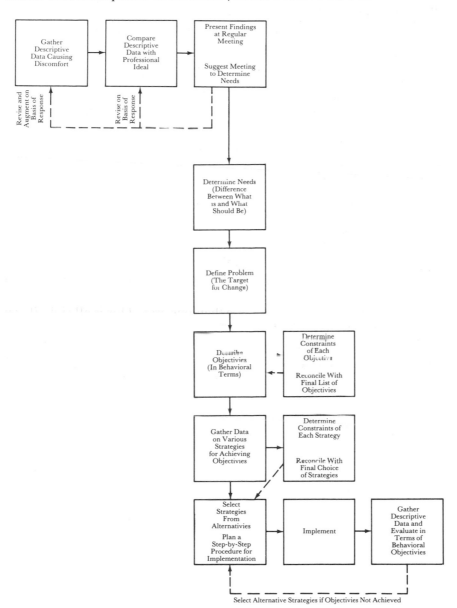

Figure 8-2.

problem based on those needs, the objectives to be achieved, and the strategies for achieving them. Feel free to add steps if you need them.

NOTES

[1] Saul Alinsky, *Rules for Radicals* (New York: Vintage Books, 1971), pp. 126–145.

[2] Ada K. Jacox and Catherine M. Norris eds., *Organizing for Independent Nursing Practice* (New York: Appleton-Century-Crofts, 1977), p. 93.

[3] *American Journal of Nursing,* Feb. 1980, p. 198.

[4] *American Journal of Nursing,* Feb. 1979, p. 205.

[5] Margaret M. Moloney, *Leadership in Nursing—Theories, Strategies, Action* (St. Louis: C.V. Mosby, 1979), p. 105.

[6] See Ronald Gross and Paul Osterman eds., *The New Professionals* (New York: Simon & Schuster, 1972).

[7] Allen B. Steckler and William T. Herzog, "How to Keep Your Mandated Citizen Board Out of Your Hair and Off Your Back: A Guide for Executive Directors," *American Journal of Public Health,* 1979, Vol. 69, No. 8, pp. 809–812.

[8] *The Role of Nurses in Primary Health Care* (Washington, D.C.: Pan-American Health Organization, Pub. No. 348, Pan-American Health Organization, Pan American Sanitary Bureaus, Regional Office of the World Health Organization, 1977), p. 7.

[9] Jacox & Norris, op. cit., p. 196.

[10] See, for example, Institute of Medicine, National Academy of Sciences, *Report of a Study: A Manpower Policy for Primary Health Care,* (Washington, D.C.), 1978.

[11] Jeffrey Merrill, "Financing Health Care: Programs and Policies," *The Emergence of Nursing as a Political Force* (New York: National League for Nursing, Pub. No. 41-1760, 1979).

[12] Leda Judd, "Nursing Politics and Trends," *The Emergence of Nursing as a Political Force,* op. cit., p. 67.

[13] Barbara S. Christy, "Nurse Power in the Federal Government: Working on the Inside," *People, Power, Politics for Health Care* (New York: National League for Nursing, Pub. No. 52-1647), p. 51.

[14] Ibid., p. 52.

[15] Mary Alice Hauser, "Attempts to Develop Alternate Nursing Practice Skills to Improve the Accessibility of Health Care Services for the Elderly," in Jacox & Norris, op. cit., p. 69.

Suggested Readings

A brief list of books is annotated to help you find additional information about some special areas of leadership.

Benson, Evelyn Rose & McDevitt, Joan Quinn. *Community Health and Nursing Practice* (2nd Ed.). Prentice-Hall, Englewood Cliffs, N.J., 1980.

Presents principles of community health and recent changes and trends in health care, and describes the variety of health settings in the community in which the nurse functions. Numerous anecdotal examples clarify issues and practices.

Brager, George & Holloway, Stephen. *Changing Human Service Organizations—Politics and Practice.* The Free Press, N.Y., 1978.

An analysis of the process of change initiated by those with limited formal responsibility for organizational problem solving, and the use of appropriate tactics for implementing change.

Clark, Carolyn Chambers. *Assertive Skills for Nurses.* Contemporary Publishing, Wakefield, Mass., 1978.

A useful workbook providing self-assessment and practice exercises for developing assertive skills. It helps the nurse identify assertive, acquiescent and avoiding aggressive behavior; control fear, anxiety and anger; and give and take criticism. It can be used by individuals or groups.

Horwitz, John J. *Team Practice and the Specialist—An Introduction to Interdisciplinary Teamwork.* Charles C Thomas, Springfield, Ill., 1970.

A discussion of the personal, professional and social factors contributing to effective functioning in an interdisciplinary team, and specific recommendations for further study in the area.

Jacox, Ada K. & Norris, Catherine M. (Eds.). *Organizing for Independent Nursing Practice.* Appleton-Century-Crofts, N.Y., 1977.

Detailed accounts, often in their own words, of the experiences of independent nurse practitioners working in a variety of models of independent nursing.

Kane, Rosalie. *Interprofessional Teamwork.* Syracuse U. School of Social Work, Division of Continuing Education and Manpower Development, Monograph No. 8, Syracuse, 1975.

A review of the literature on interprofessional team functioning; a profile of interprofessional teamwork composed of reports of 229 teams in the delivery of human services, and suggestions for further study.

Kinlein, M. Lucille. *Independent Nursing Practice with Clients,* J.B. Lippincott, Philadelphia, 1977.

A detailed account of a nurse's intellectual process toward defining a concept of nursing that justifies the establishment of the role of the independent nurse practitioner. It also presents the practical aspects of starting a professional practice in nursing.

Mager, Robert F. *Preparing Instructional Objectives.* Fearon, Palo Alto, Calif., 1962.

A programmed system for learning to write instructional objectives in behavioral terms. The reader who starts at the beginning of the book will—when reaching the last page—know how to write objectives.

Moloney, Margaret M. *Leadership in Nursing—Theories, Strategies, Action.* C.V. Mosby, St. Louis, 1979.

An overview of research in leadership and how that research relates to nursing leadership specifically. Presents the different theories of leadership and identifies the factors in individuals, systems, and situations that make for effective leadership.

Rothman, Jack. "Three Models of Community Organization Practice." In F. M. Cox, J. L. Erlich, J. Rothman, & J. E. Tropman (Eds.), *Strategies of Community Organization: A Book of Readings* (2nd Ed.). Peacock, Itasca, Ill., 1974.

A collection of "writings dealing with various aspects of community organization and social change." Includes "different approaches to community organization, a view of the nature of interorganizational linkages, . . . and a focus on the practitioner and his intellectual equipment."

Taylor, Carol. *In Horizontal Orbit—Hospitals and the Cult of Efficiency.* Holt, Rinehart and Winston, N.Y., 1970.

An excellent analysis of a hospital system by a people-oriented analyst, juxtaposing the formal bureaucratic organization with the real organization.

Verhonick, Phyllis J. & Seaman, Catherine C. *Research Methods for Undergraduate Students in Nursing,* Appleton-Century-Crofts, N.Y., 1978.

Though it is directed to undergraduates, this book is useful for anyone who is interested in beginning research in nursing. It leads the researcher step by step to the final written report—a publishable one.

Index

Aborigines, 218
Accessibility, 106
Accountability, 21
    in primary nursing, 172
    shared, 80, 89, 90, 91, 94, 107, 128
Accuracy, 106
Administration, 5, 15
    function of, 94
Administering Health Systems, 77, 102
Admission procedures, 64-65
Advisory council, 81
Advocate,
    of the aged, 205ff, 216-17
    of children, 118, 214-15, 216-17
    of minorities, 216ff
    of patients, 93
    of women, 212ff
*Affective Subjects in the Classroom: Exploring
    Race, Sex, and Drugs*, 119, 140, 178, 186,
    235, 236, 243
Aging, 68, 77, 96, 100-101, 118-19, 134,
    192, 198, 205ff, 240
Alabama State Nurses Association, 258

Alaska, 227
Alcoholism, 38
Alinsky, Saul, 247, 288
Ambivalence, 169-70
American Nurses' Foundation, 260
American Nursing Association, 259
Anatomy of an Illness as Perceived by the Patient,
    92, 102
Anderson, Elizabeth T., 188, 242
Anorectics, 196-97
Appalachia, 219, 222-23
Army, 14
Arnold, Mary F., 77, 102
Assertive Skills for Nurses, 291
Assessment, realistic, 7, 16ff, 157
"Attempts to Develop Alternate Nursing Practice
    Skills to Improve the Accessibility of Health
    Care Services for the Elderly," 270, 289
Attendant, contributions of, 82
Attitudes,
    toward change, 246ff
    toward city fringes, 235-36
    toward inner cities, 234-35

Attitudes *(contd.)*
  toward political activity, 246ff
  toward rural areas, 237
  toward suburbs, 236
Australia, 218
Authoritarianism,
  effects of, 5, 12
    on children, 11, 13
    on patients, 116
  and leadership, 9–10, 13
  and professionals, 13–14
  and rules and principles, 16
  and self-knowledge, 79
  and supervisors, 112, 169–70
Authority,
  bypassing, 122
Autonomy, 2, 5, 8, 12, 14, 53, 93, 99, 107, 112, 144,
  195, 198, 224, 248
Availability, 106
Avoidance of dying, 68

Banks, 231
Barrett, Margaret W., 172–73, 186
Bedside nursing, 150ff
Behavioral analysis, 39ff
Behavioral objectives, 31–33, 38ff, 90, 154
Beliefs and behaviors,
  inconsistency of, 70
Bell, Colin, 219, 243
Benne, Kenneth D., 16, 24, 143ff, 186
Bennis, Warren G., 143ff, 186
Benson, Evelyn Rose, 196, 243, 291
Bevis, Em Olivia, 167, 169, 169–70, 172–73, 186
Birnbaum, Max, 143ff, 186
Blankenship, L. Vaughn, 77, 102
"The Blind Men and the Elephant," 45–46, 74
Body language, 156
Brager, George, 142, 186, 197–98, 243, 291
*Broca's Brain: Reflections on the Romance of
  Science,* 65, 74
Brown, Marie S., 37, 44, 77
Bruner, Nancy A., 81, 102
Bureaucracy,
  traditional, 66
  welfare, 219
Burnham, D.H., 8–9, 24

"Can Handwashing Practices Be Changed?,"
  37, 44
Care plan, 150ff
Caring, evidence of, 134ff
Carotenuto, Rosine, 205, 206
Causes, 158

Center for Nursing, 260
Change,
  agent, 147
  asking for, 160
  of behavior, 42–44
  decisions for, 10, 53
  direct action for, 149
  education for, 104, 111–12
  fear of, 104
  function of nurse leader in, 62
  imposition of, 5, 53, 142–43
  inevitability of, 142
  involvement for, 53, 66, 90, 142, 145–46, 262
  middle class attitudes toward, 247
  mobilization for, 18ff, 66, 163
  models for, 52, 57, 60
  need for, 198
  observations on, 149
  organizational, 141ff
  a plan for, 48ff
  planning for, 3, 8, 34–36, 120ff, 142ff, 146ff
    Steps 1 through 11, 49–58
*Changing Human Service Organizations—Poli-
  tics and Practice,* 142, 186, 291
Channels, going through, 255–56
Children,
  decision making by, 262
  hitting, 143, 153
  hospitalization of, 62–63
  inadequate health care for, 214–15
  punishing, 249
  in schools, 233
  segregation of, 199
Chin, Robert, 143–46, 186
Chinese, 151–52
Christy, Barbara S., 267–68, 289
Clark, Carolyn Chambers, 291
Clark, Kenneth B., 218, 243
Classroom Management and Teaching, 243
Clinical experience, 28
Clinics,
  leadership, 257
Cold weather injuries, 38
Communication,
  circular, 137
  for change, 148–49, 162ff
  difficulties of, 80ff, 91
  hierarchical, 144
  inadequacy of, 78, 98
  need for, 4, 80ff
  skills, 77, 154ff
  for support, 108
  systems, 265

Community, 114ff, 125–26, 187ff
  defined, 203–204
  development, 188
  epidemiologic surveillance in, 128
  future of, 204–205
  health nurse, 188ff
  involvement in, 227ff, 239ff
  knowledge of, 130, 224
Community Action Programs, 218
Community Health Nursing, 205, 206, 243, 291
Community Health and Nursing Practice, 196, 243
Community Legal Services, 232
Community Organizing, 197–98, 243
Community Power Structure, 143, 186
Competency-based education, 26
Competition, 85
A Conception of Authority, 16, 24
Conflict, 97, 146, 152, 203
Congress on Racial Equality, 198
Consistency,
  of beliefs and behaviors, 70
  of objectives and needs, 70
Constitution, 70
Constraints, 63
Consumer rights, 197–98, 262
Continuum,
  feelings, 73
Contributions of team members,
  evaluation of, 95–96
Control, 53
Controversial issues, 97, 146ff, 272
Cooling of Earth, 65
Cooperator in change, 188
Coronary care unit, 65
Counseling, 114, 226–27
Cousins, Norman, 92, 102
Cowan, John, 13, 24
Cox, F.M., 292
Curriculum for community nurse practitioners, 188
Curtin, Sharon R., 101, 102

Decision makers,
  identification of, 240ff
Decision making, 107, 127, 143
  non-participation in, 66
  shared, 80, 91, 172
Defensiveness, 174
DeLapp, Tina Davis, 38, 44
Democracy,
  and control, 53
  defined, 8ff

Democracy *(contd.)*
  and efficiency, 10–11
  perfected, 70
  and self concept, 53
  and self knowledge, 79
  and values, 50
Dentist, 144–45
"Detoxification: Then What? A Community Nursing Course in Alcoholism," 38, 44
The Development and Implementation of a Curriculum Model for Community Nurse Practitioners, 188, 242
Diagnosis, 127
Diet-associated ailments, 201
Disabilities of children, 48–49, 114
Discrimination, 50, 79, 104–105, 119, 122, 143, 150, 151–52, 153, 198, 207–208, 216ff, 250, 254
"The Doctor-Nurse Game," 111, 139
Douglass, Laura Mae, 167, 169, 169–70, 186
Dying, 68, 118, 122, 272

Economic Opportunities Act, 262
Economic services, clues to, 232ff
Education,
  for the aged, 206
  for community, 197–98
  continuing, 334
  higher, 233–34
  in home nursing, 197
  objectives of, 50
  for the physician, 175–76
  preservice, 176–77
  services,
    clues to, 233–34
  and supervision, 172ff
Education for All Handicapped Children Act of 1975, 48–49
Effective Interaction in Contemporary Nursing, 116, 139
Efficiency, 10–11, 16, 54, 59, 64, 65
Ego safety, 162–63
The Emergence of Nursing as a Political Force, 222, 243, 267, 288, 289
Emergency rooms,
  use of, 65–66
Empathy, 86, 154–55, 162, 178ff
Epstein, Charlotte, 25, 44, 68, 74, 76, 102, 116, 119, 140, 169, 178, 192, 204, 207, 208ff, 219, 235, 243
Equality defined, 95
Erlich, J.L., 292
Eupsychian Management: A Journal, 93, 102
Evaluation,
  of others, 137–38

Evaluation *(contd.)*
  of outcomes, 90–91, 128, 159
  of progress, 89
"Expansions: A Pioneering Experience," 104, 139

Failure, 48
Family planning, 114
Feedback, 31, 32, 54, 58, 62, 65, 89, 128, 158, 178,
    225, 251, 256–57
  negative, 136ff
Feelings,
  disclosure of, 99ff
  identification of, 68, 70ff
  of nurses, 111–12, 119–20
Fiedler, Fred E., 3, 24
"Field Theory and Experiment in Social Psy-
    chology: Concepts and Methods," 222,
    223, 243
"Financing Health Care: Programs and Poli-
    cies," 267, 288
Flood, Daniel J., 196, 243
Follow-up, 159
Forces of change, 141–42
Formal organizations, 89–90, 145
"For the People of the Mountains: A Model Rural
    Health Center," 222, 223, 243
Fortin, Mary Lynch, 38, 44
Fragmentation,
  of care, 171, 193, 224
  professional, 75
Future shock, 104
Futurists, 204

Generalist, 128
Gerrish, Maddy, 104, 139
Gershenfeld, Matti K., 168–69, 186
Gestalt, 47
Goals (see objectives)
Governance, university, 6
Gray, Mary, 120, 140, 199
Gross, Ronald, 262, 288
Group,
  cohesiveness, dangers of, 98
  dynamics, 77, 83, 130, 178
  -oriented leadership, 3
Groups: Theory and Experience, 168–69, 186
Grunfeld, Carol C., 37, 44, 77
Guidelines, authoritative, 109
Guilt, 111, 235, 236

Handwashing, 37
Hare, Van Court, Jr., 53, 74

Harvard Child Health Project Task Force,
    117–18, 140
Hauser, Mary Alice, 270, 289
Havlovic, Marian M., 117, 140
Health,
  h. care of minorities, 216ff
  h. centers,
    commercial, 228
    community, 228–29
  continuity of h. care, 202
  education, 36, 114, 147
  and fear, 63, 201
  importance of, 191
  improvement, 195
  maintenance, 106, 110, 127, 128, 154, 206,
    224, 270
  mental, 141–42, 143–44, 201–202, 224ff
  and power, 66
  and segregation, 199
  subsidy of h. care, 196
Health Systems Agencies, 263, 267
Health and welfare councils, 193
Herzog, William T., 263, 289
Hess, John M., 77, 102
Higher education, 26, 233–34
Holism, 3, 4, 76–77
  and health care delivery, 272
  and team interaction, 85, 86
Holloway, Stephen, 142, 186, 291
Home nursing care, 196, 197, 207
Homeostasis, 9
Honesty, 4, 47
Hookworm, 201
Hopkins, Jeannett, 218, 243
Horwitz, John J., 86, 102, 291
Hospices, 272
Hospitalization, 115–17, 196–97
  costs of, 271
  reduction of, 206
Hospitals,
  admission procedures, 64–65
  availability of, 228
  coronary care unit, 65
  parental visits in, 62–63
  study of, 47
House calls, 65–66, 113
Houses, 229, 239–40
"How to Keep Your Mandated Citizen Board Out
    of Your Hair and Off Your Back: A Guide for
    Executive Directors," 263, 288
Humanism,
  defined, 8ff
  denied, 66

Humanism *(contd.)*
  and patient self-care, 106
Humanistic goals, 6
Human services delivery,
  evaluation of, 76
  holism in, 75
  inadequacy of, 193
  integration of, 224
Hunter, Floyd, 143, 186

Illich, Ivan, 195, 243
Immediate physical surroundings, 42-44
Improvability of life, 78
Independence, 50, 107, 158-59, 268-69
Independent Nursing Practice with Clients, 106,
    107, 110, 139, 207, 235, 243, 292
Independent practice, 6, 8, 103ff
  varieties of, 112ff
Industrial nurse, 192
Industries, 231-32
Informal organization, 51ff, 59-61, 137, 145
Information, 66
  accuracy of, 236
  affective, 67
  to clients, 79
  cultural, 70
  descriptive, 67
  flow of, 171
  -gathering, 3, 30-31, 47-48, 50-51, 62ff, 122,
    123, 147ff, 151ff, 221ff
    involvement in, 73-74, 221
    skills, 66ff
In Horizontal Orbit, 47, 59, 64-65, 74, 292
"Initiating Community Health Development in
    an Appalachian Community," 194, 242
Innovations in Community Health Nursing,
    222, 223, 243
In-service education, 26, 28-29
Institute of Medicine, National Academy of Sci-
    ences, 265
Institutional,
  objectives, 14, 16
  setting, 141ff
Institutions for nursing, 222ff
Instructional milieu,
  analysis of, 42-44
Integrity, 15, 16
Interaction,
  effective, 50
  interprofessional, 75ff
  observing, 51, 178ff
Interdisciplinary,
  care, 86

Interdisciplinary *(contd.)*
  collaboration, 75ff
  communication, 108
  functions of nurses, 59-60
  information, 63
  mobilization, 18ff
  model, 88ff
  problem solving, 51ff
  skills in community, 192-93
  team, 80ff, 94-95
Intergroup relations, 150
"Intergroup Relations in Occupational Health
    Nursing," 192, 242
Interpersonal skills, 77-78
Interprofessional Teamwork, 292
An Introduction to the Human Services, 25, 44,
    76, 102, 169, 186, 204, 219, 243
"Ivan Illich: Medicine is a Major Threat to
    Health," 195, 243

Jacox, Ada K., 104, 109, 114-15, 120, 139, 140, 196,
    199, 243, 256, 264, 270, 289, 292
"A Joint Practice Council in Action," 81, 102
Judd, Leda, 267, 289

Kane, Rosalie, 292
Kinlein, Lucille, 106, 107, 110, 139, 207, 235, 292
Knowledge,
  accurate, 106-107
  assessment of other's k., 161
  general k. of people, 135
  impediments to use of, 4
  interrelatedness of, 4, 75ff
  of self, 78-79
  use of k. for change, 143
Kuhtik, Nellie, 37, 44

Latin America, opportunities in, 126ff, 189ff, 264
Law,
  authority of, 142-43
  rule of, 16, 250
Lawyers, 232
Leaderless groups, 12
Leaders,
  constituency of, 251ff
  feelings of, 99, 247
Leadership,
  assigned, 5, 15
  behavior categories of, 2
  in the community, 187ff
  definition of, 2, 12-13
    implications of, 2-3
  and democracy, 10-11

Leadership *(contd.)*
  evaluation of, 16
  in forming teams, 82ff
  functions of, 3, 5, 26, 62, 81, 83–84, 90–92, 93,
    96ff, 112ff, 168–69, 214, 216, 222
  interdisciplinary component of, 75ff
  laissez-faire, 12
  in mental health, 226–27
  political, 245ff
  practice in, 2, 26–29
  in primary nursing, 172ff
  and professionals, 13–14
  qualities of, 107ff
  recognition of, 93–94
  resistance to, 6
  rewards and punishments in, 15, 249
  self-assessment for, 94
  situational, 13
  and teaching, 25ff, 163–64
  traditional study of, 1–2, 5, 8ff
  and trust, 129, 252
  values in, 6, 16
*Leadership in Nursing—Theories, Strategies,
    Action*, 15–16, 24, 261, 288, 292
Learning and fear, 63
Learning to Care for the Aged, 68, 74, 101,
    207–208, 208ff, 243
Leeser, Ilse, 205, 206
Legal services, clues to, 232–33
"Letter to the Editor," 38, 44
Lewin, Kurt, 9, 24, 141
Linking function, 191ff, 199, 232, 254
Lippett, Ronald, 9, 24
Listening, 98–99, 154, 156
Logic, 47
Love, 70
Loyalty, 6

Mager, Robert F., 292
Mainstreaming, 49
Management,
  good, defined, 8–9
  traditional goal of, 3
Management and Leadership in Nursing, 169, 186
Manipulation, 15
Marram, Gwen D., 172–73, 186
Maslow, Abraham, 21, 24, 93, 95, 102
Mass media, 239
McClelland, D.C., 8–9, 24
McDevitt, Joan Quinn, 196, 243, 291
Means and ends,
  consistency of, 249
Medical Nemesis, 195, 243

Melham, Vivian, 196–97
Mental illness, 201–202
Merrill, Jeffrey, 267, 288
Middle class,
  attitudes, 247
  communities, 189, 218ff
Migrant workers, 199
Minorities, 216ff
Mobile communities,
  problems of, 202
Mobilization, 18ff, 62, 66, 189, 217
Model Cities, 199, 218
Modeling, 28–29, 96ff, 138–39, 150, 208ff
Moloney, Margaret M., 15–16, 24, 261, 292
Monitoring, 31
Moore, Maureen, 37, 44
Motivating forces, 42–44
Motivation, 3
Motivation and Personality, 21, 24
Murder, 11
Mussolini, 11

Napier, Rodney W., 168–69, 186
National Center for Excellence in Nursing, 260
National Health Planning Council, 266
National League for Nursing, 259, 266
National Student Nurses' Association, 260
Nazis, 146
Needs,
  assessment of, 16ff, 100, 120, 127, 193, 194–95,
    200ff
  awareness of, 4
  identification of, 134ff
  satisfaction of, 6, 50, 197–98
  universal, 70, 220
  unmet, 109–110, 114, 117–18, 205ff, 270–71
Neglected groups, 109–10, 114, 117–18
Negotiation, 97
Neighborly interaction, 200
Newhy, Howard, 219, 243
The New Professionals, 262, 288
Nobody Ever Died of Old Age, 101, 102
Nonsystematic thinking, 45ff
Nontraditional competency, 131–32
Norris, Catherine Me., 104, 109, 114–15, 120, 139,
    140, 196, 199, 243, 256, 264, 270, 289, 292
Nuclear energy production, 201
Nurse,
  in the community, 114ff, 127–28, 187ff
  defining role of, 129ff
  functions of,
    in community, 127–28, 189ff
  low self-concept of, 4–5

Nurse *(contd.)*
  -patient relationship,
    decision making based on, 92
    purpose of, 106
    teaching in, 33–34
  -physical communication, 175–76
  powerlessness of, 7
  -practitioner, 48ff, 103ff, 194, 224, 264
    acceptance of, 105
    criteria of, 106–107
    hospital privileges of, 115–16, 117
    interdisciplinary functions of, 53, 127
    leadership functions of, 112ff
    leadership qualities of, 107ff
    nurses resistance to, 110ff
    philosophy of, 109
    as physician's helper, 113
  representation of n. on boards, 98, 261ff
  role change of, 127–28
  stereotype of, 105, 129, 133ff
  strategic position of, 92
  treatment of, 118
  unique contributions of, 187ff
  visiting, 194
Nursing,
  functions of, 106, 111, 123–24
  for health maintenance, 36
  homes, 205–206, 207, 271
  hospital n.,
    constraints on, 63–64
    objective of, 46–47
  institutions, 222ff
  leaving, 6–7
  objectives of, 110
  philosophy of, 110
  political problems in, 268ff
  primary, 8, 82, 171ff
  research in, 36–38
  team, 82
"Nurse Power in the Federal Government: Working on the Inside," 267–68, 289
Nursing the Dying Patient, 68, 74
Nursing Management and Leadership in Action, 167, 169, 169–70, 186
"Nursing Politics and Trends," 267, 289
Nutrition, 128

Observation,
  in the community, 227ff
  guides, 237ff
Objectives,
  for communities, 197ff
  differential o. on team, 169ff

Objectives *(contd.)*
  defining, 3, 49–50, 64ff, 90, 152–53, 217
  hidden, 14
  hierarchical, 70
  inconsistency of, 14–15, 16, 46–47, 50, 62
    in universities, 14
  organizational, 14
  patient o., 36
  restraints on achieving, 66, 70
  shared, 163
  stating o. in the team, 88–89
Office buildings, 231–32
Ojemann's equation, 42–44
Ojemann, R.H., 42–44, 44
Opposition,
  neutralizing, 146ff
Opticians, optometrists, 229
Organizing for Independent Nursing Practice, 104, 109, 114–15, 120, 139, 140, 196, 199, 243, 256, 264, 270, 288, 289, 292
Organizations, 141ff
  working with, 192
Osterman, Paul, 262, 288
Outcomes,
  evaluating, 89–90
  failure of, 261
  measurable, 46, 50, 64
    identifying, 62, 64ff, 88–89
  monitoring, 51
Outreach, 114, 147, 189, 193–94, 197, 222–23, 225

Pain, 78
Parents,
  exclusion of, 54, 58
  and hospital visits, 62–63
  nursing of, 118
  resistance of, to change, 58
Partnership, 109
"Part Time Sole-Proprietor Private Practice," 120, 140
Paternalism, 15
Patients,
  advocate, 93, 215–16
  dignity of, 6, 46
  independence of, 105, 158–59
  input of, 155–56, 158–59
  involvement in health maintenance, 128, 152–53, 158–59
  learning from, 34–35, 150ff
  needs of, 110
  powerlessness of, 46, 101, 115–16
  relationship with team, 92
  rights, 93

Patients *(contd.)*
  self-care of, 106, 158–59
  and self-worth, 46, 152
  status of, 84
  teaching, 35–36
  understanding of, 85–86, 150ff
"Patterns of Aggressive Behavior in Experimentally Created 'Social Climates'," 3, 24
Peace Corps, 200
Peer review, 109, 256
People, Power, Politics for Health Care, 196, 243, 289
Pharmacies, 229
Physician,
  in the community, 200
  extenders, 223
  lack of physicians, 193
  -nurse collaboration, 268–69
  -nurse communication, 175–76
  office of, 208ff
  traditional role of, 87-88, 94, 152
Planning, 3, 10
  organizations, 195
  for teaching, 30–33
The Pocket Book of Story Poems, 45–46, 74
Poem, 45
Police, 119, 144, 200, 232–33
Political activity defined, 248ff
Politics and professionals, 245ff
Poor people,
  hidden, 220
Poverty and health, 201, 218ff, 271
Power,
  anxiety and alienation, 220
  citizen, 262
  coercive, 250
  and democracy, 9
  élite, 143
  and management, 9
  and politics, 246, 248
  pool, 220–21
  referent, 250
  use of,
    in change, 142–43
    in team, 97
"Power is the Great Motivator," 8-9, 24
Practitioner functions, levels of, 112ff
Prejudice, 50, 79, 110, 119–20, 132, 134, 150, 151–52, 153, 216ff, 234–35, 236
Preparing Instructional Objectives, 292
Presentation of cases, 82
Primary care,
  new practitioners for, 66

Primary nursing, 8, 160ff
  in Latin America, 126ff
  need for, 103, 114, 115, 117
  problem solving in, 173ff
Primary Nursing: A Model for Individualized Care, 172, 186
Principal and change, 53, 55, 56
"Principles of Changing," 143ff, 186
"Priorities in Health Care: The Consumer's Viewpoint in an Appalachian Community," 193, 194–95, 242
Prison populations, 202–203
Problem solving, 37, 56, 78, 143, 202
  for mental health, 224–25
  methodology for nursing as, 188
Professional,
  education, 25ff, 78
    conflict in, 28
  organizations,
    leadership in, 256ff
Professionalism redefined, 77
Professional Services Review Organization, 256
Professionals, 13–14
  common areas of, 76ff
Projection, 7
"Providing Mental Health Services in Rural Alaska," 227, 243
Public Law 94-142, 48, 59
Public legal services, 232
Public transportation, 230–31

Questions,
  asking, 155–56

Rational thinking, 7
  in team interaction, 81
  requirements, of 4
Rats, 201
Ray, Carol, 38, 44
Readiness, 33
Reality oriented, 108
Referral, 193, 225
A Relevant War Against Poverty: A Study of Community Action Programs and Observable Social Change, 218, 243
"Remedies and Initiatives in Health Care," 222, 243
Report of a Study: A Manpower Policy for Primary Health Care, 265, 288
Research, 36–38, 225, 260, 273
Research Methods for Undergraduate Students in Nursing, 292
Resources, 42–44

Retrospective model, 60
Rich people, 220
Richardson, J. David, 193, 194–5, 242
Risk,
    assessment of, 124–25, 148
    taking, 136–37
Roberts' Rules of Order, 248
Role Expectations—Nurse Administrators, Governing Boards, Chief Executive Officers, 63, 74
The Role of the Nurse in Primary Health Care, 127, 140, 264, 288
Role playing, 16ff, 149, 177, 178ff, 273
Roles
    blurring of professional, 87–88
    changes in r. of nurse, 127–28
    clarification of, 88, 94ff, 129ff
    of nurse practitioners, 112ff
    social, 84
Rothman, Jack, 292
Routes to change, 120ff
Rugged individualism, 85
Rules for Radicals, 247, 248

Sagan, Carl, 65, 74
Saxe, John Godfrey, 45–46, 74
Schodde, Gretchen, 196, 242
School nurse, 48ff
Schools, 233
Scientific method, 37, 47
Scrutchfield, F. Douglas, 193, 194–95, 242
Seaman, Catherine C., 292
Secrecy, 252
Segregation, 198–99, 220–21, 233
Self-actualization, 50, 61, 64, 66, 70, 95, 107, 250
Self concept, 51, 53, 61, 157
    and control, 53–54
    damage, 152, 174
    and status, 85
Self-disclosure, 96, 100ff, 154–55, 156, 161–68
Self-doubt, 99–100
Self-expression, 11
Self-fulfillment, 167–68
Self-health, 188, 195, 206
Selective perception, 4, 7–8, 124
The Self-Reliant Manager, 13, 24
Self-understanding, 4, 78–79, 96, 234ff
    in groups, 83
Sensitivities, 51, 178ff
Sensors, 89, 98
Sexism, 105, 110, 213–14, 247
Shingles of professionals, 228
Sickle-cell anemia, 156ff, 201

Simulation, 177
Singer, Lillian E., 81, 102
Skill development (see last section in each chapter)
    self-assessment in, 26–27, 176–77, 273ff
Social Darwinism, 85
The Sociology of Community, 219, 243
Solutions, alternative, 48
"Some Priorities in Appropriations for Health Care Delivery," 196, 243
"Soulside, Washington, D.C. in the 1960's: Black Ghetto Culture and Community," 219, 243
Specht, Harry, 197–98, 242
Special children, 49
Staff development, 172ff
Status, 84–85, 95
    desire for, 110
Status quo,
    maintenance of, 5
Steckler, Allen B., 263, 288
Stein, Leonard, 111, 139
Stevens, Warren F., 169, 186
Stillner, Marianne, 227, 242
Stoiber, Susan, 222, 242
Stores, 230
Strategies of Community Organization: A Book of Readings, 292
Stress, 65
Stumbo, Jan, 222, 223, 242
Supervision, 5, 15, 172ff
    education in, 29, 32
    functions of, 89–90, 94
    inadequacy of, 177
Supervisor,
    exclusion of, 59
    resistance of, 112
Support, need for, 108
Surgery, 271–72
Survival, 70
    system, 65
Sussman, Leila, 53, 74
Sweets, preference for,
    in babies, 37
System,
    universal, 46
Systems,
    approach, 3, 37, 45ff, 88ff
    circumventing, 66
    dehumanization of, 54, 59
Systems Analysis: A Diagnostic Approach, 53, 74

"Taking the Bite Out of Frostbite and Other Cold-Weather Injuries," 38, 44

Tales Out of School, 53, 74
Targeting change, 147ff
Task-oriented leadership, 3
"Taste Preferences of Infants for Sweetened and
    Unsweetened Foods," 37, 44
Taylor, Carol, 47, 59, 64–65, 74, 292
Tay-Sachs disease, 201
Teacher Corps, 200
Teachers, 118, 143, 145, 148, 157
Teaching, 25ff
  in the community, 195ff, 200
  functions of, 3
  patients, 35–36, 86
  planning for, 30ff
  for professional competence, 25ff
Teaching of Community Health Nursing, 189ff,
    242
Team,
  cohesiveness, dangers of, 98
  collaborative, 86–87
  equality of t. members, 95
  evaluation of contributions of t. members,
    95–96
  expectations in, 168
  feelings of t. members, 83, 95, 96, 99, 168–69
  functional roles in, 223
  and holism, 85
  impetus for organizational change, 91
  integrative, 86–87
  interaction, 80–81
  interdisciplinary, 82ff, 91ff, 129–30
    goals, 89
  involvement of all personnel on t., 92, 130–31
  management t., 223
  meeting, 164ff
  model of t. functioning, 88ff
  negotiation, 97
  nursing, 82, 167, 169–70
  power,
    t. use of, 97
  sports, 85
  survival of, 93
*Team Practice and the Specialist—An Introduc-
    tion to Interdisciplinary Teamwork,* 86,
    102, 291
Technology, 47

A Theory of Leadership Effectiveness, 3, 24
Third party payment, 269–70
"Three Models of Community Organization
    Practice," 292
Toffler, Alvin, 104
*Toward a Primary Medical Care System Respon-
    sive to Children's Needs,* 117–18, 140
Training, 128
Tropman, J.E., 292
Trust, 100, 101, 154–55, 194, 199, 252
Tuchalski, Claire, 205, 206

Ulcer,
  cause of, 153
Unions, 192
Unit manager, 160ff
University goals, 14
Untermeyer, Louis, 45–46, 74

Values, 6, 15–16, 50, 130–31
  clarification, 68, 70ff, 217
  community, 68
  identification of, 70ff
  inconsistency of, 14–15, 70
Verhonick, Phyllis J., 292
Vicarious experiences, 178ff
Vietnamese, 150ff
Vista, 200

War on Poverty, 218, 232, 261, 262
Warner, Anne R., 222, 223, 227, 243
Wattleton, Faye, 187
Welfare agency, 145, 219
Welsh, Kenneth S., 194, 242
Whistle-blowing, 112
White, Robert K., 9, 24
Winning at Wellness, 196
Women,
  attitudes toward, 212ff
  stereotype of, 105
Work,
  dissatisfaction, 15
  -related diseases, 200
World Health Organization, 189ff, 264
Writing, 38, 125, 129